Mastering

otography

Macmillan Master Series

Accounting
Advanced English Language
Astronomy
Arabic
Banking
Basic Management
Biology
British Politics
Business Communication
Business Law
Business Microcomputing
C Programming
Catering Science
Catering Theory
Chemistry
COBOL Programming
Commerce
Computer Programming
Computers
Databases
Economic and Social History
Economics
Electrical Engineering
Electronic and Electrical Calculations
Electronics
English as a Foreign Language
English Grammar
English Language
English Literature
English Spelling
French
French 2
German
German 2
Hairdressing
Human Biology
Italian
Italian 2
Japanese
Manufacturing
Marketing
Mathematics
Mathematics for Electrical and Electronic Engineering
Modern British History
Modern European History
Modern World History
Pascal Programming
Philosophy
Photography
Physics
Psychology
Pure Mathematics
Restaurant Service
Science
Secretarial Procedures
Social Welfare
Sociology
Spanish
Spanish 2
Spreadsheets
Statistics
Study Skills
Word Processing

Mastering

Photography

Gordon Roberts

First published 1995 by
MACMILLAN PRESS LTD
Houndmills, Basingstoke, Hampshire RG21 2XS
and London
Companies and representatives
throughout the world

ISBN 0–333–61704–5

A catalogue record for this book is available
from the British Library.

10 9 8 7 6 5 4 3 2 1
04 03 02 01 00 99 98 97 96 95

Typeset by TA Tek-Art, Croydon, Surrey

Printed in Hong Kong

Contents

List of figures and plates x
Introduction xvii

1 History and development 1
1.1 Camera obscura 1
1.2 Self-test exercise 4
1.3 Chemistry and photography 4
1.4 Thomas Wedgwood 5
1.5 Joseph Nicéphore Niépce 5
1.6 Louis Jacques Mandé Daguerre 6
1.7 William Henry Fox Talbot 7
1.8 Frederick Scott Archer 13
1.9 Richard Leach Maddox 16
1.10 George Eastman 17
1.11 Colour photography 19
1.12 Instant pictures 20
1.13 Oskar Barnack 20
1.14 Victor Hasselblad 21
1.15 35 mm SLR 21
1.16 Mini-labs 21

2 The camera 22
2.1 Pinhole cameras 22
2.2 Simple cameras 24
2.3 Compact cameras 24
2.4 35mm single lens reflex (SLR) cameras 27
2.5 Autofocus cameras 32
2.6 Medium format cameras 33
2.7 Large format cameras 35
2.8 Camera technique 39

3 Lenses 41
3.1 Simple lenses 41
3.2 Spherical aberration 43
3.3 Chromatic aberration 44

3.4 Coma 44
3.5 Distortion 45
3.6 Astigmatism 46
3.7 Resolving Power 46
3.8 Compound lenses 46
3.9 Focal length 47
3.10 Self-test exercise 50
3.11 Critical focus mark 50
3.12 Apertures 54
3.13 Depth of field 55
3.14 Depth of focus 57
3.15 Infra-red focus 58
3.16 Close up accessories 58
3.17 Other accessories 61
3.18 Lens uses 62

4 Film **64**
4.1 Structure 64
4.2 Choice 68
4.3 Sensitivity (speed) 70
4.4 Contrast 71
4.5 Film size 72
4.6 Care and storage 73
4.7 Film faults 74

5 Exposure **76**
5.1 Determining exposure 76
5.2 Self-test exercise 77
5.3 Exposure values 78
5.4 Light meters 79
5.5 Camera modes 80
5.6 Hand held meters 81
5.7 Exposure compensation 83
5.8 Reciprocity failure 86

6 Light **83**
6.1 Wavelength 88
6.2 Colour temperature 88
6.3 Daylight (natural light) 91
6.4 Artificial light 93
6.5 Electronic flash 94
6.6 Direction 94
6.7 Quality 95
6.8 Contrast 95
6.9 Self-test exercise 99

7 Composition 101
7.1 Rule of thirds 102
7.2 Golden means 102
7.3 Golden section 105
7.4 Lines 105
7.5 Leads 106
7.6 Blocks 109
7.7 Patterns 111
7.8 Colour 112
7.9 Shape 112
7.10 Background 112
7.11 Movement 115
7.12 Scale 115
7.13 Colour or black and white 115
7.14 Self-test exercise 116

8 Flash 118
8.1 Guide numbers 118
8.2 Setting up 119
8.3 Dedication 122
8.4 Red eye 122
8.5 Bounce flash 122
8.6 Fill flash 123
8.7 Multiple flash 125
8.8 Close up 125
8.9 Flash for effect 127
8.10 Studio flash 128

9 Filters and accessories 130
9.1 Filter factors 130
9.2 Contrast filters 131
9.3 Correction filters 133
9.4 Effect filters 135
9.5 Colour back filters 136
9.6 Homemade filters 138
9.7 Tripods 138
9.8 Cable release 139
9.9 Monopods 140
9.10 Pocket supports 141
9.11 Grips 141
9.12 Levels 141
9.13 Camera bags 141
9.14 Odds and ends 142

10 The Darkroom 143
10.1 Setting up 144
10.2 Equipment 145

11 Film processing 148
11.1 Film processing 148
11.2 Developers 151
11.3 Stop baths 152
11.4 Fixers 152
11.5 Washing 152
11.6 Drying 153
11.7 Compensation development 153
11.8 Faults 154
11.9 Self-test exercise 154

12 Printing 155
12.1 Printing paper 155
12.2 Safelights 158
12.3 Photograms 158
12.4 Contact prints 159
12.5 Enlarging 160
12.6 Drying 162
12.7 Self-test exercise 163
12.8 Printing control 163
12.9 Trouble shooting 167
12.10 Self-test exercise 168
12.11 Special effects 168

13 Finishing and presentation 172
13.1 Negative filing 172
13.2 Print storage 173
13.3 Enlargements 174
13.4 Framing 175
13.5 Slide storage 176
13.6 Retouching 177
13.7 Toning 177

14 Disciplines 179
14.1 Portraiture 179
14.2 Landscapes 185
14.3 Buildings 190
14.4 Action and movement 197
14.5 Still life and close up 201
14.6 Photo essay 204

14.7 History of photography 204
14.8 Natural history 206
14.9 Black and white 207

15 Examination requirements **211**
15.1 Planning and research 211
15.2 Technical quality 212
15.3 Visual quality 213
15.4 Evaluation 215
15.5 Other requirements 215

Glossary 217
Recommended reading 223
Index 225

List of figures and plates

Figures

1.1 A seventeenth-century contemporary drawing of a camera obscura 1
1.2 A camera obscura at Clifton, Bristol 2
1.3 One of the panoramas from the camera obscura at Clifton 3
1.4 The Oriel Window at Lacock Abbey 9
1.5 The exterior of the Oriel Window at Lacock Abbey 10
1.6 The entrance to Lacock Abbey 11
1.7 The cloisters of Lacock Abbey 12
1.8 Ambrotype, 1870 14
1.9 Rouen, taken in the 1860s using the wet collodion process 15
1.10 Cartes de visite 17
1.11 Typical box camera photograph, India, 1943 18
1.12 Recording our daily life 18

2.1 Making a pinhole camera 23
2.2 A negative produced using a pinhole camera, with the positive print made from it 23
2.3 Parallax error 25
2.4 A range of box cameras, 1932 to 1980 25
2.5 Artistic photograph using the box camera 26
2.6 Cross-section of a modern 35mm SLR 27
2.7 Inside a 35mm SLR, showing mirror, pentaprism and computer 28
2.8 Loading the film into the camera 30
2.9 Cross-section of 35mm camera, showing autofocus sensors 32
2.10 Voigtländer Brilliant and Superb cameras, 1932 33
2.11 Cross-section of a twin lens reflex roll film camera 34
2.12 Cross-section of a medium format single lens reflex camera 35
2.13 TLRs and some medium format SLRs produce square images 36
2.14 Large format camera movements 37
2.15 Keeping distortion to a minimum 38
2.16 First lessons in good camera technique 40

3.1 A lens and its travelling trunk, 1870s 42
3.2 Refraction 42
3.3 Simple positive and negative lens elements 43

3.4 Spherical aberration 43
3.5 Chromatic aberration 44
3.6 Coma 45
3.7 Distortion 45
3.8 Astigmatism 46
3.9 A segmented Nikkor 35–105mm zoom lens 47
3.10 Focal length of a lens and its relationship with image area 48
3.11 The same view taken with 35mm wide angle and 210mm telephoto lenses 49
3.12 Photographs taken with 35mm, 50mm, 70mm, 105mm, 150mm and 210mm lenses 51–3
3.13 Typical lens markings 50
3.14 Stand and *f*/number sequence 54
3.15 Depth of field chart 55
3.16 Three photographs of the same subject showing increase in depth of field from *f*/2.8 to *f*/8 and *f*/22 56
3.17 Avoiding a cluttered background 57
3.18 Depth of focus either side of the film plane 58
3.19 Photograph taken using extension tubes 59
3.20 Extension tubes and bellows 59
3.21 Photograph taken using close up lens 60
3.22 Cross-section of a typical mirror lens 63

4.1 Cross-section of black and white film 64
4.2 Typical silver halides 65
4.3 Photographic film's response to light 66
4.4 The eye's response to light 66
4.5 Cross-section of colour film 67
4.6 A small selection of films available 69
4.7 DX coding on 35mm film cassettes 71
4.8 Film sizes available 72
4.9 Information on the film box 74

5.1 Shutter speed/aperture combinations 77
5.2 Exposure value table 78
5.3 Correct exposure indications 79
5.4 Centre weighted metering 80
5.5 Partial metering 80
5.6 Spot metering 80
5.7 Integrated metering 80
5.8 The Weston meter 82
5.9 Backlit photographs exposed for the background and for the subject 84
5.10 Night shot lit only by the street lamps and using the ground as a camera support 85
5.11 Night shot with 2½ minutes exposure time 87

6.1 The electromagnetic spectrum 89
6.2 The visible spectrum 90
6.3 Bright sunlight to create mood 91
6.4 Mist obscuring the background 92
6.5 Photograph taken using artificial lighting only, with extended exposure time 93
6.6 A portrait taken using directional flash 94
6.7 Side lighting 96
6.8 Shadows created by side lighting 96
6.9 How the scene changes with lighting 97
6.10 The shot in Figure 6.9, under an overcast sky 97
6.11 High contrast lighting 98
6.12 Harsh lighting 100

7.1 The image area divided into thirds 103
7.2 Vertical thirds 103
7.3 Unequal or unequally shaped thirds 103
7.4 Unequal horizontal thirds 103
7.5 Dividing the frame equally 104
7.6 A landscape with the horizon line dividing the image in two 104
7.7 The four golden means 104
7.8 Hand and face placed on the golden means 104
7.9 The golden section rule 105
7.10 The golden section rule applied from the left 105
7.11 Vertical, horizontal and diagonal lines 106
7.12 Vertical lines 106
7.13 Diagonal lines 107
7.14 Leads drawing the eye into the picture 107
7.15 Leads taking the eye to the top of the picture 107
7.16 Leads taking the eye across the picture 108
7.17 Repetitive lines 109
7.18 Blocks used to hold the viewer's attention 110
7.19 Blocks blanking out a bland sky 110
7.20 Blocks completely framing the image 110
7.21 Regular patterns 111
7.22 The same view treated horizontally and vertically 113
7.23 Messy cluttered background 114
7.24 Blur in movement shot 114
7.25 People as an indication of size and scale 116
7.26 Simplicity in black and white photography 117

8.1 Rear view of a typical small flashgun 119
8.2 Selecting flashgun power output 120
8.3 Hammerhead flashguns 121
8.4 Bounce flash off a ceiling 123
8.5 Bounce flash for softer lighting 124

8.6 Fill flash 124
8.7 Manual flashgun firing 126
8.8 Candle effect created by flash 127
8.9 Multiple flashes fired manually with the camera shutter open on brief 128
8.10 Studio flash 129

9.1 Coloured filters 131
9.2 The same scene taken without filtration, with yellow and with red filter 132
9.3 Using a polarising filter 134
9.4 Starburst filters 137
9.5 Grey graduated filters 137
9.6 A tripod with stays between the legs and central column 139
9.7 A 'G' clamp 140

10.1 The ideal layout of a darkroom 144
10.2 Cross-section of a daylight film processing tank 145
10.3 The condenser and diffuser enlarger 146

11.1 Starting a film on the spiral 149

12.1 Cross-section of fibre base and resin coated paper 155
12.2 Cross-section of colour printing paper 157
12.3 A photogram 158
12.4 A contact print 159
12.5 A test strip 161
12.6 The final print 161
12.7 A cascade washing system and proprietary print washer 163
12.8 Three prints from the same negative using grade 1, 3 and 5 paper 164
12.9 A straight print and one 'burnt in' 165
12.10 A straight print and one with 'dodging' 166
12.11 Solarisation 169
12.12 Lith transfer 170
12.13 Sandwiching a lith negative and a lith positive just out of register 171

13.1 Layout of photo album page 174

14.1 Formal portrait with strong sinister mood 180
14.2 Formal portrait with strong mood 181
14.3 Using props 182
14.4 Supporting background information and objects 183
14.5 Photographing children 184
14.6 Traditional landscape 186
14.7 Landscapes with buildings 186
14.8 Landscapes with maximum depth of field 187
14.9 Simple abstract compositions 188

14.10 The sky in landscape photographs 189
14.11 Converging verticals 190
14.12 Strong vertical lines 191
14.13 Environment of a photograph 192
14.14 Record shot and more intimate view of the same building 193
14.15 Interior shot with articicial light and fill flash 194
14.16 Interior shot with limited artificial light and fill flash 195
14.17 Adjusting camera position to alter mood 196
14.18 Blur in action shots 198
14.19 Panning to show movement 199
14.20 Pre-focusing 200
14.21 Still life shots 201
14.22 Photographing flowers using the macro facility 202
14.23 The photo essay 203
14.24 Natural history photography 205
14.25 Imagination and experimentation 208
14.26 More artistic images 209
14.27 Lith transfer from black and white image 210

15.1 Finding suitable subject matter 212
15.2 Technical quality 213
15.3 Visual quality 214
15.4 Evaluation 214

Plates

1. Market stall
2. Seaside shelter
3. Louvre ceiling
4. Pebbles on sand
5. Pigeons
6. Street lamps and seats
7. Punts on river
8. Upturned boat
9. Sunlight on yacht
10. Eiffel Tower
11. Fireworks over water
12. Class 4 yacht
13. Kites
14. Dancing light
15. Frosted leaves
16. Reflection in engine
17. Reflection of boat
18. Sunset over corn
19. Seascape
20. Loch Lomond

Plates (continued)

21. Cottage on river
22. Sludge on water
23. Stained glass reflection
24. Piano in window
25. Room in mirror
26. Male portrait
27. Female and cat
28. Female artist
29. Gypsy caravan
30. Girl in tree
31. Lamp and flowers
32. Tulip in basket
33. Motorbike
34. Aeroplane spraying
35. Whiskey bottle
36. Red mat
37. Coins
38. Pencil shavings
39. 50p coin
40. Rusty iron
41. Lozenges
42. Candles and glasses
43. Fungi
44. Damselfly
45. Harvest mouse

Introduction

In this age of mass communication with images being scattered world-wide via satellites, the population has become blasé towards image making and reproduction. Maybe it is for this reason that photography no longer holds the esteemed position that it once had.

Photography is the most accessible medium for the creation of artistic works and one which most people can cope with quite easily, it crosses all social and ethnic barriers. Able bodied and disabled people are capable of gaining the same sense of achievement and satisfaction. Even the most handicapped person can participate with the help of a few specially designed aids.

Today the modern automated camera makes taking a photograph as simple as pressing a button. Once the film is finished it is handed over to a high street minilab and another automatic process produces colourful prints of one's endeavours. This has led to a misconception by a large majority of people that photography is easy and anyone with a grain of sense can do it. This in turn has led to the acceptance of very inferior imagery under the guise of photography and photographic art.

Within all of us there is an artist trying to get out and for those of us who struggle with pencil and brush, photography is an ideal outlet for the imagination and self-expression. To begin with little thought may be given to artistic interpretation but with progression comes a raising of expectation, requiring an improvement in artistic and technical quality. Imitation is said to be the sincerest form of flattery and maybe this is the easiest route towards improving standards, although trying to emulate some of the great works may result in frustration and demoralisation. It therefore follows that each new goal should be obtainable, stretching one's abilities by just the right amount so that success is assured.

To be successful at anything one needs to have an understanding of the materials and techniques involved. Just as an artist has to be able to use a brush in different ways and understand what happens when various colours are mixed, so the photographer should have a knowledge of camera equipment and the processes that enable images to be recorded. That is what this book aims to do, to bring an understanding of the hardware and software involved, plus an insight into the artistic requirements to make a success of photography.

To begin with photography is a mechanical process which records an instant in time and as such can be achieved with little or no artistic talent. Once a scene has been committed to film it becomes an historic document, providing future generations with an insight into that moment. The vast majority of photographs taken are for record purposes be they professional or amateur in origin. Holiday snaps are records designed to stimulate the memory in years to come and evoke the pleasure or heartache of the time. They may not be high art but as long as they achieve what they set out to do then they can be considered successful.

Regrettably, as with art, there is an awful lot of snobbery in photographic circles, human nature being what it is this is always likely to be the case. Photographic clubs and societies, large or small, tend to perpetuate this by having an hierarchical structure which makes the newcomer feel uncomfortable. Competition judges and old sages holding court can destroy a beginner's morale by their ill considered comments. Photography is a very personal craft or art and at the end of the day as long as the photographer is happy with the result then that is all that matters. The professional has to satisfy two masters in the client and themselves, often leading to a compromise, but then isn't life about compromise?

Gordon Roberts

1 History and development

1.1 Camera obscura

The principles of photography go back into history much further than most people would appreciate. The ability of light to form images was well known to scholars as long ago as the fourth century BC. The Greek philosopher Aristotle was the first person to comment on the practical use of this phenomenon in the study of astronomy. By using a darkened room and allowing the light to pass through a small hole, an image of the sun was created on the opposite wall. He had also noticed that the size of aperture through which the light passed had a direct effect on image sharpness. Some 1300 years later, Hassan ibn Hassan, a tenth century Arabian scholar, wrote an account of a solar eclipse in which he commented on

Figure 1.1 A seventeenth-century contemporary drawing of a camera obscura.

Figure 1.2 In the seventeenth century this building at Clifton, Bristol, was a snuff mill, the windmill tower was turned into a camera obscura in 1829 and is maintained in working order, one of three in Britain.

the effect of different size holes, the smaller the hole the sharper the image. By the thirteenth century Roger Bacon was familiar with the ability of light to form images of scenes, as well as being used to observe solar activity. The term 'camera obscura' comes from the Latin and means dark room, and that is exactly what the first examples were, and as such their application was limiting. The first known published reference to one appeared in 1544. Several fixed camera obscuras exist around the world; now mainly tourist attractions they do afford the visitor an idea of the basic principles of photography (see Figure 1.1). In Britain there are three open to the public, one in Bristol, one in Edinburgh and one at Builth Wells in Wales (see Figures 1.2 and 1.3). In the original camera obscura the image appears upside down and back to front, in later versions where a mirror was introduced the image appeared the right way up but still back to front. With the three existing cameras in Britain a prism is fitted in the lens housing and the image appears the right way round.

By the late 1500s the camera obscura was part of everyday life for artists. It was instrumental in the formation of the Renaissance period in art, helping artists to

Figure 1.3 One of the panoramas from the camera obscura looking out at the Clifton Suspension Bridge spanning the Clifton Gorge, Bristol, well worth the 61-step climb to the top.

understand true perspective. Portable examples, complete with simple lenses, began to appear in the early 1600s. They ranged in size from large rooms mounted on bearers, tent arrangements with a rotatable lens and mirror at the apex, to specially equipped sedan chairs and portable boxes with mirrors and viewing screens. By the middle of the century the camera obscura was a common sight and in use throughout Europe. Much of the design and development of the camera obscura was carried out in Switzerland at Altdorf University and Würzburg in Germany. In 1685 Johann Zahn, a monastic scholar, described several types of camera consisting of wooden boxes with adjustable lenses and a mirror reflecting the image onto an opal screen or oiled drawing paper. Viewing was improved by fitting a shade around the screen. This is considered by photographic historians to be the first viable reflex camera suitable for photography, all that was missing was the chemistry to record the image.

The wider acceptance of the camera obscura by artist and scientist alike led to improvements in both the camera and optics over the next hundred years or so. The name of John Dollond is familiar to all of us living in Britain as his name is carried by one of the country's largest chain of opticians. In 1758 he introduced a new lens which overcame the problem of chromatic aberration, the breaking up of light into spectral colours.

1.2 Self-test exercise

Visit one of the major art galleries where they have a range of work, particularly pre-Renaissance paintings (before 1500), and compare the various periods, taking note of how techniques improved with the introduction of the camera obscura, especially the understanding of perspective. One can get a feel of the camera obscura by setting up an over head projector so that the lens looks out of the window in a darkened room. Place some tracing paper over the platen and focus the image using the focus adjustment on the lens column. This will give a full colour moving image of the scene outside.

1.3 Chemistry and photography

Photography relies on the action of light on silver salts to record an image, something we fully understand today. Although it was known that silver salt blackened as far back as the middle ages, there was no understanding of the reasons for it. It was not until 1614 that Angelo Sala recognised that the action of the sun turned silver salts black, although he did not know whether it was the light or heat which caused the reaction. It was to be more than another century before Johann Schulze, a professor at Altdorf University, discovered that it was light from the sun that caused the change. This came about by accident in 1725 whilst performing an experiment, but so struck was Schulze that he investigated further, finally arriving at the conclusion that the sun created darkness. Regrettably he made no connection between this phenomena and the camera obscura already in use at the university.

Fifty years later in 1777 Carl Scheele, a Swedish chemist, confirmed that it was light that reacted with silver salts. In an effort to discover if the blackened salts were metallic silver, Scheele poured ammonia onto them finding that some were dissolved, the salts most affected by light, i.e. the blackest, remained. Taking this one stage further Scheele then experimented with various coloured light and discovered that the sensitive silver salts took varying times to react according to the colour of that light. Jean Senebier from Geneva took these experiments further and established times for exposures. He found that the salts reacted quickest to the blue end of the spectrum, turning black within seconds, where as it took twenty minutes to react to red light. Senebier also experimented with some resins and found that they too reacted and hardened when exposed to light.

In 1800 the Astronomer Royal, Sir William Herschel, discovered the existence of heat rays beyond the visible red band, these would later be identified as infrared and used in specialist types of photography. J.W. Ritter discovered other invisible rays beyond the violet rays in 1801, these we now know as ultra-violet. Although UV rays are invisible to the eye they can be seen by film. Sir David Brewster worked on the polarisation of light and stereoscopy in the early years of photography and many other scientists were working independently along similar lines. A large number of papers and books were published on the nature of light and its effects on silver salts, but nobody made the connection with the camera obscura.

Had that connection been made the world would have had photography at least 100 years earlier and possibly before that. Just imagine that if Angelo Sala had continued with his experiments, photography could have been a fact by the mid-sixteen hundreds. The Great Plague and The Great Fire of London, The Boston Tea Party and American War of Independence, The French Revolution and Battle of Trafalgar, Waterloo and the Industrial Revolution could all have been recorded for posterity. From a personal aspect that would mean seven or eight generations of one's family life. It is ironic that the greatest means of communication since the written word should have taken so long to come to fruition.

1.4 Thomas Wedgwood

Thomas Wedgwood was the youngest son of Josiah Wedgwood of English pottery fame and, as befitted a child of the Industrial Revolution, had a strong inclination towards the sciences. In fact it was his father who started the investigations into the use of a camera obscura to assist with designs for decorating pottery, having taken an order from the Empress of Russia for 952 pieces of creamware depicting 1244 different scenes. Transfers had been invented some 40 years earlier by John Sadler and Guy Green, two Liverpool printers, and Wedgwood was hoping to combine this with images from the camera obscura.

After leaving university in 1788 Thomas Wedgwood spent a couple of years investigating the properties of light. This in turn led to experiments with the camera obscura and paper coated with silver salts. He received much encouragement from members of the Lunar Society, a body of eminent personalities to which his father belonged, in particular Dr Joseph Priestly. It was 1799 when Wedgwood began his trials and over the next couple of years struggled to obtain an image using silver nitrate coated on paper. Humphry Davy, with whom Wedgwood had struck up friendship in the late 1790s, suggested that he try using silver chloride as it was more sensitive. Together they worked on various materials and discovered that leather was far more sensitive than paper. It had been thought for years that this was due to the presence of gallic acid in the leather, but this has since been proved wrong. Davy later went on to expand on Wedgwood's work but neither succeeded in obtaining an image through the camera obscura. Wedgwood died in 1805 and with him the incentive to push these findings further.

1.5 Joseph Nicéphore Niépce

The story now moves to France where this son of a King's Counsellor began experiments with a camera obscura in 1816 at his home in Meursaûlt, near Chalon-sur-Saône. Today the Niépce family still own the vineyards on which the family fortune is based.

It was not long before Niépce succeeded in obtaining an image on sensitised paper, but as his brother had suggested, the image was reversed in tones. Two major problems confronted him, how to obtain a positive image and how to make the negative permanent. Nitric acid provided a short-term solution to the latter but he never did succeed in obtaining a print. In 1822 Niépce managed to make a permanent image of an engraving using bitumen of Judea coated on glass and then dissolving it in oil of lavender, a process known as Heliography; no examples of these first 'photographs' exist. From glass he moved to zinc and pewter and after a number of years of experimentation succeeded in fixing an image from nature through the camera obscura. The year was 1827 and the pewter plate shows a view from the window of his workroom after some eight hours' exposure and is the world's earliest surviving photograph. The image was very faint and Niépce was unable to etch it in the usual manner.

Further successes followed but all these experiments had taken their toll of the family finances and Niépce found himself impoverished. In 1829 Niépce entered into a partnership with Louis Daguerre in order to perfect Heliography. Daguerre had dabbled with image making but had not achieved any notable successes. Joseph Niépce died in 1833 and was succeeded in the partnership by his son Isidore. Today Joseph Niépce is recognised as the inventor of photography and there is a museum to his memory in Chalon-sur-Sâone, where he was born, halfway between Dijon and Lyon in France.

1.6 Louis Jacques Mandé Daguerre

In 1822 Daguerre had been involved in a venture known as the Diorama, a novel combination of painted scenery and lighting techniques. The camera obscura was a prime implement in obtaining the painted images for the Diorama so it was only natural that Daguerre should turn his mind to trying to obtain images directly. After entering the partnership with Niépce the two men worked independently, but corresponded by coded letter to avoid their findings falling into the wrong hands. Before Joseph Niépce died he had begun to use silvered copper plates coated with various chemicals in an endeavour to obtain an image. After Niépce's death it was a long time before Daguerre felt he could continue the work using the same materials. The system they had been working on was eventually to produce a direct positive image with no negative involved. Because of the expense of the plates they were stored for cleaning and resensitising after each failure. In 1835 he wrote to Isidore Niépce asking him to come to Paris to witness his latest discovery which had come about purely by accident. On opening the cupboard one day Daguerre noticed that one of the unsuccessful plates had acquired a distinct image. After a lengthy process of elimination he discovered that the latent 'invisible' image had been 'developed' by a few drops of mercury from a broken thermometer.

This discovery now meant that exposure times could be reduced from hours to as little as thirty minutes, the plate being developed by vapour of mercury. A fixing agent had still not been found but that did not stop Daguerre announcing that he had fixed an image from the camera obscura. It was to be a further two years before a suitable fixer was found in table salt (sodium chloride). Daguerre insisted that the process be called after him in spite of protestations from Niépce. The next stage was to raise capital, and to this end Daguerre toured Paris trying to interest people in buying shares in the Daguerre-Niépce company. The move failed miserably so he turned to influential friends for ideas, in particular Francois Arago. Arago gave a short paper to the Académie des Sciences on 7 January 1839, the date recognised as being the birth of photography.

Arago went on to convince the French Government that they should take this very important new invention onboard and recompense the two partners. This they eventually did and awarded pensions to both men in return for which they would prepare a manual on the process, henceforth to be known as the Daguerrotype. By the end of the year the government had published this in six languages and donated it to the world, although Daguerre had previously taken out patents in London, thus denying England of the free use. Daguerre was made an Officer of the Legion of Honour and received many other decorations from foreign countries. In 1840 he retired to the country and left others to perfect this far from perfect imaging system, dying in 1851.

The Daguerrotype had several drawbacks; firstly the mirrored surface made it difficult to see, secondly being a direct positive the image was laterally reversed; in fact this turned out to be something of an advantage in portraiture, because of course we all see our own reversed image in a mirror. Finally being produced on copper plate it could not transmit light and was therefore unique and unable to be copied; this was overcome to some extent by the introduction of a multiple imaging camera. Although expensive, having your portrait taken soon became very fashionable world-wide, the finished image being presented in a gilt frame supplied in a red Moroccan leather case lined with embossed red velvet. Multi exposure cameras produced up to twelve thumbnail images which proved popular for lockets and putting together in 'family' frames.

Once the process was taken up throughout the world improvements were not long in coming, in particular the use of a prism in front of the lens to correct the laterally reversed image. Exposure times were still counted in terms of tens of minutes but with further experimentation these were reduced to between one and five minutes by 1841. To ensure that the sitter remained still for the required time head and body clamps were introduced, perhaps that is why you never see a Victorian smiling. Antoine Claudet, a Frenchman who had settled in England, took out the first patent for the Daguerrotype in that country in 1840, and by 1853 was appointed 'Photographer-in-Ordinary to Her Majesty Queen Victoria'. The first studio in Britain was opened by a one-time coal merchant Richard Beard in 1841 in London. The Daguerrotype lasted until the introduction of the wet plate in 1851 and as late as 1860 in a few countries.

1.7 William Henry Fox Talbot

Whilst Niépce and Daguerre were concentrating on the direct reversal process in France, an Englishman was working quietly away at another method of obtaining images through the camera obscura. Fox Talbot was the grandson of the Earl of Ilchester and in 1833 was the Member of Parliament for Chippenham, Wiltshire. Fond of foreign travel he spent the best part of that year travelling Europe with his new wife. Lake Como, in Italy, was a favourite spot with artists and Fox Talbot spent some time there sketching with the aid of a camera lucida, a form of portable camera obscura designed especially for the artist. He had achieved some commendable sketches in the past and it was whilst using the camera lucida at this location that he turned his thoughts to fixing nature's own image.

Having given up his seat in Parliament early in 1834 he put his mind to the processes of creating images on high quality paper coated with silver nitrate. These first pictures were called 'photogenic drawings', known today as photograms, objects laid on the paper and exposed to light creating a white silhouette. Initial attempts to gain an image through the camera obscura failed even after several hours' exposure. Talbot discovered that if the camera was miniaturised, exposure times were dramatically reduced. He had a number of tiny cameras, which his wife nicknamed 'mouse traps', made by the estate carpenter. Success came with exposures of just thirty minutes and a negative image resulted, this was a 'printing out' process in which no developing chemicals were used. By 1835 he found that sodium chloride provided adequate fixing of the image, two years before Niépce and Daguerre. From these negatives he obtained a positive, by laying another sheet of sensitised paper in contact and exposing it to daylight. Other more pressing events took Talbot's mind away from his experiments and it was not until the announcement of Daguerre's process that he was jolted back into action.

Talbot protested that he had invented the process long before the French pair and presented a paper to the Royal Society at the end of January 1839. The reaction to this paper and the images displayed was one of complete indifference both on the part of the Institute and the public. Talbot felt that he deserved better treatment and even some form of recognition, although there was no precedent for this, even the likes of Watt or Stephenson had not received such an honour. So it was with some bitterness that he published a booklet on the process of photogenic drawing in the February.

Encouraged by Sir John Herschel (he coined the terms 'photography', 'negative', 'positive', and 'snapshot'), and Daguerre's success, Talbot concentrated on perfecting imaging through the camera obscura. In September 1840 he made a discovery that astonished him, like Niépce and Daguerre with their copper plates, Talbot decided to try and resensitise his failures. This he did with gallo-nitrate of silver and to his surprise an image began to appear. This now reduced exposure times to as little as three minutes and made portraiture a viable proposition, with the aid of head clamps. In February 1841 Talbot patented his improved 'Calotype' process, from the Greek meaning beautiful. The negatives and resultant positives were now being fixed in bromide of pottassium which gave them the familiar sepia colouring. He pursued infringers of the patent with vigour and this must have had an influence on the very low level of interest shown. The patent laws did not apply in Scotland and Robert Adamson opened a studio in Edinburgh by 1843 using the Calotype, and was joined later by David Hill. It was largely due to their success that Talbot opened his own studio in Russell Terrace (now Baker Street), Reading in 1844 supplying portraits and landscapes. It was during this time that Talbot embarked on the first photographically illustrated book *The Pencil of Nature* published in June 1844. Under the direction of Talbot's valet Nikolaas Henneman the establishment flourished and in 1847 he undertook the management of a new studio in Regent Street, London. This led to Henneman being appointed the 'Photographer on Paper to her Majesty Queen Victoria'. The following year the

Figure 1.4 The Oriel Window at Lacock Abbey, still much the same as when Fox Talbot took his first photograph of it in 1835.

Figure 1.5 The exterior of the Oriel Window above the mediaeval cloisters at Lacock Abbey.

Figure 1.6 The entrance to Lacock Abbey, home of Fox Talbot, 'father of the modern photographic process', now in the hands of the National Trust.

Figure 1.7 The cloisters of Lacock provide excellent material for photographs.

Regent Street studio was bought from Talbot by Henneman and his partner Malone, despite the fact that it was losing money.

Talbot was forced to relax his patent restrictions which were having a detrimental effect on the progress of photography in Britain. Financial considerations also forced him to close the Reading establishment but he continued to work on in photography for a few years until his process, now known as the Talbotype, was overtaken by events. The fibrous writing paper used as the base for the Talbotype gave the image a less than satisfactory result due to a general lack of sharpness, even after waxing in an attempt to reduce the effect of the paper's structure. This problem was compounded when prints were also made on quality writing paper. However, the process did lay the foundations of the modern negative/positive system of photography that is still in use today.

The Calotype process required longer exposure times than the Daguerrotype and gave a much softer, romantic image. However, it was very much cheaper and more convenient, particularly for location work, its greatest advantage being that a negative was produced enabling endless prints to be made. Very few people had the opportunity to travel outside their local community and images from around the world gave the public an insight into countries and cultures that would otherwise have remained largely unknown.

Fox Talbot is regarded as the Father of Modern Photography and his home of Lacock Abbey near Swindon, Wiltshire, is in the hands of the National Trust and open to the public along with a small museum. A visit is to be recommended as not only is it educational but the building with its medieval cloisters is very photogenic.

1.8 Frederick Scott Archer

1851 was the year of the Great Exhibition at Crystal Palace, London, which displayed the best of Victorian ingenuity. Photography played an important part in this with displays of photographs and equipment. It was in this atmosphere that photography took a great leap forward.

Although other pioneers had tried glass as a base for the sensitive emulsion it was Scott Archer, an English sculptor, who came up with a solution that would be universally adopted. The process was known as 'Wet Collodion' and involved spreading a syrup like mixture onto glass. Nitrocellulose dissolved in ether and alcohol was coated onto the glass plate and when set floated on a bath of silver nitrate. The plate then had to be placed in a light tight container and exposed in the camera immediately. The latent image was developed whilst the emulsion was still damp and fixed in a number of different chemicals, one of which was the highly toxic potassium cyanide. On drying, the collodion formed a tough and flexible emulsion that was impervious to liquids when dry. Nitrocellulose is also known as 'Gun Cotton' and used, as the name suggests, as an explosive charge. A highly volatile mixture combined with a poisonous fixer made this improvement in photography a more risky business than using the mercury vapour of the Daguerrotype.

The ritual of coating plates was tedious and messy, however, the new system

Figure 1.8 This Ambrotype, with gilt frame and wooden case, was taken in Epsom, England around 1870.

increased the sensitivity of emulsions and was hailed as a major advance, bringing exposure times down to a few seconds. The glass plate gave clearer images and allowed higher quality prints to be made. In spite of the drawbacks of having to coat plates immediately before exposure, the system found favour with location photographers who would either push a hand cart, or drive a horse and wagon containing the darkroom. Bearing in mind the volatile nature of the chemicals employed one might think twice before embarking on a photographic expedition, even more so if the location was a war zone. In 1855 Roger Fenton set out to cover

Figure 1.9 The French town of Rouen taken in the 1860s using the wet collodion process.

events in the Crimea and in doing so became the world's first war photographer. Fenton returned to Britain after the war to become a successful portrait photographer. Six years later Mathew Brady, a New York photographer, took the camera to the front line and was nearly killed for his trouble when his wagon was caught in cross fire. Not to be put off his team continued recording the events of the American Civil War using the wet collodion process.

Between 1856 and 1860 an Englishman by the name of Francis Frith made three journeys to the Holy Land in order to record the sights of biblical fame. Suffering intense heat and aggravation from locals he recorded some of the finest images of the time. He later went on to travel the length of Britain photographing towns and villages, copies of which are still available today. Julia Margaret Cameron used the wet collodion process to challenge the stuffy formal portraits of the time by producing relaxed, informal photographs of friends, many of whom were famous figures. In effect, she became the first photographic stylist producing innovative, romantic portraits.

An interesting hybrid resulted from the use of a deliberately under exposed collodion negative which gave the appearance of a Daguerrotype. The negative was coated with a black lacquer or placed against a dark background, thus giving a positive image. These were then placed in frames and cases in the style of the Daguerrotype and marketed as Ambrotypes (see Figure 1.8). Another Daguerrotype imitator was the Tintype, this was a small sheet of black japanned iron coated with a collodion emulsion. The tough emulsion combined with the strength of the base made these photographs very popular and were instrument in bringing portraiture within the reach of the populace. The wet collodion process would remain in use for twenty years or more until another Englishman took the next logical step (see Figure 1.9).

1.9 Richard Leach Maddox

The next logical step in the development of photography was to come up with a dry emulsion that could be used at the photographer's convenience. In 1871 an English doctor at Southampton University came up with a solution of cadmium bromide, silver nitrate and gelatine coated on glass for negatives. The same mixture could also be used on paper for print making. This now made it possible for photographic plates to be mass produced and for the photographer to be relieved of the burden of carting a darkroom around. Initially these new plates were less sensitive than the wet collodion ones. Requiring long exposure times. Further development soon brought them in line and eventually they became highly sensitive with exposure times measured in fractions of a second. The introduction of the dry plate also had an effect on the design of cameras with plate sizes being standardised and miniaturised. These factors meant that photography was no longer a messy and scientific process, making it more acceptable to the keen amateur. In spite of these improvements many photographers remained with the wet collodion process for a number of years.

Figure 1.10 Carte de visite are a typical product of the dry plate process, popular throughout the world. These examples from Europe also show some of the ornate styling used on the back.

1.10 George Eastman

In the late 1800s George Eastman was manufacturing dry plates for the photographic trade and with one of his employees, W. Walker, began experiments with flexible film. Celluloid had been invented in either 1861 or 1865, depending on which history books you read, and was used as the base for this new type of film using existing technology of silver halides suspended in gelatine for the emulsion. In 1888 a French company went into production with a new flexible film based on celluloid. The same year the Eastman company produced the first camera using a flexible roll film.

George Eastman was aware of the international potential of his product and looked for a name that could be pronounced in every language without difficulty. The name Kodak was chosen for this first camera which contained a roll of film giving 100 exposures. When all the exposures were taken the camera was returned to the company where the film was processed and printed and the camera reloaded with more film. The advertising campaign coined a catchy phrase which let the

Figure 1.11 Subject matter has not changed. A typical box camera photograph (India, 1943), one of the countless millions taken around the world.

Figure 1.12 Photography is used to record all manner of events that affect our daily lives.

purchaser know exactly what happened: 'You press the button, we do the rest.' At $25 it was not cheap but it was the beginning of the age of 'Snapshot' photography for unskilled amateurs.

The name of Kodak became synonymous with amateur photography, and in 1900 the first of a long line of box cameras under the brand name of 'Brownie' was produced. The Brownie cost just $1 and a roll of film 15 cents, well within the reach of the average person. The concept spread rapidly and soon the box camera was in production world-wide capturing images of family life. Recreational and happy events in the family were recorded from weddings and christening of children, outings and holidays to treasured possessions. All life could now be recorded and the gates were opened for an unprecedented wealth of pictorial information to be gathered (see Figures 1.11 and 1.12). Since those early days Kodak has introduced a number of different concepts in cameras including the 'Instamatic', 'Disc' and more recently the photo 'CD'.

1.11 Colour photography

Colour photography did not become generally available until after the Second World War, but it must not be assumed that it was unknown before that time. The earliest example of a colour image was taken in 1861 by James Clark Maxwell, using the trichrome technique. Three black and white photographs were taken using the primary colour filters, red, green and blue. The negatives were then printed separately onto glass producing transparencies, these were projected through three magic lanterns each illuminated by light of one of the primary colours, thus producing a superimposed coloured image. Prior to this and right up until the late 1950s, coloured images were produced by hand colouring black and white prints with either oil paints or water colours. Some of the best examples of this can be seen on the early Daguerrotypes and during the 1950s and 1960s on photographs produced in Hong Kong. It was this colouring of small portraits that killed off the business of painting miniatures.

Experiments continued throughout the latter half of the nineteenth century using the tri-colour techniques, still the basis of modern colour photography. In 1868 Charles Cros and Louis Ducos du Hauron both proposed the same method of recording colour, unaware of the other's work. Five years later Professor Hermann Willhelm Vogel announced his discovery of colour sensitisation using dyes. Grains of transparent coloured material were laid on a glass base and covered with a sensitive emulsion, thus acting as filters. The negative image was then printed to produce a positive and when viewed with back lighting gave an acceptable recreation of the original colours. In 1903, using the same principles, Auguste and Louis Lumière began production of a transparency emulsion coated on glass known as 'Autochrome' plates. By 1912 Agfa were producing both colour film and plates, becoming the first of the major manufacturers to do so.

Stable colour transparency film was being mass produced by the Lumière, Agfa and Dufay factories in the 1930s. In 1935 Kodak came up with a new system for the manufacture of colour transparencies and launched 'Kodachrome' onto the market. Using the chromogenous system (where substances are chemically converted to dyes), the film outclassed everything before it giving high colour saturation and fine grain.

Agfa were the first on the scene with a negative/positive process using complementary colours (yellow, cyan and magenta) which they launched in 1939, Kodak followed with their version in 1942. Around the same time Kodak also introduced a reversal printing material for use with Kodachrome transparencies. Because of the hardships of the war little colour material was available outside the USA or Germany and it would be another twenty years before it became generally available.

1.12 Instant pictures

We are all familiar with the instant photograph which proves such fun at parties and other informal gatherings. It was Edwin Land who produced the first positive black and white instant picture back in 1947 under the name of Polaroid. Expensive and messy to use they were not an immediate success, but they did find a market in professional photography. In 1961 the first instant colour positive picture was introduced taking two minutes to develop. Development was started by pulling the film through rollers, breaking the sachet of chemical which was spread over the film. The early versions required a certain temperature in order to develop properly and the most convenient place was under the armpit. A metal folder was provided to place the film in and this gave rise to the term armpit development. The majority of Polaroid images are direct positives with no negative and therefore unique, thus linking us with the Daguerrotype of the 1840s. Edwin Land was also responsible for giving photography the polarising filter, which he first produced in 1934.

1.13 Oskar Barnack

An apprentice precision machinist Oskar Barnack was a keen amateur photographer working for the Zeiss company. As early as 1910 he was working on his prototype 35mm camera developed to use the standard movie film. On offering the design to his company it was turned down as being of not much use. In 1911 he moved to the Leitz company and again put his design forward, this time it was accepted with more enthusiasm. Encouraged, Barnack developed the design but it was not until 1925 that it eventually went into production as the Leica. The camera had a focal plane shutter with a limited number of shutter speeds, a retractable lens and combined film wind and shutter tensioning. No viewing system was incorporated and a separate viewfinder had to be fitted. The film was contained in cassettes similar to those still in use today, although the Leica took 36 pictures while other makes that arrived on the scene over the next couple of years took up to 100 frames.

The miniature camera was taken up with enthusiasm by the various sections of the photographic trade, particularly the photojournalist. The camera enabled a much more candid and interpretative style of photography to develop. Today the Leica is still considered by some to be the best 35mm camera on the market.

1.14 Victor Hasselblad

Although reflex plate and roll film cameras had been around for some years, Victor Hasselblad came up with a design that would revolutionise the roll film camera. 1948 saw the launch of the Hasselblad 1600F, a single lens reflex (SLR) camera incorporating interchangeable lenses and, more importantly, interchangeable film magazines. This meant that the photographer could now shoot pictures on different film stock using the same camera body; before this the photographer would have had to carry another camera for each type of film in use. It did not take long for the Japanese camera industry to imitate the Swedish design and there are now four or five different makes using the same principles. Should you fancy picking up a second-hand Hasselblad then the next time you are passing the Moon stop off for a few minutes, there are several just lying around up for grabs.

1.15 35mm SLR

The Hasselblad principles were rapidly adopted by the manufacturers of 35mm cameras and 1957 saw the appearance of the Pentax single lens reflex. In 1959 Nikon introduced the Nikon f, a 35mm SLR fitted with a pentaprism and instant return mirror. The pentaprism corrected the reversed image normally associated with reflex cameras and the instant return mirror meant that the image was only blacked out for a very short time during exposure. The 35mm SLR soon became the industry standard taking over from the Leica and similar cameras, used by amateur and professional alike. Today's SLRs have taken photography onto a new plateau with auto exposure and auto focus facilities, leaving the photographer free to concentrate on picture structure.

1.16 Mini-labs

Probably the most significant recent advance in technology is the advent of the high street mini-lab; prior to this films would take anything up to fourteen days to process and print, through the local chemist or photographic store. Now with a conveniently located colour photo-lab in most towns, prints can be collected just one hour after the films are deposited. Intense competition means that the consumer benefits from low prices and quality guarantees. The down side to this is that it is very difficult to get black and white films processed and printed, and if one is lucky enough to find somewhere that can deal with them the price is high.

2 The camera

Everyone is familiar with cameras of one sort or another; from our early childhood we have cameras pointed at us to record our birth, first steps and other important events throughout our lives. At some stage we will want to try taking photographs for ourselves and this usually comes about by using the family camera. The first contact is likely to be a simple compact where we just point and shoot. No thought will be given to composition or the moment of exposure. The end result will be less than pleasing and we may just start asking why the picture does not come up to our expectations. The first step in improving your photography is to have an understanding of the equipment being used. In essence all cameras are simply a light tight box with a lens to focus the image, an iris diaphragm to control the amount of light and a shutter to expose the film at the required time.

2.1 Pinhole cameras

We mentioned in Chapter 1 that the first cameras were just dark rooms and later boxes. A very simple camera can be made using some basic materials and skills. One will need some black card or stiff paper, double sided sticky tape, a piece of greaseproof paper and a small piece of tin foil (see Figure 2.1).

Fold along the score lines as accurately as possible and then open out again. Using sticky tape stick the piece of tin foil over the circular hole so that it ends up on the inside of the camera. The front and back panels can now be folded into place and stuck bringing the sides round and ensuring that the final flap ends up inside the camera. This just leaves a square hole at the back of the camera over which the greaseproof paper should be stuck. Now fold and stick the hood; when in position this will enable the image to be seen very much more easily. The final task is to make the pinhole in the foil at the front of the camera. Find the centre of the hole and make a single small hole with a needle or pin. It should now be possible to obtain an image through the pinhole camera, an image that will be reversed and upside down. Taking this one stage further, in order to take a photograph, a light proof cover to fit over the back of the camera will be required.

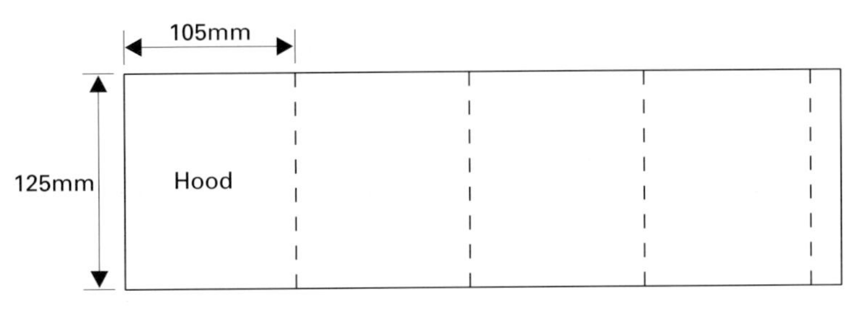

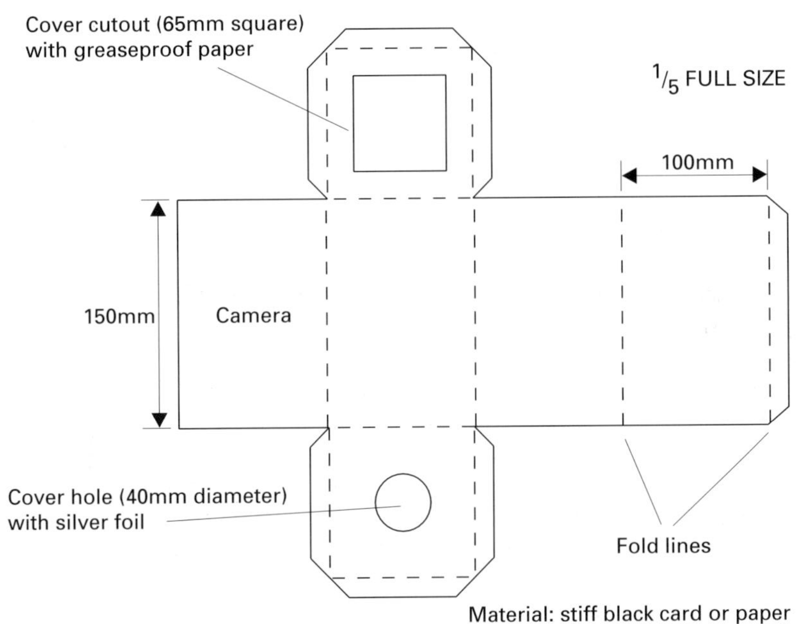

Figure 2.1 Making a pinhole camera.

Figure 2.2 A negative produced using a pinhole camera, with the positive print made from it.

The greaseproof paper is removed and replaced by a piece of photographic printing paper in a dark room, the back cover is placed over to prevent fogging and the pinhole covered up. A firm support will be needed for the camera as the exposure time will be quite long, this could be outside or on a windowsill looking out, the exposure should be made in bright sunlight in order to keep this time to a minimum. Once the camera is positioned the pinhole is uncovered and the paper left to expose for a few seconds, between 15 seconds and 1 minute depending on the brightness of the day. The paper is then removed from the camera in the dark room and processed in print developer, giving you a negative. To convert this into a positive the negative is placed on top of another piece of paper and covered by a sheet of glass; this is then exposed to light, either under the enlarger or by ordinary household lamp. Exposure calculation is achieved by making a test strip (see Chapter 12 for printing and processing methods). The construction of the paper will obviously have an effect on the quality of the image, but none the less it should be a remarkable result for such a basic camera. The resultant camera is a simple version of the first box cameras of the turn of the century, and if this exercise is carried out the results achieved will be very similar to the first efforts of Fox Talbot (see Figure 2.2)

2.2 Simple cameras

Todays simple cameras are somewhat more sophisticated but not that far removed from the pinhole version. A simple lens has been introduced along with a shutter, aperture control and viewfinder. The viewfinder is placed near the top right hand corner of the camera and is therefore displaced both laterally and vertically from the lens which is usually in the centre of the camera. This causes 'parallax' error, where the lens does not see the same view as the photographer (see Figure 2.3). Fixed focus, where the lens is set at the 'hyperfocal' distance giving acceptably sharp focus from 2 metres to infinity, is normal. Exposure is set for use with ISO 100 or 200 film giving a shutter speed of around 1/40 second, therefore requiring a steady hand to avoid camera shake. On the more expensive models there is limited control over the aperture and focus, two or three positions indicated by very simple symbols. Their lineage starts with the wood and metal roll film box cameras of the turn of the century, remaining relatively unchanged throughout the 1930s and 1940s. With the advent of bakelite a smoother, more streamlined version appeared after the Second World War, leading to the introduction of modern plastics in the instamatic cameras of the early 1970s. Today's simple cameras use 110 cartridges or 35mm film but still use the same principles as their predecessors (see Figures 2.4 and 2.5).

2.3 Compact cameras

The 35mm compact camera is the next step up the equipment ladder and contains a few added features. The viewfinder viewing system remains and therefore the camera still suffers from parallax, however, there is usually some form of

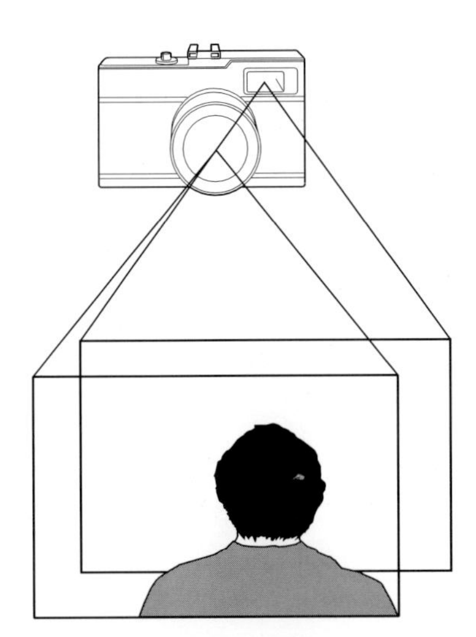

The viewfinder may have 'parallax compensation' marks when photographing a subject nearer than 2 metres

Figure 2.3 Parallax error, where the viewing system and taking system of a camera see different views.

Figure 2.4 A range of box cameras from 1932 to 1980.

Figure 2.5 Artistic photographs could be produced using the box camera.

adjustment guide built-into the viewfinder. Many will still be fixed focus and manually operated, but the trend is towards more automation with focusing, exposure and film transport all carried out by the camera. Even the film speed will be set automatically using the DX coding system (see Chapter 4 on film). For high contrast lighting conditions backlight compensation is available, increasing the exposure by two or three times. This eliminates human error and leaves the photographer free to concentrate on picture structure.

Many accessories can be fitted, such as filters, close up lenses and flash guns, although many cameras come with built-in flash. The top of the range have the facility to give very long exposure times for night time photography, with the option to switch the flash off. A self-timer is often included to enable the photographer to leave the camera and appear in the picture. Traditionally these cameras are fitted with a short focal length lens, some will have the ability to switch to a built-in long focal length lens, but power zooms are becoming more popular giving the camera a versatility close to that of an expensive 35mm SLR. Another useful feature introduced in the past couple of years is the ability to take long thin images, ideal for landscape work, as well as the standard size frame. For the forgetful among us a data back, giving date and sometimes time, is offered on some models.

For the beginner who has serious intentions this is probably the best buy, providing a reasonable quality image with a lightweight, convenient size camera at a moderate price. The film is readily available world-wide and easily processed in any town.

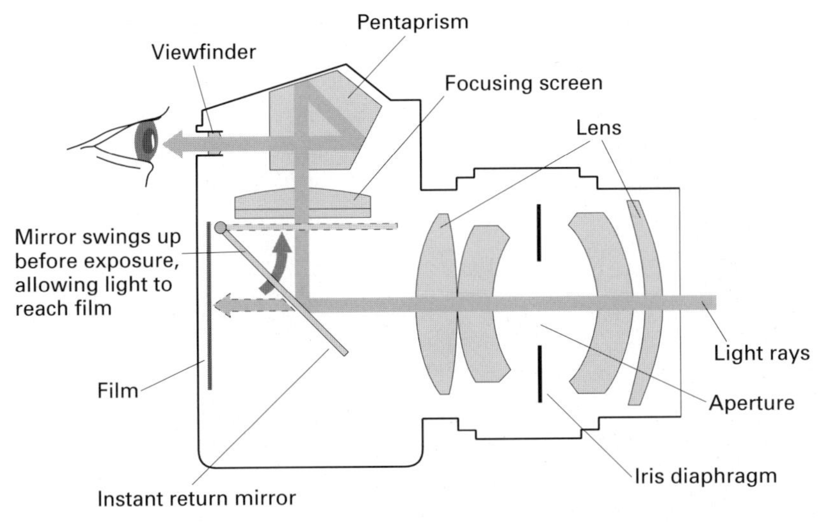

Figure 2.6 Cross-section of a modern 35mm SLR.

2.4 35mm single lens reflex (SLR) cameras

The 35mm SLR camera is very versatile and has become the standard tool of amateurs and many professionals alike. A viewing and focusing system through the taking lens avoids parallax problems and interchangeable lenses make it highly flexible (see Figure 2.6).

Light passes through the camera lens and is reflected by a mirror onto the focus screen. The image is viewed through an eyepiece via the pentaprism, this allows the subject to be seen the right way round, and shows approximately 90–95% of the image that will appear on the film. Focusing is achieved by use of the fresnal screen just below the pentaprism, this often incorporates a split image to assist in sharp focus. The image is lost for a split second during exposure as the mirror lifts to allow the light to reach the film. Because the subject is viewed through the taking lens the camera does not suffer from parallax, which means you photograph what you see, particularly important in close up photography.

Film sensitivity is set on the ISO dial or by using the DX coding system, this enables the light meter in the camera to calculate the correct exposure. This is known as through the lens (TTL) metering and the sensors for the light meter are situated around the pentaprism close to the focus screen. There are four options available for taking exposure readings through the camera: (1) Manual, here there is usually a needle or illuminated + and – signs that need to be centred on an 0, where the photographer adjusts the shutter speed and aperture to achieve this. (2) Shutter priority, where the photographer sets the shutter speed most suited to the type of picture being taken, and the camera works out the aperture. (3) Aperture priority, here the photographer selects the aperture according to the depth of field required and the camera will set the appropriate shutter speed. (4) Program, where the camera works everything out; the more expensive cameras have a system whereby the photographer can tell it the sort of picture being taken, i.e. portrait, landscape, etc.; This enables the camera to choose between shutter speed or aperture

Figure 2.7 Inside a 35mm SLR, showing mirror, pentaprism and computer.

as being the most important (see Figure 2.7).

The 35mm SLR is fitted with a focal plane shutter, so called because it is situated immediately in front of the film plane, giving a range of speeds from one second to 1/12 000 second and these are set on a shutter speed dial, or a liquid crystal display (LCD). The typical full range is as follows 1, 2, 4, 8, 15, 30, 60, 125, 250, 500, 1000, 2000, with some cameras giving 4000, 8000, and even 12 000. With the exception of 1 all the figures represent fractions of a second. Many electronic cameras will also give whole seconds up to 30s and even speeds in between the normal range, such as 1/90, 1/45, etc.

Fabric blinds have largely been replaced by metal shutter blades, the direction of travel depends upon the manufacturer, either vertically or horizontally. Such a large selection of shutter speeds enables the photographer to chose the one most appropriate for the job in hand. For hand held photography a speed of 1/125 second is adequate for most tasks when using a standard 50mm lens, for longer lenses a shutter speed equal to the focal length should be used, i.e. 1/500 second for a 500mm lens. Never use a speed slower than 1/60 second when hand holding the camera as camera shake will result unless you have an extremely steady hold. For all slow shutter speeds and long lenses a tripod, or some other form of support, should be used in conjunction with a cable release. For inanimate subjects the shutter speed will be dictated by the depth of field required, see Chapter 3 on lenses. If one is out to capture shots of moving objects then a high shutter speed will be required, the choice will depend on the speed and direction of travel of your subject. A higher speed will be needed if the subject is moving across your field of vision as against coming towards you. Subjects up to 15 kilometres per hour (kph) head on 1/125, across your view 1/500, up to 100kph head on 1/500, across your view 1/1000. Although one can give guidelines, it is far better for you to experiment with different speeds and decide for yourself which suits your purposes. Another setting found on the shutter speed dial is B, this is brief, sometimes called bulb, where the shutter will remain open as long as pressure is maintained on the shutter release button. Used in conjunction with a locking cable release very long exposure times, minutes or even hours, can be achieved. The shutter release button is normally found on the top of the camera alongside the shutter speed dial and will often have a small threaded hole in it for a cable release. If there is no hole then the cable release will fit elsewhere on the body, very often being an electronic connection and costing a small fortune. On a very few models there is no facility for a cable release; this can be overcome by the use of an adaptor which fits over the top of the shutter release button.

Alongside the shutter speed dial is the film advance lever, not found on motor-drive models. As the name suggests it winds the film on by one frame after each exposure and also tensions the shutter ready for the next photograph. A motor wind will enable the photographer to take single pictures or a continuous run, up to six frames per second. On a few more expensive models there is a facility which enables the photographer to tension the shutter without moving the film on for double or multiple exposures. Whilst the camera manufacturer will not guarantee that the film will not move at all, it works well enough for most practical purposes.

At the other end of the camera is the film rewind knob which rewinds the film into the cassette after exposure; on many cameras this is done by motor. Once the leader of the film is engaged in the take up spool the shutter release button must be fired and the film advanced until both sets of sprocket holes are engaged on the sprocket wheel drive. If this is not done one risks the film becoming detached and taking all the pictures on the first frame. Once the film is engaged correctly the camera back can be closed and the tension taken up by rewinding the film rewind knob. When the first two or three shots are fired to clear the fogged film from the gate the rewind knob will also rotate, letting one know that the film is transporting through the camera properly (see Figure 2.8).

Around the film rewind knob or within the shutter speed dial can be found the film ISO settings. These must be set according to the ISO of the film in use, failure to do so will result in incorrect exposure and poor quality pictures. On electronic and some manual cameras this is done using the DX coding system. Within the LCD display or around the film rewind knob the exposure compensation dial can be found (see Chapter 5 on exposure). On top of the pentaprism housing is the hot shoe, for fitting small flash guns. The term comes from the fact that the electrical connection to fire the flash is situated within the shoe. Although all 35mm SLRs are fitted with a hot shoe for flash operation many also have a separate flash synchronisation socket on the front of the camera, often protected by a rubber cap. This enables off camera operation, essential for the more serious photographer. Referring back to the shutter speed dial the flash synchonisation speed will be found either picked out in red or with an X or ϟ symbol alongside it.

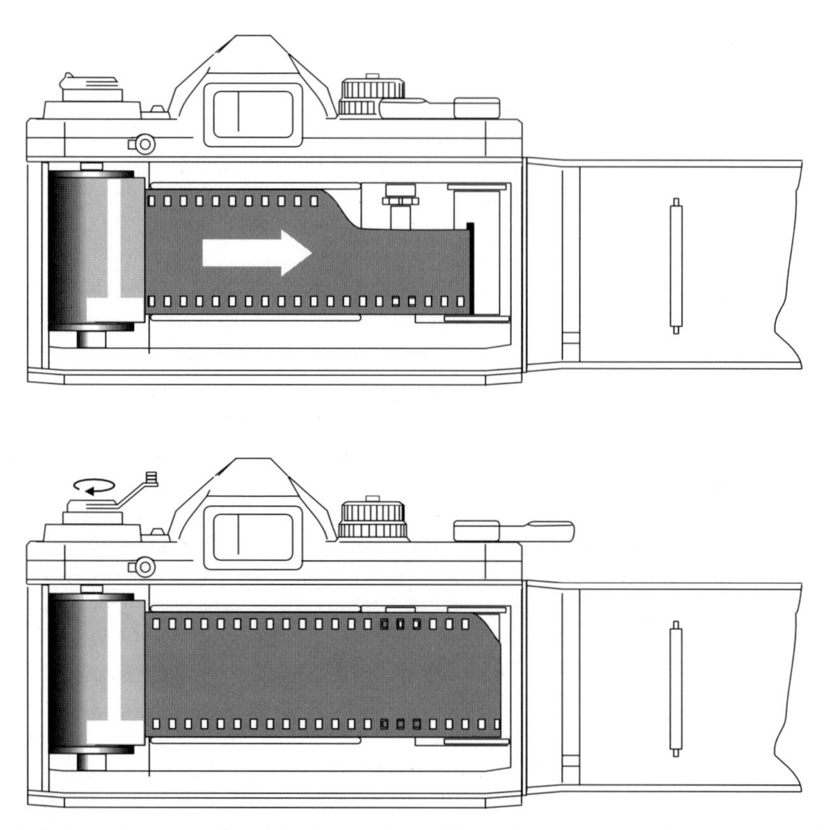

Figure 2.8 Loading the film into the camera: Open the camera back in the shade by pulling the film rewind knob up. Place cassette into left hand compartment and push rewind knob back down. Insert film leader into take-up spool and wind film forward until both sets of sprocket holes are engaged on the sprocket wheel teeth. Close back of camera and tension film by turning rewind knob clockwise, now fire three shots to bring counter to number 1.

After the film has been exposed it has to be rewound into its cassette. On the bottom, rear and sometimes front of the camera you will find the sprocket wheel release button which must be pressed before film rewind is attempted. Failure to do this will result in the sprocket holes of the film being torn off rendering the film useless, because it is impossible to process. Two common mistakes made on a regular basis by beginners are that of forgetting to release the sprocket wheel before rewinding the film and being unaware that the film is finished by not watching the counter and then using excessive force to wind on thereby ripping the film out of the cassette. When rewinding the film there should be a resistance, if the rewind knob is free and not under tension then the film has been pulled out of the cassette. To check, put the lens cap on and fire the shutter and wind the film on, if the rewind knob does not move this confirms that the film is no longer connected. DO NOT OPEN the back of the camera as this will ruin all the film. Instead take the camera and a film pot into a totally dark room, open the back and pull the film off the take up spool, roll gently and place in film pot, close lid and seal with tape. Mark the outside of the film pot with make and ISO rating of film and be sure to tell the process house what has happened. I watched one amateur open the back of his friend's camera to find that it had been pulled out of the cassette and state, 'you've ruined your film', whereas in truth he had done so by opening the back.

If the camera does not have a built-in motordrive then a quick look at the bottom of the body will tell you if one can be fitted. A keyway under the sprocket drive and series of electrical contacts will be found.

Other useful facilities include the self-timer or delayed action function. Here the firing of the shutter can be delayed by ten or more seconds to enable the photographer to appear in the picture. The position of this will vary quite considerably and take the form of a turning knob or switch. Most will provide an audible indication of working and some will also provide a flashing light, both of which will increase in speed as the time expires. On the base of the camera there is a larger threaded hole for the fitting of tripods or flash gun brackets, this is an industry standard bush common to all manufacturers.

Moving to the inside of the camera, on the back of the door is the film pressure plate which holds the film flat during exposure. This must not be touched for fear of damaging the springs or transferring grease to it. On the left of the camera is the cassette compartment possibly with the DX coding sensors. In the middle the shutter blades can be seen, again these must not be touched as buckling may result causing inaccurrate operation. Grease from fingers could also cause the blades to stick and give incorrect speeds or cease operating altogether. The inside of the camera should be kept clean with a blower brush, being careful not to get hairs trapped in the shutter blades. This should be carried out before loading every film, as minute particles of film and dust will be deposited as the film transports through the camera. Taking the lens off gives access to the mirror compartment and this should also be kept clean by light brushing. The mirror is very often a silvered metal plate rather than glass so a proprietary glass cleaner must not be used otherwise the surface will be destroyed. Should the mirror become misty then a gentle wipe with a small piece of very soft chamois is sufficient. The bottom of the focusing screen can also be cleared of dust by a light brushing. Some people may prefer to use compressed air instead of a brush but remember that compressed air is always damp and the force of it could also cause problems by forcing dust into spaces between the pentaprism and focus screen.

More general care of the camera during operation is a matter of common sense. Never leave your camera near a window where it will get very hot, or in a moist atmosphere. When photographing on or near water place the body in a plastic bag with just the lens protruding and sealed either with tape or an elastic band. The same trick applies for beaches or deserts to keep the sand out, whereever you are always keep the camera bag closed when not in use. All modern cameras have batteries and some form of condition check which should be used regularly. If the camera is going to be out of use for extended periods of time then the batteries should be removed. The life of a battery will depend on how many films are put through the camera and how many functions it operates, but on average they will last between 18 months and two years. Many will cease to function in low temperatures, below –5°C, and if they are on their last legs the cold will finish them off. It is therefore advisable to carry spares in the camera bag and on your person in cold conditions. Even a good battery might fail once it gets too cold but can often be brought back to life by warming, so by frequent changing of batteries the camera will continue to operate in very low temperatures. The business of always leaving the shutter untensioned is open to question, cameras have been in use for twenty years or more with the shutter left tensioned to no ill effect.

2.5 Autofocus cameras

It is traditional to focus the camera image manually using a fresnel focus screen or split image finder, however, more and more cameras are being fitted with autofocus. Two types of autofocus are used in cameras, active and passive, using either infra-red or sonic signals to operate. The active system focuses on the subject and will continue to search for optimum focus as the camera is moved. The drawback to the system is that it has a narrow angle of acceptance and will only focus in the centre of the viewfinder. That, of course, will present problems when the subject is situated towards one side of the frame and the camera is focusing in the centre, leaving the subject blurred. A focus lock can be found on some models enabling one to focus with the subject in the centre of the frame, lock the focus, and then recompose the picture.

With the passive system the autofocus only works on demand and once focused on the subject will not change when the composition is altered. This version allows much more freedom with picture structure and is likely to give better results. An indication of correct focus is often given in the viewfinder by way of an LED. A similar system is used on some manually focused cameras where an LED lets the photographer know when correct focus is achieved.

On the more sophisticated cameras the autofocus function is coupled with the various picture programs available to give maximum depth of field (see Chapter 3 on lenses) in the landscape mode, or restricted depth of field for portrait work.

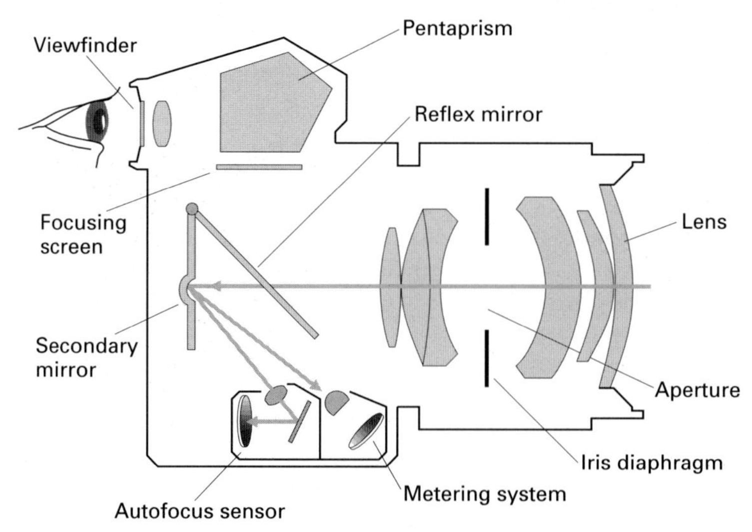

Figure 2.9 Cross-section of 35mm camera, showing autofocus sensors.

Autofocus should be more accurate and reliable than manual focus and relieve the photographer of the often tiring task of focusing, particularly with long lenses and in low light conditions (see Figure 2.9).

2.6 Medium format cameras

This is the term given to a series of cameras that take roll film (120) and give a selection of image sizes. The first of these is the twin lens reflex (TLR) which first came onto the market in 1932. As the name suggests the camera is fitted with two lenses, one for viewing and one for taking. The lenses are mounted on a common panel one above the other, the image from the viewing lens reaches the focusing screen via a mirror, making it laterally reversed. The distances between lenses and focus screen and film are equal, so that when the image is in focus on the viewing screen it will also be in focus on the film. The viewing screen is surrounded by a hood to shield it from excess light, this usually incorporates a magnifier for ease of focusing. All these types of cameras suffer from parallax when taking close up pictures, however some models do overcome the problem by having geared lenses, where the viewing lens dips towards the taking lens. The vast majority of TLRs have fixed standard focal length lenses with between the lens shutters, giving a maximum speed of 1/500 second (see Figure 2.10).

Figure 2.10 Voigtländer Brilliant and Superb, two of the first twin lens reflex cameras made in Germany in 1932.

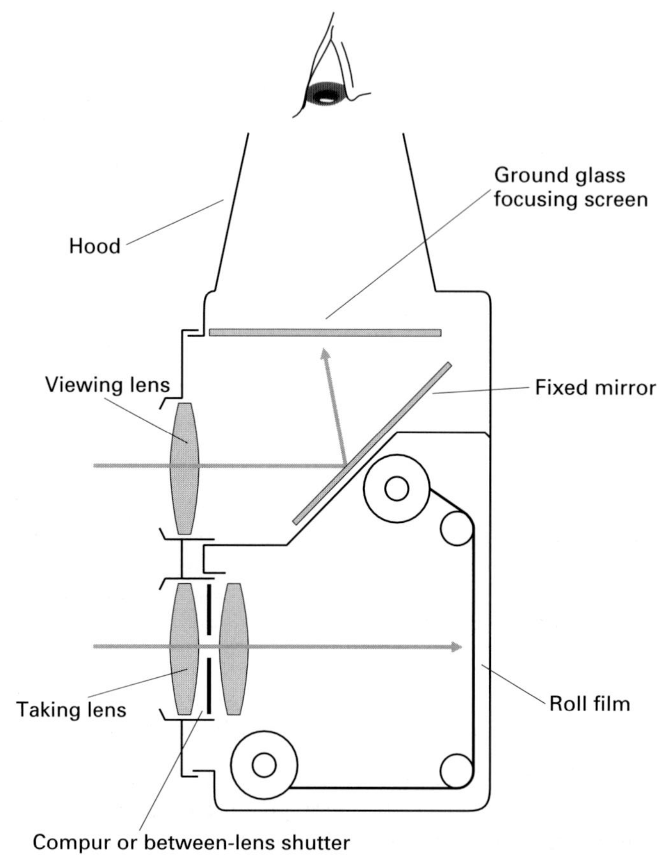

Figure 2.11 Cross-section of a twin lens reflex roll film camera.

One or two models are available with interchangeable lenses, this means of course that both the viewing and taking lens have to be changed making it a rather expensive option. The major advantage is that they are fitted with a bellows unit enabling close up photography to be carried out without the addition of close up lenses. Having separate viewing and taking lenses means that the subject is in view at all times, a very important consideration in portraiture. The shutter is very quiet in operation and this has distinct advantages when undertaking any informal or candid portraiture (see Figure 2.11).

Still preferred by many professionals, these cameras are manually operated with shutter speeds and apertures being set by hand. Film advance is also a manual operation as is exposure calculation by use of an off camera light meter, although one or two are fitted with a built-in meter. The laterally reversed image makes it difficult, if not impossible, to use this sort of camera on its side or upside down, hence the reason for a square format.

To achieve the versatility of the 35mm SLR and quality of medium format cameras it is logical to combine the two systems; this is exactly what has happened with the medium format single lens reflex (see Figure 2.12). Introduced in 1945 by Hasselblad there are now many different types on the market. The image size

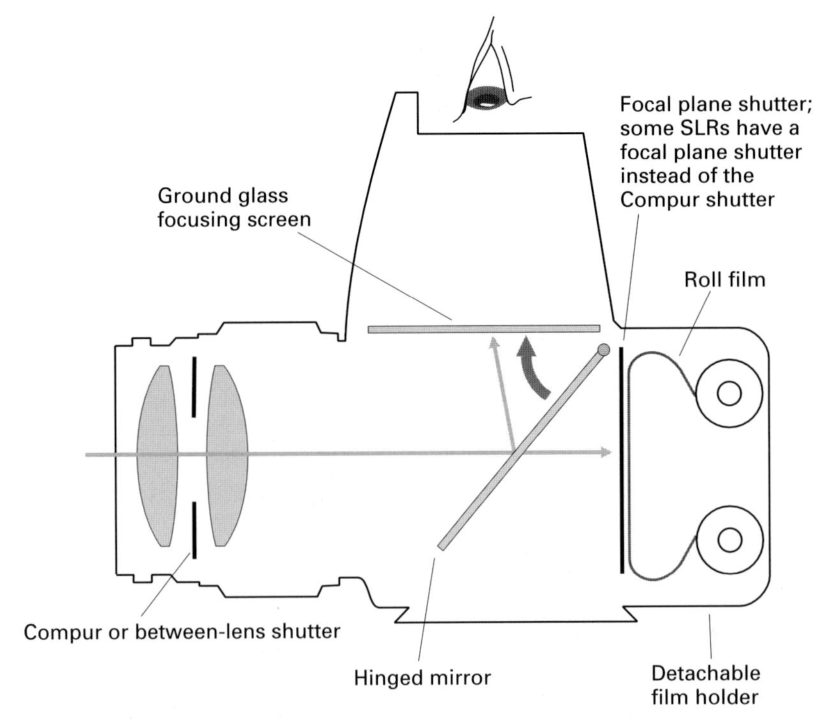

Figure 2.12 Cross-section of a medium format single lens reflex camera.

remains 6cm wide but the length will vary according to the model in use, typically 6 × 4.5cm, 6 × 6cm, 6 × 7cm and 6 × 9cm, giving 15, 12 or 8 shots per roll. Like its smaller brother the camera comes with interchangeable lenses, most are fitted with between the lens shutters and give a maximum speed of 1/500 second, some incorporate the focal plane shutter and give speeds up to 1/2000 second. Greater versatility is achieved by virtue of the fact that the camera body can be fitted for either reflex viewing, as with the TLR, or pentaprism as with the 35mm SLR. Added to this, they also come with interchangeable film backs, enabling the photographer to change film types part way through a roll. They are obviously more bulky and heavier than their 35mm counterpart, but most people who use them appreciate that little extra weight for stability. Motorwind for film advance for single shot or continuous run can be fitted as can an autoexposure facility.

2.7 Large format cameras

These cameras are direct descendents of the original camera obscuras and have evolved from the plate cameras in use over 150 years ago. Film sizes range from 5 × 4 to 20 × 16 in, but the glass plate has been replaced by sheet film. Two types of large format cameras are available today, the baseboard and the monorail. The baseboard camera is built around a box housing with a drop down front, the lens being pulled out on runners. The lens panel is interchangeable and each has a between the lens shutter. At the back is the ground glass screen onto which the

Figure 2.13 TLRs and some medium format SLRs produce square images.

image is projected, this is shielded by a collapsable hood. A direct viewing system means that the camera does not suffer from parallax error and you take what you see, unfortunately what you see is upside down and back to front. The viewing screen is fitted on springs and is moved out to enable the film holder to be placed for exposure. Sheets of film are placed in a light tight double dark slide containing two sheets and once placed in a camera a sheath is withdrawn to allow exposure, the slide is then reversed and the second exposure made.

These cameras are considerably more versatile than either the 35mm or medium format types by virtue of their movements (see Figure 2.14). Camera movements allow the lens panel and the film panel to be moved about a central or base axis thus controlling the shape and focus of the image.

The other type of large format camera is a monorail, here the camera is fitted to a

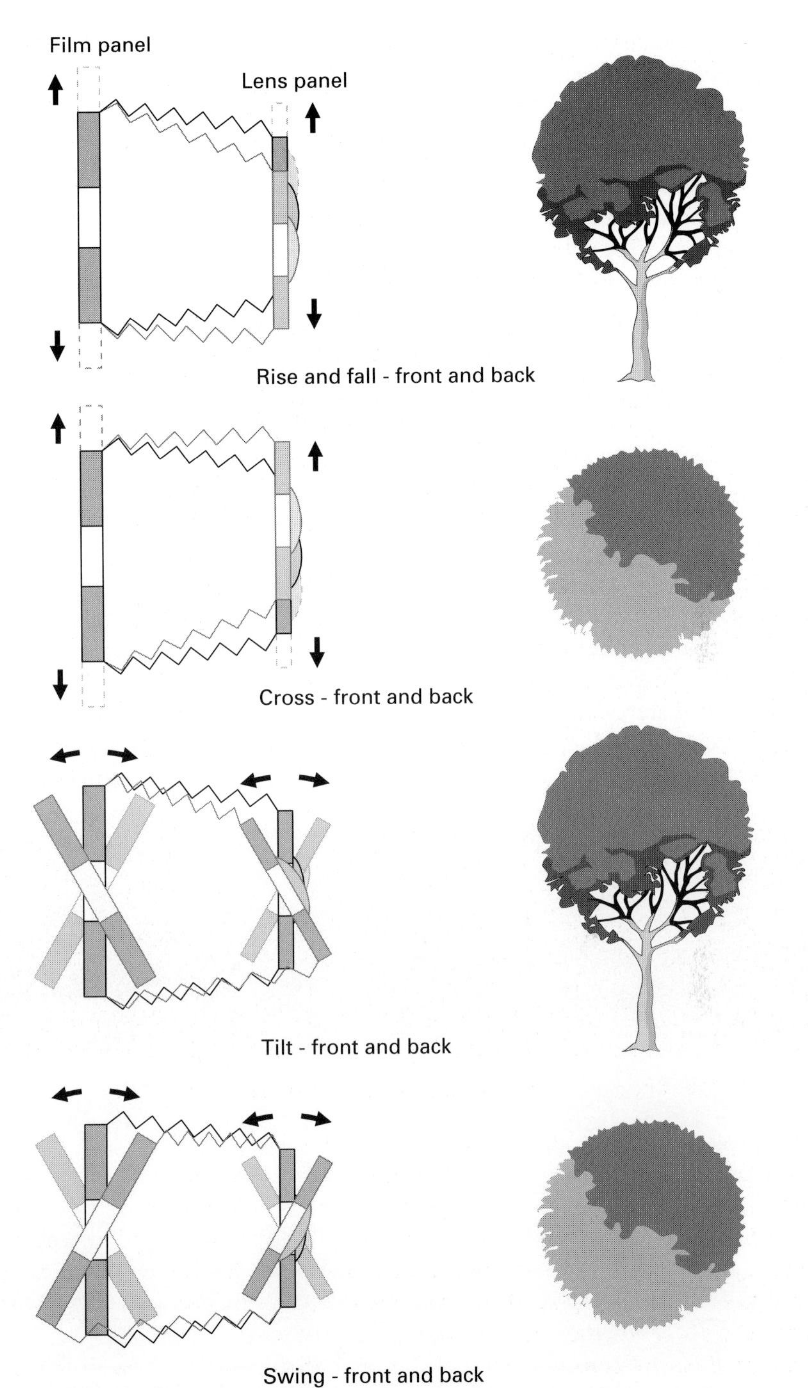

Figure 2.14 Large format camera movements.

single central rail instead of a baseboard. All the movements are made around central vertical and horizontal axes. There are five movements for both the lens and film panels which can be used independently or in combination with each other.

- *Rising front is where the lens is moved upwards remaining parallel to the film plane.*
- *Falling front is moving the lens downwards whilst remaining parallel to the film plane.*
- *Cross front is where the lens is moved either to the left or right of the central axis remaining parallel to the film plane.*
- *Swing front enables the lens to be turned left or right about the central vertical axis.*
- *Tilt front is the pivoting of the lens to look up or down about the horizontal axis.*

Other terms are used to describe these movements, for instance drop front instead of falling front and swing front is sometimes used to describe movement about both the vertical and horizontal axes. Exactly the same names are applied to the movement of the film panel, rising back, swing back, etc.

When photographing any tall object with a 35mm or medium format camera the camera has to be tilted upwards in order to get the top in. This results in converging verticals with the sides of the object tapering into the distance. Rising front has a similar effect to raising the whole camera up enabling the top of the object to be included in the picture and at the same time keep the sides parallel. If there is insufficient movement in the lens panel then the film panel can be dropped giving the effect of further rise front. Care must be taken to ensure that the edges of the image do not start darkening as this means that the limit of the lens covering power has been reached. To ensure sharp focus the front and back panels must be kept parallel during this operation. All actions have an opposite reaction and

Figure 2.15 By using camera movements, distortion within a picture can be kept to a minimum.

the price paid for using this movement is an elongation of objects near to the edges of the image area.

Falling front is used in exactly the opposite way where the camera viewpoint needs to be lower without tilting the camera and again suffering from converging verticals. The occasions for using this movement in the field are limited and it is much more common to find it in use in the studio.

Cross front is used for similar reasons as rising front but on the horizontal plane. If a square on viewpoint cannot be achieved then the use of cross front will enable a parallel image to be gained from an oblique viewpoint. This is useful when photographing glass, to prevent the camera's own reflection being seen.

Swing front affects the depth of field, by turning the lens panel towards the plane of the object being photographed a greater depth of field can be achieved. Again there is the risk of cut off at the edges so care must be taken in using it, however, combining this movement with swing back can minimise the cut off. Tilting front works in the same way as swing front but in the vertical plane.

If swing and tilt front are in use the plane of focus will be changed and no longer be parallel to the film. Using swing and tilt back in the corresponding combination with front movements will bring the film back into the plane of focus. Back movements can also alter the shape of the image quite dramatically, so as with everything in photography, it is a matter of compromise. Although movements are used on their own it is much more likely that they would be used in combination; practice and experimentation is the only way to gain a full understanding of such things.

So why the need for larger formats? Well simply quality, the larger the original negative or transparency the better the definition and image sharpness, the more information that can be recorded, and of course the larger the negative the less magnification required when printing.

2.8 Camera technique

When using any type of camera smooth operation is the key to sharp clear photographs. With small hand held cameras the support will normally be the photographer so it is important that a steady posture is taken up. The feet should be between 45 and 60cms apart and flat on the ground, the camera held in both hands firmly ensuring that the fingers are clear of the lens. With the viewfinder placed at eye level the arms should be kept vertical and the elbows tucked into the side of the chest. Holding the camera with just the finger tips and arms stuck out like wings is asking for trouble. The shutter release is squeezed gently so as not to induce any downward movement of the camera. Although a medium format camera can be hand held, it is to be recommended that a tripod be used whenever possible, and of course large format cameras have to be used on a tripod at all times. If nothing else, it will make the photographer take time over setting up the photograph.

Try not to take too long in arranging photographs of people as they will soon become bored and wander off. On the other hand, having set the camera up for a landscape or building shot, one may have to wait for some time for right lighting, or unwanted 'bodies' to move out of the way.

Figure 2.16 It is never too early to learn good camera techniques.

3 Lenses

The camera is just a light tight box which has little effect on the quality of the final image, in spite of ever more sophistication. The lens, on the other hand, does make the difference between poor and excellent technical quality in a photograph. It is far better to have a middle of the range camera fitted with the best lens that can be afforded than to spend a disproportionate amount on the body leaving little for the lens. Modern lenses are designed and built to eliminate the faults so common in the early days and there is not a great deal to choose between the best makes. Since the earliest days of photography the lens has been, and continues to be, looked after with tender loving care. As with all things photographic, cleanliness comes before godliness and steps must be taken to protect and keep the glass clean (see Figure 3.1).

3.1 Simple lenses

The first thing to understand is what happens to light when it passes through a glass surface. Light travels in straight lines and when it strikes any surface three things will happen, if the object is solid then some of the light will be reflected and some absorbed, if the object is transparent then the third thing will also occur, transmission. Using a thick piece of glass two of the three are observable, reflection and transmission, absorption is perhaps noticeable in the fact that the light passing out the other side is less intense. Light travels at 300 000 k per second (kps) but when it enters another substance it is slowed down, in glass by one third to 200 000 kps. Something else also occurs with light striking the surface obliquely and that is the bending of the rays, called refraction; light entering at right angles is not affected (see Figure 3.2). With a flat surface the ray is always bent towards the normal, an imaginary line at right angles to the surface being entered, on exiting the ray is bent away from the normal.

Modern lenses are designed and manufactured to such a high standard that almost no light is reflected or absorbed and therefore the film receives the

Figure 3.1 Care of the lens has always been important; this is a lens and its travelling trunk from the 1870s.

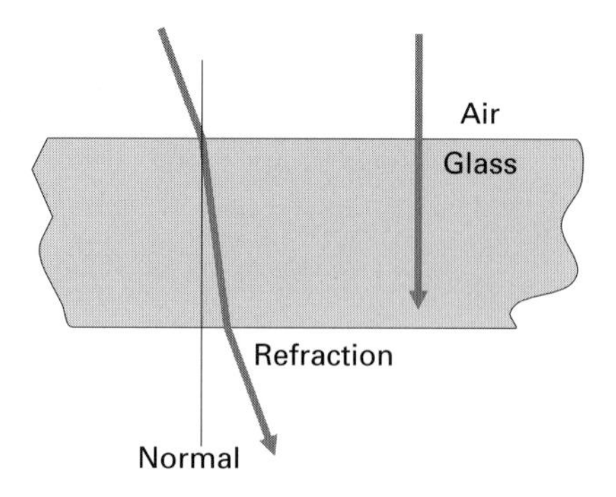

Figure 3.2 Refraction: light entering a glass surface obliquely will be bent towards the normal, on exiting the light is bent away from the normal. Light striking at right angles is unaffected.

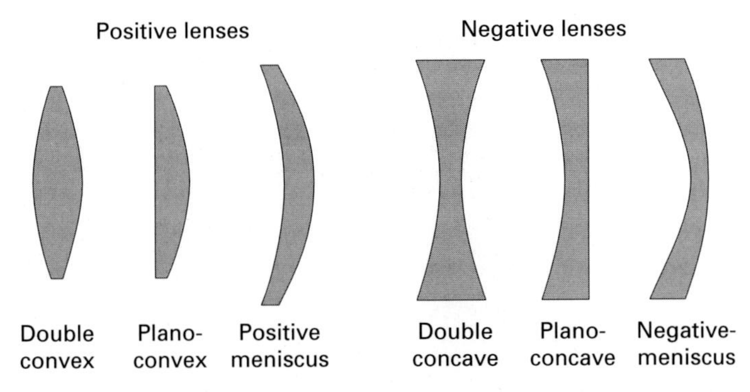

Figure 3.3 Simple positive and negative lens elements.

maximum available for exposure. In poor quality lenses other things may also happen to the light and these are known as aberrations.

3.2 Spherical aberration

The surface of a lens element is nearly always curved and this is a major factor in the way in which an image is formed. Single element lenses are by far the most economical to produce but not the ideal for image formation. With spherical aberration rays of light passing through the centre of the lens come to a focus further away than those passing through the edges (see Figure 3.4). This results in an unsharp image which can be minimised by closing the aperture down. In a compound lens it is cured by introducing a negative surface of equal power.

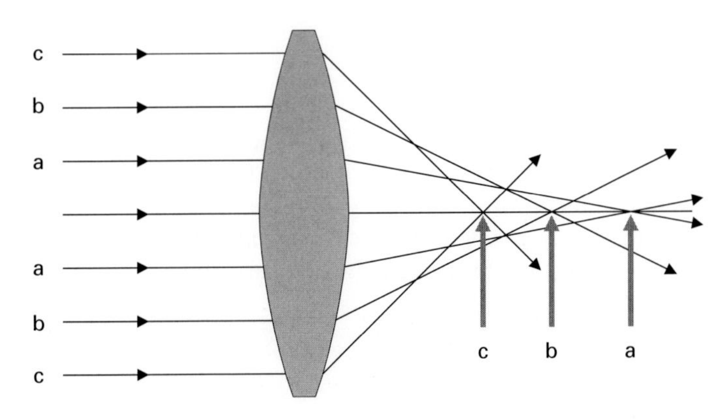

Figure 3.4 Spherical aberration.

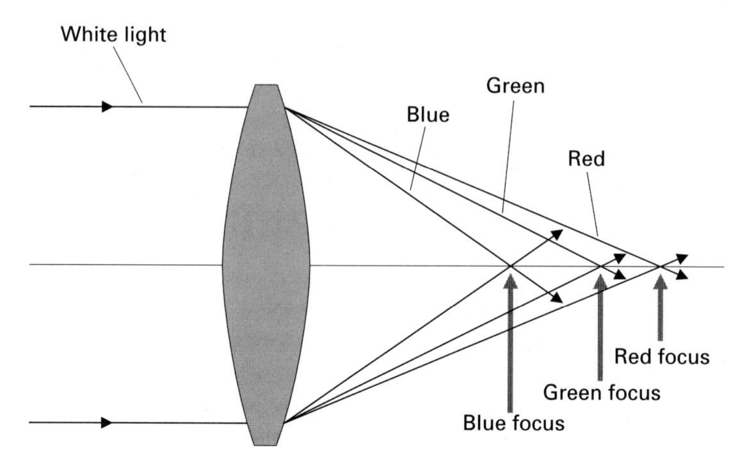

Figure 3.5 Chromatic aberration.

3.3 Chromatic aberration

This is where white light entering the lens is split into the spectral colours each of which is brought to a different focus (see Figure 3.5). The blue end of the spectrum is brought to a focus closer to the lens than the red end. The eye has its maximum sensitivity in the green band so when a lens suffering from chromatic aberration is focused the red and blue bands will be out of focus. Again this can be overcome to some extent by closing down the aperture or by introducing another element with a negative surface. In 1757 John Dolland did just that, producing what he termed an achromatic lens.

3.4 Coma

This form of aberration is similar to spherical aberration but concerns rays of light entering a lens obliquely. Although all the rays focus on the same plane they do so at different distances from the lens, giving the image an elongated appearance (see Figure 3.6). This is easily overcome by restricting the area of the lens through which the light passes, i.e. by closing the aperture down.

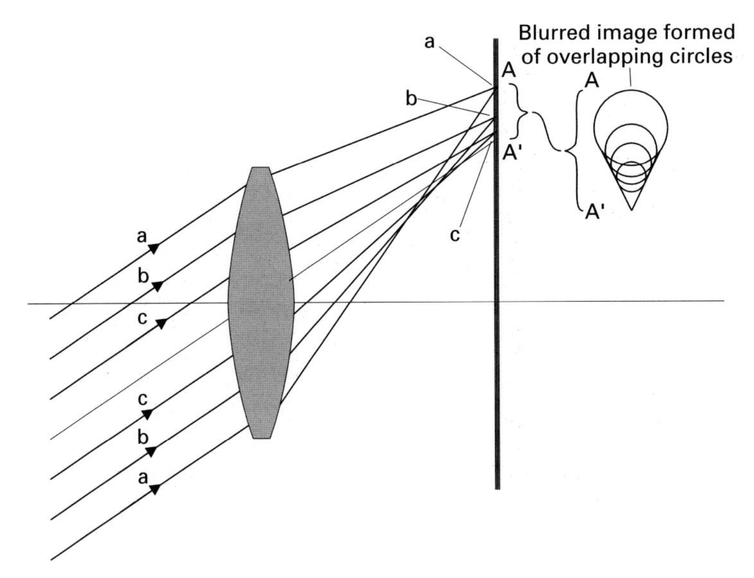

Figure 3.6 Coma.

3.5 Distortion

This form of aberration affects the shape of the image and not the sharpness. With barrel distortion lines are bent inwards and become progressively more distorted towards the edge of the image area, with pincushion distortion the lines are bent outwards (see Figure 3.7). The problems can be overcome by using a symmetrically constructed lens where one element produces barrel distortion and the other pincushion distortion, thus cancelling each other out.

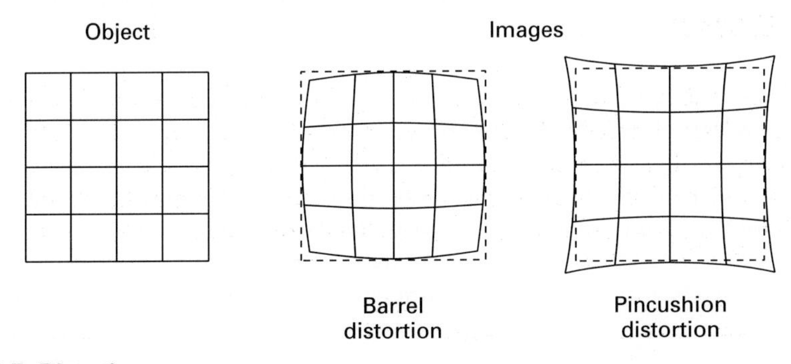

Figure 3.7 Distortion.

3.6 Astigmatism

As with the human eye astigmatism affects only the edges of the lens rendering point objects as either lines or larger circles. The rays of light passing through the lens will come to a different focal point on both the horizontal and vertical axes. Therefore, depending on the relationship of the object to the lens axis, either the vertical or horizontal lines will be out of focus while the other will be sharp (see Figure 3.8).

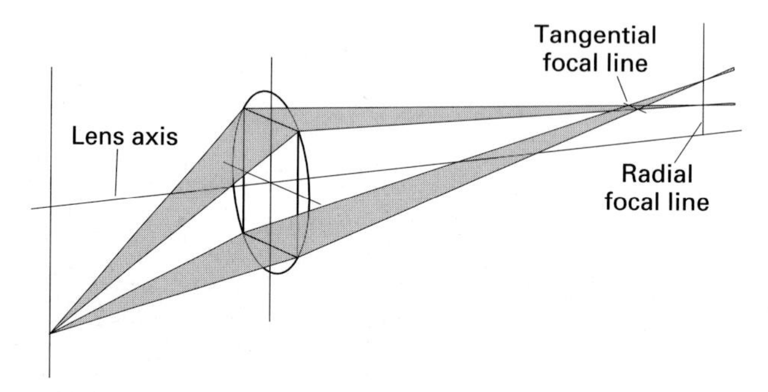

Figure 3.8 Astigmatism.

3.7 Resolving power

A lens's ability to define fine detail is termed its resolving power, this is expressed in terms of lines per mm. A lens's resolving power is affected by all the aberrations, some will affect the image at large apertures and others at small apertures. Thus a lens will operate at its best in the middle of the range, around *f*/8. In terms of photography, resolving power is also affected by the ability of the film to record those lines.

3.8 Compound lenses

A compound lens is one which is made up of several elements which when combined, eliminate or reduce the effect of aberrations and determines the focal length and angle of view of that lens. Simple elements are used on their own or together, where two or more elements are stuck together they are known as a group (see Figure 3.9). With advances in lens technology manufacturers have largely overcome aberration problems, or learnt to control them in modern compound lenses and resolving power is of the highest order. Perhaps the most common aberration is distortion, particularly among the cheap and very wide angle lenses.

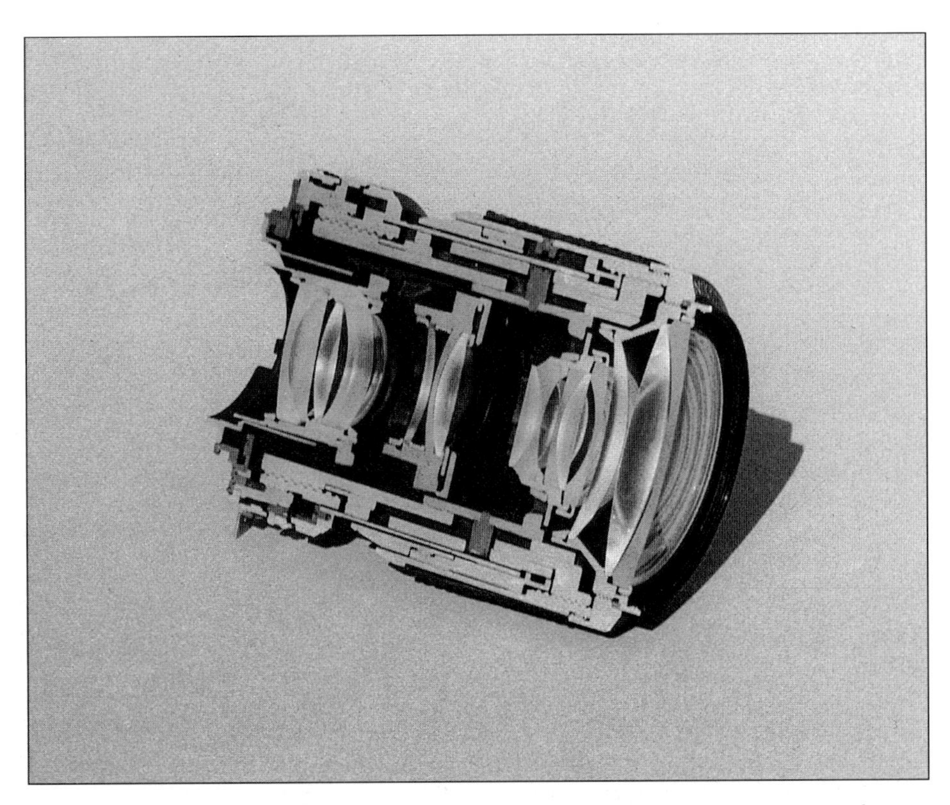

Figure 3.9 A segmented Nikkor 35–105mm zoom lens, showing various elements in use.

3.9 Focal length

'Focal length' is the term used to define the magnifying power of a lens and is today measured in mm, the longer the focal length the greater the magnification. The focal length of a lens is the distance between the lens 'node' and the film plane, when that lens is focused at infinity. On a simple lens the node will be in the centre of the element where the rays of light cross, for compound lenses it will vary according to construction. As the subject comes closer to the lens so the distance between the lens and film plane increases; look at your camera and see how the lens move in and out as you turn the focusing ring. A standard focal length lens is one where the measurement between the lens and film equals that of the diagonal of the image on the film (see Figure 3.10). A standard focal length lens also has an angle of view and perspective similar to that of a human eye (not both) when held still, approximately 53°. Try this for yourself, it will be quite difficult because of the brain's ability to be selective.

A standard focal length lens for 35mm format should be 43.3mm, but most manufacturers standardise on 50mm, for medium format cameras standard focal lengths are 75mm for 6 × 4.5, 84.8mm for 6 × 6 which is rounded down to 80mm and 108mm for 6 × 9 rounded up to 110mm. For the large format 5 × 4in it should be 6.5in but this is rounded down to 150mm.

Any lens with a focal length of less than the standard is termed a short focal

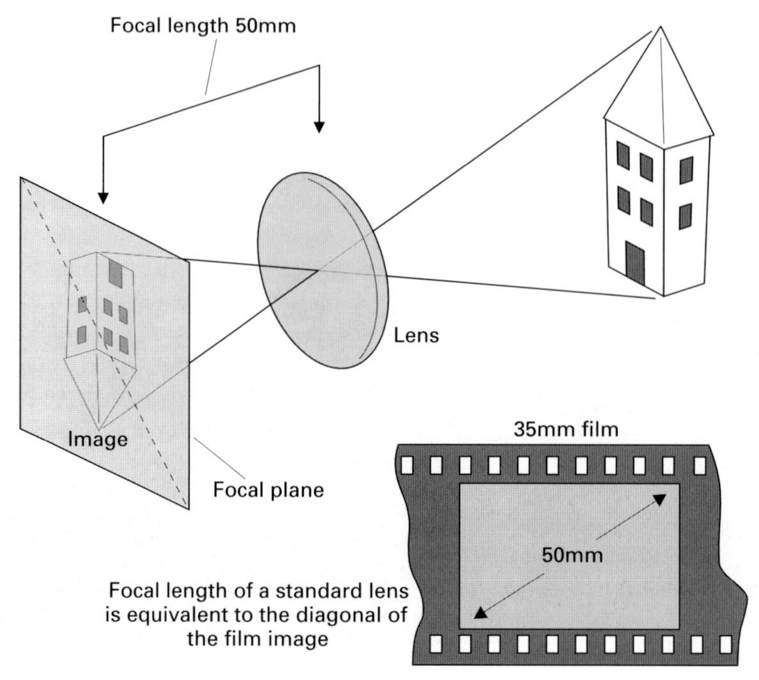

Figure 3.10 Focal length of a lens and its relationship with image area.

length lens, but because they have a greater angle of view they are commonly called wide angle lenses. Perspective is exaggerated, with distant objects being diminished and subjects close to the lens becoming enlarged and distorted (see Figure 3.11a-b). A lens with a focal length greater than the standard is known as long focal length lens, telephoto lenses come within this group but are correctly found at the extremely long lengths, 200mm plus for the 35mm format. The angle of view is narrower than the standard and as the focal length increases so the angle of view becomes narrower still. Again perspective will change, this time being diminished or flattened, reducing the relative differences in the sizes of objects. Lenses that have a fixed focal length are known as prime lenses and are of extremely high quality, particularly the standard lens.

A zoom lens is one whose focal length can be varied and can be either short or long focal length or a mix of both, for instance a 24mm–50mm, 70mm–210mm or 35mm–300mm for a 35mm format. In the past photographers only used them as a last resort because of the indifferent quality, today however, zoom lenses are very nearly as good as prime lenses as far as quality is concerned. Their main advantage being that one or two zoom lenses will cover a wide range of prime focal lengths, as well as a large number of normally unobtainable ones in between. The biggest disadvantage is that they tend to be slow, i.e. with small maximum apertures around *f*/5.6, restricting their use in low light.

The focal length of a prime lens can be changed by using teleconverters, these fit between the lens and camera body and change the focal length by increasing it. Thus a × 2 will double the focal length of the lens in use and a × 3 will treble it. These are really only usable with standard and long focal length lenses and as with

Figure 3.11a

Figure 3.11b

Figure 3.11a–b The same view taken with 35mm wide angle and 210mm telephoto lenses. There obviously had to be a change in camera position in order to keep the framing the same. Study these shots carefully to get an appreciation of the change in perspective and relative position of objects.

other forms of lens attachments there is a substantial loss of light. Being glass there is a degrading of image quality, but with high quality zoom lenses now available there is little need for teleconverters.

3.10 Self-test exercise

To get a full appreciation of the effect of different focal length lenses on a subject, both for angle of view and perspective, the photographer should set a camera up on a tripod and take a series of pictures using a variety of focal lengths. Probably the easiest way is to fit the camera with a zoom lens that covers a range between 35mm and 200mm. A control photograph could be taken using a prime 50mm lens. Detailed notes will need to be taken as to the focal length used on each photograph and the prints laid out side by side for analysis. Compare Figure 3.12a–f.

From this simple exercise the photographer will gain a greater understanding of the effects of focal length and also be able to judge the amount of distortion, if any.

3.11 Critical focus mark

At the top centre of the lens is a red or orange line or diamond, this is the mark at which the focus distance can be read off. These distances are usually marked out around the lens barrel in both feet and metres (see Figure 3.13). For the average amateur there will be no need to refer to them and many may not have noticed them. They will become more important as your photography progresses, particularly when referring to depth of field and using flash.

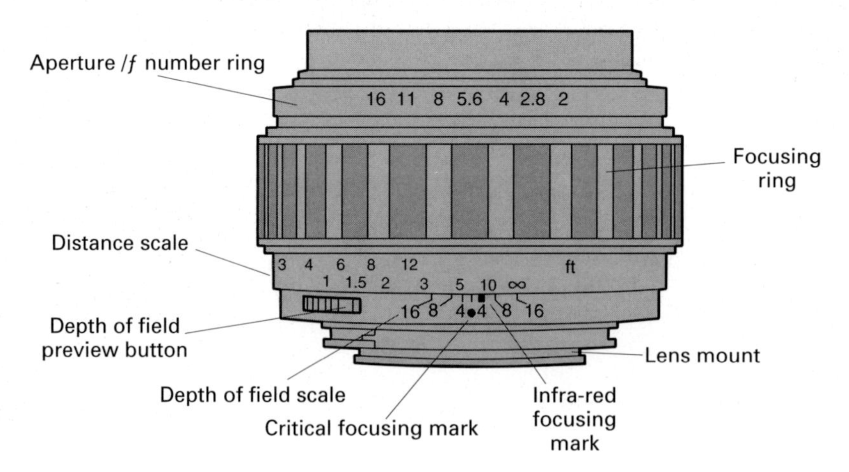

Figure 3.13 Typical lens markings.

Figure 3.12a

Figure 3.12b

Figures 3.12a–f Photographs taken with 35mm, 50mm, 70mm, 105mm, 150mm and 210mm lenses. There was no change in camera position, so no change in position of objects relative to each other, but perspective has changed.

Figure 3.12c

Figure 3.12d

Figure 3.12e

Figure 3.12f

3.12 Apertures

The aperture is the opening in the lens created by the iris diaphragm through which light passes to the film. The diaphragm can be a simple device such as a hole in a metal plate or the more common series of metal blades which overlap. The size of the hole is determined by the *f*/number which can be found around the lens barrel. The definitive range of numbers are as follows: 1, 1.4, 2, 2.8, 4, 5.6, 8, 11, 16, 22. The smallest number is known as the maximum aperture and the largest the minimum aperture and are often referred to as stops. Many lenses will have different maximum apertures at the bottom end of the range, such as 1.8, 2.4, or 3.5, this is because the hole created does not correspond to one of the definitive range, measuring the lens's maximum light gathering ability and suitability for low light work and is entirely at the discretion of the manufacturer. Each number lets in exactly half the amount of light as its predecessor, i.e. 8 lets in half the amount of 5.6. The correct way of writing the numbers is *f*/8, *f*/5.6 and so on (see Figure 3.14). There is a direct relationship between the aperture and the focal length of the lens which is as follows: *f* = focal length of the lens, / is a division line as in maths and the number represents itself, this equation giving the size of the hole created by the diaphragm. Therefore, taking a standard lens of 50mm divided by an *f* number of 8 gives 6.25mm which will be the size of the aperture in the lens. However, if a 200mm lens is used then the answer will be different, 200mm ÷ 8 = 25mm, making the hole four times as large. However, the amount of light reaching the film in each case will be the same, this is because of absorbtion and refraction reducing the light's intensity as it travels down the longer lens barrel. On the other hand taking a 35mm lens, the opening will be 35 ÷ 8 = 4.375mm, reflecting the fact that light has less distance to travel through a wide angle lens, and consequently more reaches the film.

Most lenses have the ability to be closed down to a position between the definitive numbers, these are known as half stops and written as *f*/5.6–8 or *f*/6.3 which is the actual number. Electronic cameras will give a read out on the liquid crystal display but with manual settings the aperture ring is set at a position in between two numbers.

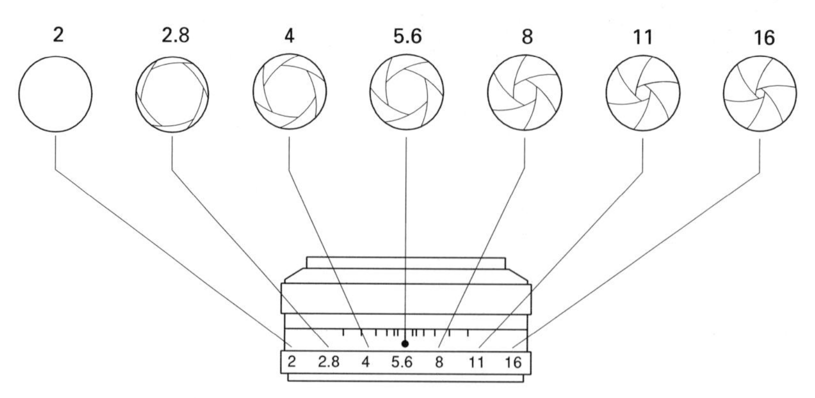

Figure 3.14 Standard f/number sequence; variations may be found at the lower end.

3.13 Depth of field

One of the most important functions of the aperture is that it controls the depth of field, this is the distance in front and behind the main subject that is in acceptably sharp focus. Depth of field increases with the *f* number, so the larger the number, the smaller the aperture, the greater the depth of field. Conversely, the smaller the number, the larger the aperture, the less the depth of field. With normal photography, as the depth of field increases it does so both in front of and behind the point of critical focus, to the ratio of 1/3 in front and 2/3 behind, with close up work the ratio is more equal. Only the point of critical focus will be 100% sharp, the sharpness of the rest of the image will deteriorate gradually until it becomes unacceptable (see Figure 3.15 and 3.16).

Maximum depth of field can be obtained by focusing on what is called the hyperfocal distance, this will vary according to the aperture in use but means that everything from infinity back to half the hyperfocal distance will be in acceptably sharp focus. This is the technique used on fixed focus cameras to ensure reasonable sharpness throughout the picture. The same system is used by press photographers, knowing the limits within which their subject must appear, they set their cameras up to ensure that they have sufficient depth of field thus dispensing with the need to focus. The shorter the focal length of lens the greater the depth of field, because the aperture is smaller at any given *f* number, and the longer the focal length of lens the less the depth of field, because the aperture is larger at any given *f* number

A depth of field scale can be found on the top of the lens, it consists of the *f* numbers repeated either side of the critical focus mark. The distance over which the subject is acceptably sharp can be assessed at a given aperture by looking at the scale after focusing on the main subject. On some large format cameras a scale

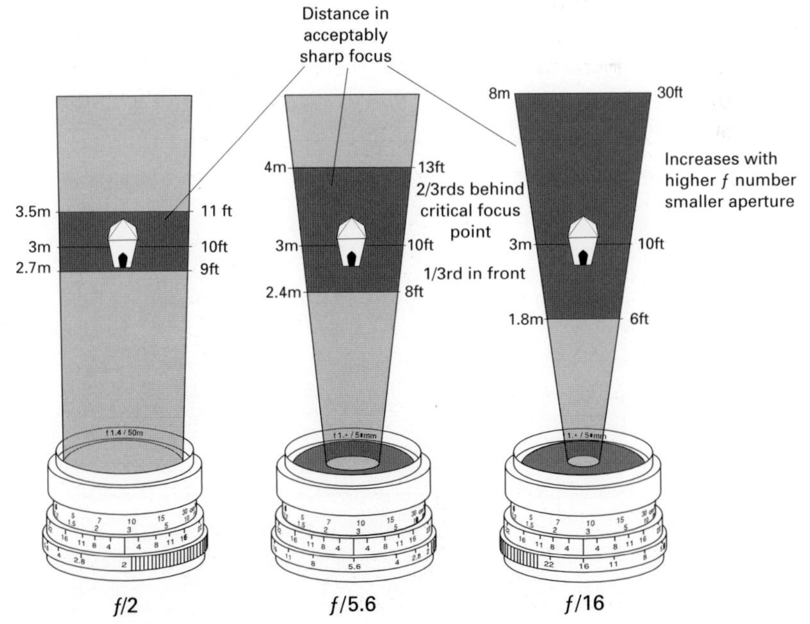

Figure 3.15 Depth of field chart, showing increase in D or F with smaller aperture.

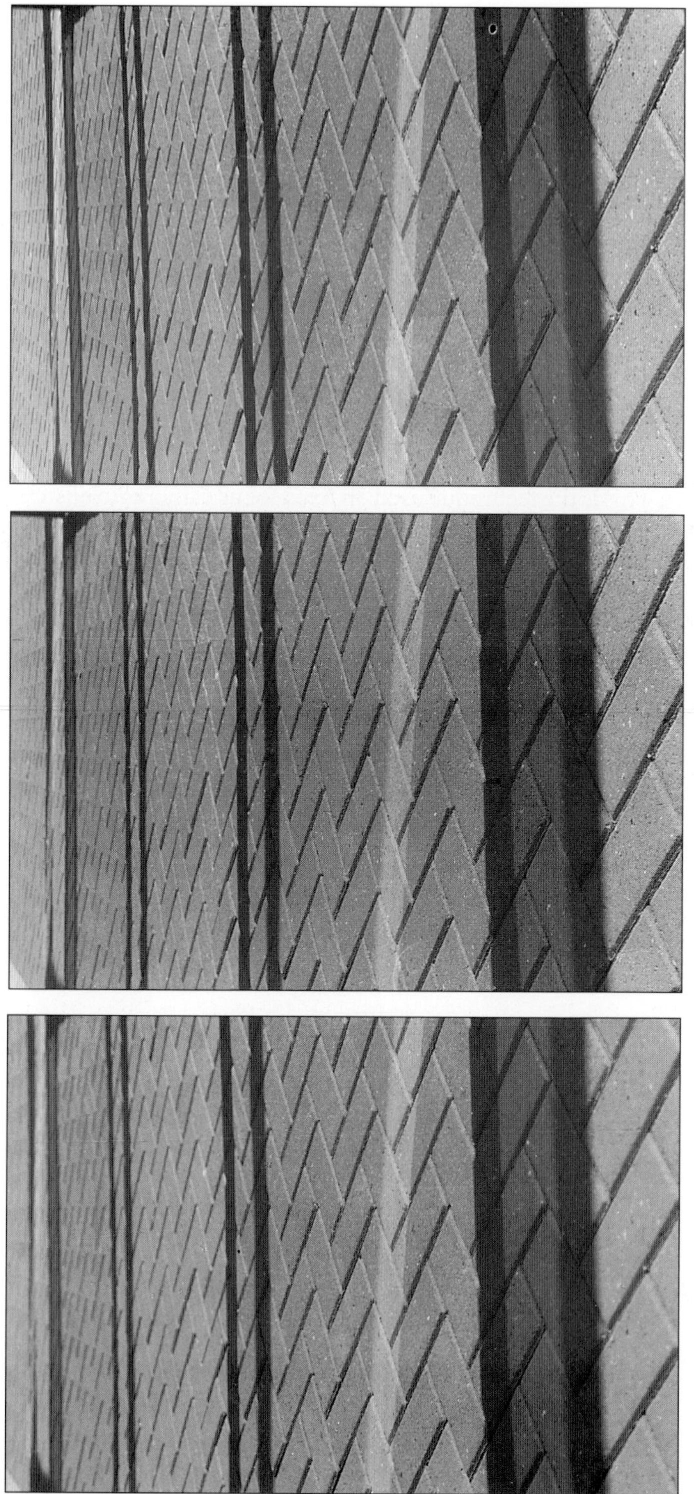

Figure 3.16 Three photographs of the same subject showing increase in depth of field from *f*/2.8 to *f*/8 and *f*/22.

Figure 3.17 A cluttered background can be pushed out of focus by using a large aperture (small f/number) to limit depth of field.

can be found along the baseboard for use with a standard lens only, otherwise there are charts available for guidance, though never definitive. Unfortunately most modern electronic cameras do not have a depth of field scale, neither do the majority of zoom lenses. On fully programmed cameras the photographer can still control the depth of field by using electronic chips according to the type of photography being undertaken. A landscape chip will give maximum depth of field whilst a portrait one will minimise the depth of field. Another way of ascertaining depth of field is by using the depth of field preview button sometimes found on the lens or camera body. This closes the iris down to the pre-selected *f* number and although the image in the viewfinder becomes darker, once the eye has become accustomed to the weaker image, the depth of field can be seen easily. As will be seen in Chapter 7 on composition, depth of field becomes a very important consideration when photographing different subjects.

3.14 Depth of focus

Depth of field is concerned with limits of sharpness outside the camera, whereas depth of focus is concerned with the same limits inside the camera. Depth of focus is the distance either side of the plane of sharp focus that the film can be moved and still record an acceptably sharp image. As with depth of field the smaller the aperture, the larger the *f* number, the greater the depth of focus. In contrast to

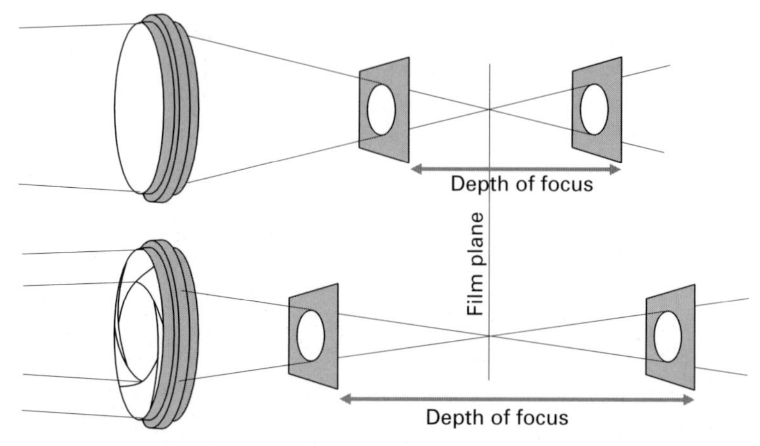

Figure 3.18 Depth of focus either side of the film plane increases the closer the lens is to the subject, the longer the focal length of lens and the smaller the aperture.

depth of field, the closer the camera is to the subject the greater the depth of focus and, to some extent, the longer the focal length of lens in use the greater the depth of focus (see Figure 3.18). Although on modern 35mm cameras the film is held firmly in the film plane and depth of focus is of little concern to the user, it does become more important to the medium and large format user where the film is more flexible and camera movements are used.

3.15 Infra-red focus

Close to the critical focus mark on the lens, or on the depth of field scale, a red mark can be found, either a dot or *R*, this is the focus position when using infra-red film. Infra-red light has a different wavelength and therefore, focuses at a different distance to visible light, and as we focus using visible light the focus of the lens has to be adjusted to ensure a sharp image. Once the subject is focused visibly the distance is read off the distance scale and then set against the red *IR* mark. On some zoom lenses there is a red focus line which curves out along the lens barrel corresponding to the varying focal lengths of the lens.

3.16 Close up accessories

At their closest focusing distance most standard lenses will give a magnification of around 1:10, one tenth life size. In order to increase this ratio the lens must be moved further away from the camera and film plane. At some stage all photographers will want to get closer to their subject than the minimum focus of the lens will allow. One way around this is to purchase a lens with macro facility, this enables the lens to focus closer than would usually be the case with a prime lens. A standard macro lens will give a magnification of 1:4, i.e. quarter life size, at the closest focusing distance. The scale of magnification can normally be found on the lens focus ring along with the word macro.

Figure 3.19 Photograph taken using extension tubes to produce a 1:1 image on film.

Figure 3.20 Extension tubes and bellows used for macro photography.

If a magnification of greater than 1:4 is required then a set of extension tubes will be needed (see Figure 3.19). These consist of a set of three hollow tubes, each of a different length, with the appropriate connections to operate the iris diaphragm in the lens. They fit between the lens and the camera body and because there is no glass involved there is no degradation of the image, unlike supplementary close up lenses. When used singly or in pairs they give a variety of magnifications, when used all together they should give a magnification of 1:1, life size. Extension tubes can be used with standard and long focal length lenses, but not with wide angle lenses. There is a marked loss of light but the metering system in the camera will allow for this.

Another method of achieving large magnification is the extension bellows (see Figure 3.20). Again this fits between the camera body and lens and contains no glass. The bellows are fitted to a central column and infinitely variable, but this time there is no connection for the iris diaphragm and this has to be operated manually. With the lens focus turned to minimum a magnification of greater than 1:1 can usually be achieved, particularly if used in conjunction with a macro lens. Again there is loss of light, up to two stops, but the camera will allow for this when metering. Because of the greater extension available with the bellows care has to be taken not to get cut off by taking the lens too far away from the camera. A more

Figure 3.21 Close up lenses allow the photographer to fill the frame with the subject.

sophisticated version that allows the lens to be raised and swung is available for some models of camera. Bellows can be used with standard and long focal length lenses but not wide angle. There is an attachment available for slide copying that fits on the front of the bellows extension.

Reversing rings are a cheap and viable option to either of the above, they fit onto the camera body and the lens is fitted to them back to front. The iris diaphragm will not operate and has to be set by hand either before or after setting the camera up. There is much less loss of light with this system but focusing may have to be carried out by moving the camera back and forth.

Supplementary or close up lenses fit in front of a standard lens and enable the lens to focus closer than normal (see Figure 3.21). This is achieved by shortening the focal length of the prime lens with supplementary lenses measured in dioptres. Like extension tubes they usually come in sets of three, 1, 2 and 3 dioptres, the higher the number the greater the magnification. Loss of light is insignificant and there is normally no need to change the exposure, but being glass there is a slight degrading of quality. With fixed lens cameras such as compacts and twin lens reflexes this is the only option open for close up work. With both supplementary lenses and extension tubes or bellows there is a problem with extremely limited depth of field which necessitates using small apertures and a tripod.

3.17 Other accessories

One of the most important accessories for use on lenses is all too often not used or not known about. This is the lens hood, a plastic or rubber hood that screws onto the front of the lens. The function of the hood is to shield the lens from non-image forming light which manifests itself as lens flare. In its worst form it shows up as orange hexagonal shapes which will appear in pictures taken into the sun, otherwise there may just be a general weakening of colour saturation and contrast. Although modern lenses are coated to reduce lens flare, if filters, which are not coated, are put on the lens then this will nulify the lens coating. It is surprising how much difference the regular use of a hood can make to the finished photograph. Two types of hood are available for most lenses with the exception of the extreme wide angle ones. There are the solid plastic variety which must be matched to the focal length of lens, and the collapsable rubber ones which can be extended to suit wide angle, standard and long focal length lenses. Some telephoto lenses come with an integral hood which is pulled out from its housing in the lens barrel. A more elaborate version which holds filters and other effect devices, known as a matte box, might prove useful for the still life photographer.

When a new lens is purchased it should come complete with two lens caps, one for the front and one for the rear. It is essential that these are in place to protect the lens when not in use, when fitted to the camera always keep the front lens cap on unless a lens hood is fitted.

Keeping the lens clean and free from dust is essential and to this end the photographer should have a cleaning kit. This consists of a blower brush for removing dust, a bottle of lens cleaning fluid and a very soft fibre free cloth for removing finger marks and grease. The paper tissues as supplied for glasses are not really very suitable as they are very fibrous and more trouble than they are worth. Far better to use a very old soft handkerchief or thin piece of chamois. All lenses should have a skylight filter permanentely attached to protect the front element of the lens; replacing a damaged filter is a lot cheaper than having a lens repaired.

3.18 Lens uses

Having looked at the design and construction of the lens it is now time to consider its use. Taking the standard lens first we have already established that it has the same angle of view and perspective as the human eye and this makes it ideal for most photographic purposes, from portraiture to landscape. Its high quality makes it ideal for use in close up work particularly in conjunction with extension tubes or bellows. Both the GCSE and City & Guilds examinations can be undertaken successfully with just the standard lens.

The short focal length or wide angle lens will give a greater angle of view whilst some distortion can be expected. It proves very popular for landscape work because of the extended perspective and greater depth of field, this enables objects to be placed in the near foreground and still be in focus. They come into their own where space is restricted such as when photographing a building in the confines of a built up area or even an interior. The greater the angle of view the greater the distortion, with straight lines close to the edge of the frame bending severely. This may prove unacceptable when trying to photograph a building with strong straight lines, unless it is being done as part of the artistic interpretation. Extreme wide angle lenses, fisheyes, so called because of the large bulbous front element, use this distortion to great effect, although it is falling from favour now. The very short fisheye gives a circular image on the film while the longer focal length one fills the frame. Using a wide angle lens for portraiture will lose friends and upset people rapidly, as features close to the lens, such as noses, will be made very prominent.

Long focal length lenses are like telescopes, for use when the subject is a great distance away and one cannot physically get closer. Because of the flattening of perspective they are ideal for serious portraiture, most photographers using between 100 and 150mm for the 35mm format. The smaller depth of field at a given aperture is also useful particularly for lifting the subject away from the background. Because of their extra length and weight care must be taken in use, especially in regard to camera shake. Even with high shutter speeds it is very difficult to hold a telephoto lens steady so a monopod or tripod is essential.

Zoom lenses are probably the most convenient for the average photographer giving as they do an infinite variety of focal lengths. With the high quality modern lenses it would pay to have a couple of zoom lenses covering a range of between 35mm and 300mm for 35mm format, rather than a bag full of prime lenses. Most zooms should be focused at maximum focal length and then adjusted to the desired position. There is a danger that the photographer might be tempted to use the zoom facility instead of getting closer to the subject, better quality can be expected at the lower end of the focal length. One major drawback to the zoom is that the maximum aperture is fairly small, usually around *f*/3.5–*f*/5.6, requiring longer exposure times.

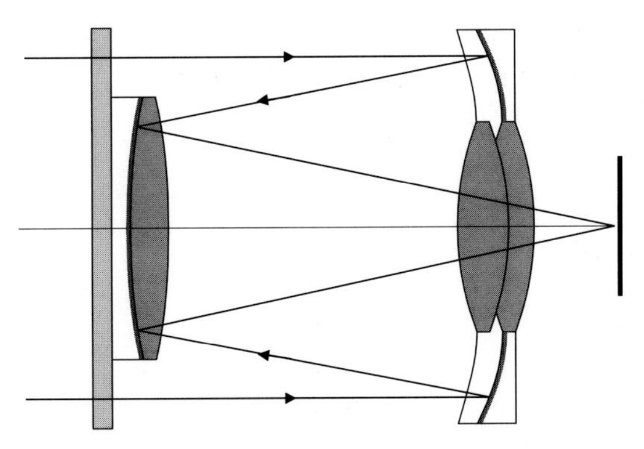

Figure 3.22 Cross-section of a typical mirror lens.

Mirror lenses are long telephoto lenses that use the binocular principle of internal reflection to achieve the desired focal length (see Figure 3.22). Although considerably shorter than a conventional lens of the same focal length they are very much bulkier. Because of the internal construction an iris diaphragm cannot be fitted and all mirror lenses have a fixed aperture, usually around *f*/8. This limits the depth of field and usefulness of the lens quite considerably, but they do tend to be slightly cheaper than a prime lens.

Shift lenses are specialist lenses for the architectural photographer giving a limited amount of upward movement to reduce the effect of converging verticals. Usually of standard or short focal length they are very expensive and not worth investing in unless a great deal of architectural work is undertaken.

The final choice of lenses that will be carried will depend on the type of photography being undertaken and the amount one can afford to spend. Buying anything secondhand is risky so if used lenses are considered take great care to inspect them ensuring that the glass is not chipped or scratched and that the iris diaphragm operates correctly and quickly. It is probably worth that little extra to buy from a reputable dealer offering a three or six month guarantee.

4 Film

After the camera equipment the choice of film is the next most important factor affecting quality. There are a number of film manufacturers and all produce high quality material. Names which spring to most people's mind will be Agfa, Fuji and Kodak, but beyond these there are others such as Ilford, Konica and 3M. Outside these proprietary brands there are very many own brands sold by major retailers. These should not be dismissed as inferior because the majority are made by the leading film manufacturers.

4.1 Structure

Before looking at the various types of film available it is as well to see how film is constructed. Essentially when one exposes a picture in the camera light passes through the lens and excites the silver halides in the light-sensitive emulsion. This forms a latent or invisible image which needs to be made visible by processing.

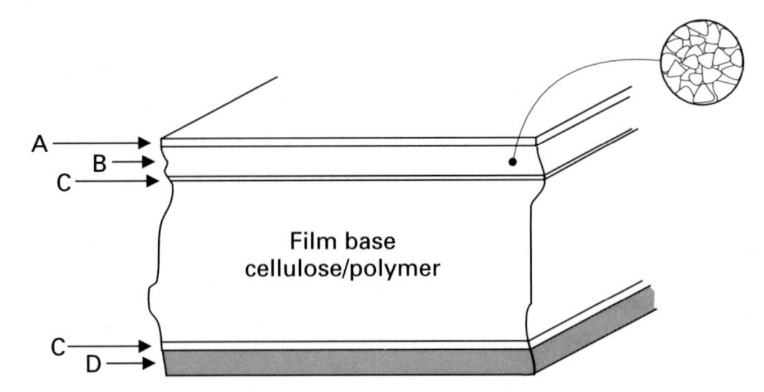

Figure 4.1 Cross-section of black and white film.

A anti-scratch coat,
B emulsion (light sensitive silver salts in gelatine),
C subbing (adhesive),
D anti-halation backing.

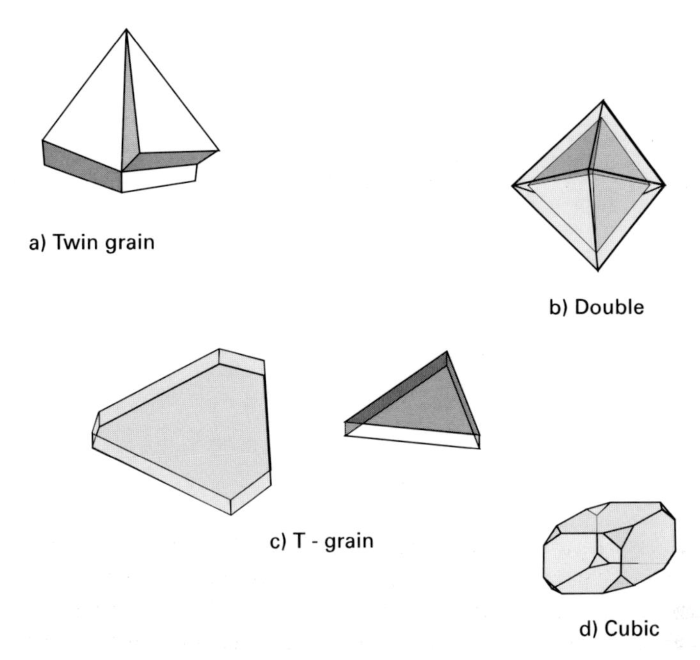

Figure 4.2 Typical silver halides found in films.

Silver halides are minute grains of silver salts, most commonly silver nitrate, suspended in gelatine which makes up the light-sensitive emulsion of the film. The gelatine carrier is the same as that used in cooking, extracted from animal skin and bone, but has to be of the highest quality. The film base, at one time celluloid, is now a cellulose acetate for roll films and polymer for larger sheet films (see Figure 4.1). There are two types of grain structure used in film manufacture, first the traditional ones which are of irregular shape but uniform in size and increasingly, the modern grains which are regular in both size and shape (see Figure 4.2). The more sensitive (faster) the film the larger the grain structure. When viewing a black and white print the graininess that can be seen is not made-up of single grains but of clusters.

As will be seen in Chapter 5 on exposure, white light is made up of three primary colours, red, green and blue, and all film varies in its sensitivity to it. Looking first at black and white there are two types available at present. Orthochromatic is only sensitive to green and blue light and can therefore be handled in standard darkroom red safe-lighting, and panchromatic which is sensitive to all three colours and has to be handled in total darkness. Black and white film has its peak sensitivity in the blue band of the spectrum and therefore sees things differently to the human eye, which peaks in the green band (see Figure 4.3 and 4.4).

Colour films are more complex than black and white and their structure varies between manufacturers. But essentially there are three emulsion layers each of which is sensitive to one of the primary colours. All colour films will tend to have a bias and this is caused by the differing levels of sensitivity between the emulsion layers, added to which the order in which those layers appear in the film will also have an affect on the bias. Most colour film gives a direct silver image coupled

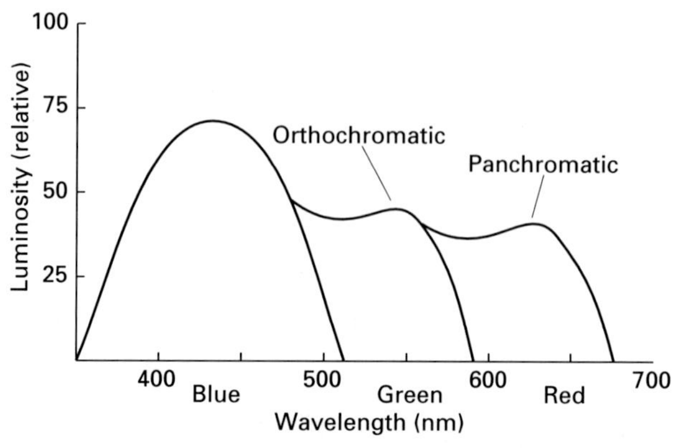

Figure 4.3 Photographic film's response to light, peaking in the blue band.

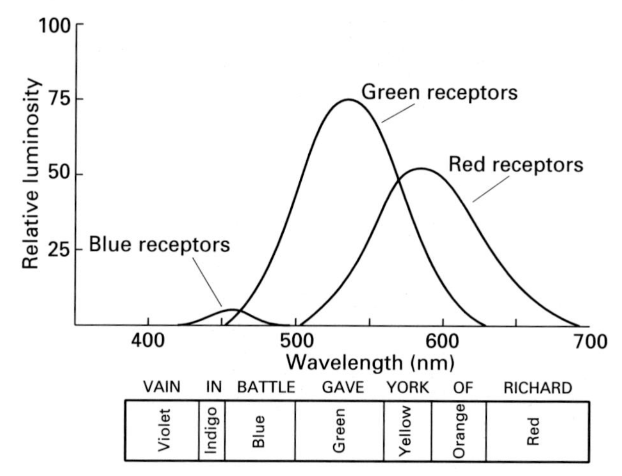

Figure 4.4 The eye's response to light peaking in the green band.

with colour dyes, but there are a selection of films which have the silver image replaced by dyes during processing and these tend to be known as high resolution with the prefix VR or HR. The advantage of these types of film is that the dye structure remains constant no matter what the speed of the film. An ISO 1000 film will appear to have the same size dye matrix as an ISO 100, both will seem to be as 'grainy' as a standard ISO 400 film. Another advantage of this film is its exposure latitude, its tolerance to over and under exposure. It is this ability that was seized upon by Ilford when they produced their XP1 black and white film. Colour dye transfer technology has been applied to this film and as a consequence it can be processed in colour chemistry. Replaced by XP2 and nominally rated at ISO 400 the film can be exposed anywhere between ISO 50 and 1600 on the same roll, i.e. over and under exposing, without detriment to the image. Figure 4.5 shows the structure of two different types of colour film.

FUJICOLOUR REALA

Before development

Blue sensitive emulsion and colourless yellow coupler

Cyan sensitive emulsion

Green and blue sensitive emulsion and yellow coloured magenta coupler

Red and blue sensitive emulsion and red coloured cyan coupler

Protective layer

Yellow filter layer

Interlayer

Image controlling layer

Interlayer

Image controlling layer

Interlayer

Anti-halation layer

Safety film base

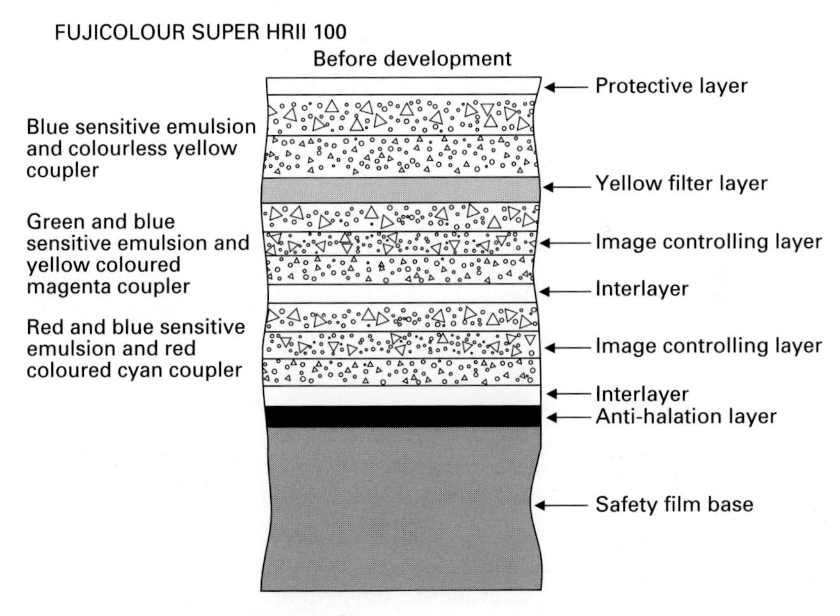

Figure 4.5 Cross-section of colour film.

4.2 Choice

Looking first at factors which will affect your choice of film, the decision has to be made as to whether it should be colour or black and white, negative or transparency. The question of colour or black and white is one of personal choice and aesthetics. Many people consider black and white to be the poor cousin of colour while others think that it is the only true medium for artistic photography. Certainly black and white can often be far more expressive than colour and many photographers prefer the greater control they feel they have over it. Obviously if the object of the photograph is to record colour then the choice is made for you, but where colour is of little importance then the arguments for and against become, like photography itself, highly subjective.

The question of negative or transparency is easier; if one requires prints then negative film is the obvious choice. Transparency film produces a positive image and although prints can be made from transparencies the quality is less than satisfactory and often very disappointing. Should there be a need to reach a larger audience then transparencies shown through a slide projector are the answer. If the work is to be published then printers prefer transparencies, although many will now accept prints. Whatever the pros and cons, the arguments should be weighed up carefully. There is a further consideration to be made with colour film, that of daylight or tungsten lighting balance. For photography outside, daylight film is the answer, this can be used inside under artificial light but the result will be orange or green depending on the light source. The 'warm glow' encountered is often acceptable but to achieve correct colours a blue correction filter should be used on the camera. Taking the reverse situation, if tungsten film is used out of doors the result will be very blue and totally unacceptable, correction can be made with an orange filter.

Choice of film is highly subjective and there is a wide selection available, although many high street outlets restrict their stock to the more popular range. A simple way to distinguish types is that all colour negative films, giving prints as the final result, end in the words 'colour' or 'print', i.e. Kodacolor, Truprint, etc. Transparency/slide/reversal are all terms for films which produce slides for projection and end in the term 'chrome', such as Kodachrome, Agfachrome and so on. Black and white films may require some detective work to find out what they are, there often not being any indication in the name, though the term 'pan', for panchromatic, as in Agfapan or Neopan is used. In the past black and white film was known as 'Monochrome' but this confusing term has largely been dropped (see Figure 4.6).

As already mentioned, colour film is very particular about the light source that is used and so there are two types available, daylight and tungsten. There will not normally be any indication on colour negative film as to whether it is daylight or tungsten balanced until you open the box and read the instructions. However, as a guide one can assume that film below ISO 1000 is daylight and faster films are tungsten. Colour transparency film is easily identified with the vast majority being daylight balanced. Tungsten colour transparency film will always carry a T suffix i.e. Ektachrome 160T. Processing and mounting costs are included in the pur-

Figure 4.6 A small selection of films available; note the use of the terms 'chrome', 'colour' and 'print'.

chase price of some colour transparency films. Black and white film does not mind what the light source is and will even accept a mix of daylight and tungsten. For an explanation of colour balance see, Chapter 6 on light.

Beyond standard colour and black and white films there are a number of specialist films which provide a different viewpoint on subject matter. Infra-red film can be obtained in black and white and what is known as false colour, having a sensitivity beyond the red section of the spectrum and therefore, outside the range of the human eye. Infra-red radiation is emitted or reflected by a number of living and inanimate objects. With colour film a yellow/orange filter is generally used giving quite unnatural results.

Vegetation reflects infra-red and comes out red on colour film – the healthier the plant the brighter the colour, very useful for determining growth problems. Archaeologists use this phenomena to study buried foundations by using infra-red aerial photography. For the most spectacular results in black and white the film is used in conjunction with a red filter. Manufacturers will not give an ISO rating for infra-red film and therefore several exposures will be required to obtain a good result. Once a working procedure has been established exposures becomes easier. Another interesting film is Line or Lith, a very slow, high contrast orthochromatic black and white film. Because of its high contrast the intermediate grey tones are limited and a highly graphic image results. Normally used in the darkroom to make derived images it can be exposed in camera, although with an ISO rating of just 4 it needs very long exposure times.

Some retail outlets offer 'Professional' films alongside the standard range and to the amateur it may appear advantageous to use these, assuming better quality.

However, professional films are designed to be exposed and processed within a very short time scale and as soon after leaving the production line as possible. They have a much shorter shelf life and it is therefore essential they are kept refrigerated both by the retailer and photographer. On top of this they are also more expensive. Amateur films are designed to be kept at normal room temperatures after manufacture and perhaps prolonged periods in camera. There is little difference in quality and unless you are likely to use all the film quickly there is no advantage in purchasing professional stock.

As already mentioned, there is a bewildering selection of films on the market today from the four or five major manufacturers plus a lot of lesser brands. This has created some snobbery regarding film usage: film choice is highly subjective, if it suits your purposes and the final print or slide quality suits your needs then that is all that is important. Standard film takes time to process and print so for the impatient there is the instant picture. There are as many as ten types of instant film on the market, some for use in their own special cameras, others for use in holders that attach to larger format cameras, plus 35mm film. Black and white print, colour print and colour transparency are available in speeds ranging from ISO 200/24 to ISO 3200/36.

4.3 Sensitivity (speed)

Sensitivity is the reaction of film to light and has been measured in a number of different ways over the years; the term 'speed' is also used to denote the rate at which the emulsion reacts to light. The first system of measurement was introduced by photographic pioneers Hurter and Driffield in 1890.

There is a wide range of sensitivity in all types of film and this is donated by the term ISO (International Standards Organisation). This nomenclature is derived from the old ASA/DIN (American Standards Association/Deutsche Industrie Normen) system which had been the standard since the 1930s. The relationship between the two older systems is very simple, as the ASA doubled so the DIN increased by 3.

25ASA/15DIN becomes ISO 25/15
50ASA/18DIN becomes ISO 50/18
100ASA/21DIN becomes ISO 100/21
200ASA/24DIN becomes ISO 200/24, etc.

Eventually the DIN number will be dropped and the new ISO standard will be the same as the old ASA. There are a number of films that fall in between the round ASA numbers and these equate to single DIN figures, for instance 64ASA is 19DIN, 80ASA is 20DIN, 125ASA is 22DIN, and so on. These figures are represented by a dot on your camera film speed dial. The film speed must be dialled into your camera when loading the film so that the computer can work out the correct exposure. An increasing number of cameras save you the trouble by using the DX coding system (see Figure 4.7). DX coding applies only to 35mm film and is found on the cassette in the form of black and silver squares which are read by sensors in the camera cassette compartment. The coding tells the camera the

1 and 7	Common return
2 - 6	ISO rating
8 - 10	Number of exposures
11 and 12	Exposure latitude

Figure 4.7 DX coding on 35mm film cassettes.

ISO rating of the film, how many exposures there are on the roll and the film's exposure latitude. The vast majority of films now carry the DX coding but a few of the lesser brands and bulk loaded films will not, for these occasions packs of coding stickers can be purchased. If no coding information is available the camera will resort to a setting of ISO 100/21. Whilst most compact cameras only operate on the DX coding the better SLRs will also have a manual override system, ideal for when the film has no coding or when you want to change the film's effective rating by special processing.

The terms that are used to describe film speeds are historical and now dating somewhat. More important though are the characteristics associated with the various film speeds. A slow film, ISO 80 or below, will have high contrast and a fine grain structure, ideal for recording fine detail. A medium speed film, between ISO 100 and 200, will have medium contrast and grain and is a good general purpose film suitable for most types of photography. Fast films, ISO 400 and above, tend to have low contrast and coarse grain structure and will be used mainly in low light conditions. Grain size has a direct bearing on the films resolving power, its ability to record fine detail. The finer the grain the greater the resolution, the finer the detail that can be recorded and the sharper the image, so the lower the ISO the better the resolving power, though with advancing technology the distinction between slow and fast films is becoming less noticeable. The thickness of the emulsion also has a bearing on resolution but this is of little significance today, as all modern emulsions are very thin.

4.4 Contrast

Contrast in a subject can come from either its own colour or tonal ranges, such as very light and very dark colours alongside each other, or from the lighting, as with strong directional sunlight. However, contrast can be introduced by using a slow speed film, where in extreme cases with black and white film only blacks and whites are recorded. In colour it is the brightness and richness of the colours which is affected, known as colour saturation. Conversely, if one wanted to reduce the contrast of a subject or reduce the separation between colours then a high speed film will do the job.

The choice of film speed will be dictated by the task to be undertaken. With a finely detailed subject where this detail needs to be recorded accurately, a slow speed fine grain film will be required for maximum quality. On the other hand in low light conditions where you need to stop action and are prevented from using flash you will need a high speed film. However, if the subject is inanimate a slow film could be used with a tripod and long exposure time. Grain in film can also be used for artistic effect so one may wish to use a high speed film in bright daylight conditions. For most students starting out on either the GCSE or City & Guilds exams the initial work will be done in daylight and a medium speed film will suffice if the lighting conditions are good. Black and white film ranges in speed from ISO 25 to 3200, colour negative film from ISO 25 to 6400 and colour transparency film from ISO 25 to 1600.

4.5 Film size

Film still comes in a number of different sizes and shapes to match particular cameras (see Figure 4.8). Starting with the smallest and most insignificant, disc film, this is made specifically for the disc camera and consists of fifteen very tiny negatives around a disc of plastic. Next comes 16mm film as used in the compact 110

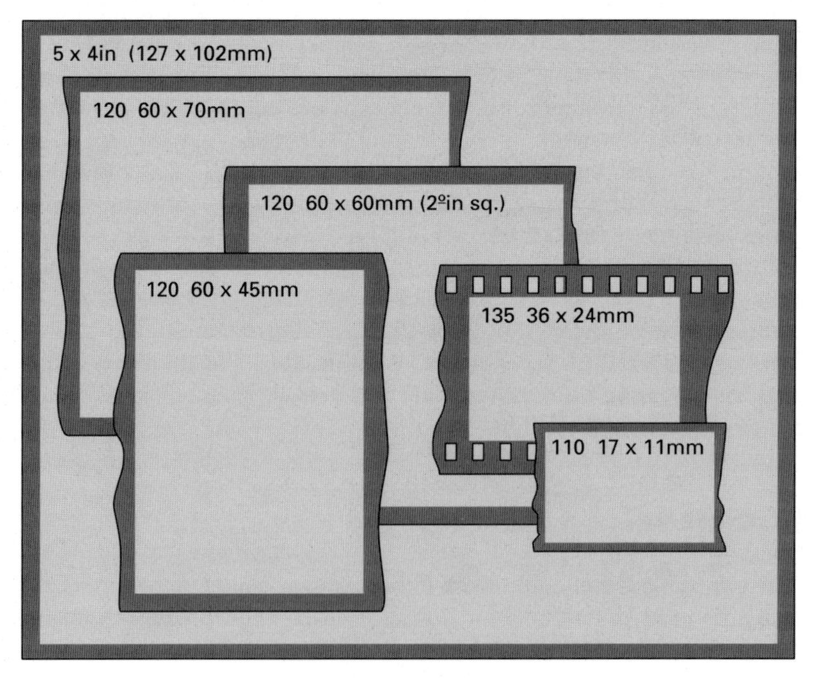

Figure 4.8 Film sizes available up to 5 in × 4 in, to scale.

camera and many of the so called 'spy cameras'. Then come two films in the 35mm category, 126, which fitted the cartridge loaded Instamatic cameras and 135, the standard cassette for 35mm cameras. The 35mm cassette comes in various lengths, 12, 24 and 36 exposures, bulk lengths of 30 metres can be obtained and loaded into cassettes, but care must be taken as film damage can occur when re-using cassettes. These are followed by sizes known as roll films, first 127, 45mm wide and dating from the days of box cameras, very rare these days. The standard roll film today, which again dates from the early box cameras is the 120, 60mm wide and used in all modern medium format cameras. The size and number of images on a roll film will depend on the camera used. Another version of 120 roll film is 220, giving twice as many exposures per roll, now going out of popularity. These are followed by sheet film sizes that replaced the glass plates of yesteryear. The modern sizes are 5in × 4in, 7in × 5in, 10in × 8in and 20in × 16in, as used in large format cameras by professional photographers. The reason for having larger films is quite simple, quality: the bigger the image the better the reproduction.

4.6 Care and storage

There are several pieces of information on a film box that should be noted and understood (see Figure 4.9). The most obvious will be the film type, colour negative, colour slide or black and white, followed by the ISO rating. Next comes size and number of exposures, i.e. 135–20, 35mm 20 exposures. Other data will indicate whether the film is daylight/flash or tungsten, plus a 'process by' date and emulsion batch number. This 'process by' date is the latest recommended date by which the film should be used, although if stored under ideal conditions this can be exceeded without any problems. The batch number will help the manufacturer identify the film should there be any fault with it. It is therefore a good idea to hold onto the box until after having the film processed.

When buying in bulk films should be stored in a black polythene bag on the top shelf of a domestic fridge. The film should be removed from the fridge a couple of hours before using to prevent condensation forming on the emulsion. Once exposed the film should be processed as soon as possible, as latent image degradation will begin. If this is not practical, for instance, when on holiday, then the film should be returned to the fridge, sealed in a plastic bag.

Another important consideration is the transport of film; never leave it to roast in the glove box of a car, or leave it lying around in the sun. When travelling abroad your film will have to go through security checks and this means X-ray machines. In the west film up to ISO 1000 should be safe, but remember the affect is cumulative and it may be advisable to have the faster films processed before coming home. Fewer and fewer customs points are prepared to check film by hand, so if you have ideas of using very fast film then it would be as well to buy it on arrival. The lead bags that are available for putting your film in vary in quality and some customs posts will take the film out before passing it through X-ray machines. Problems can occur in third world countries where machinery is wound up full and will damage even the slowest of films.

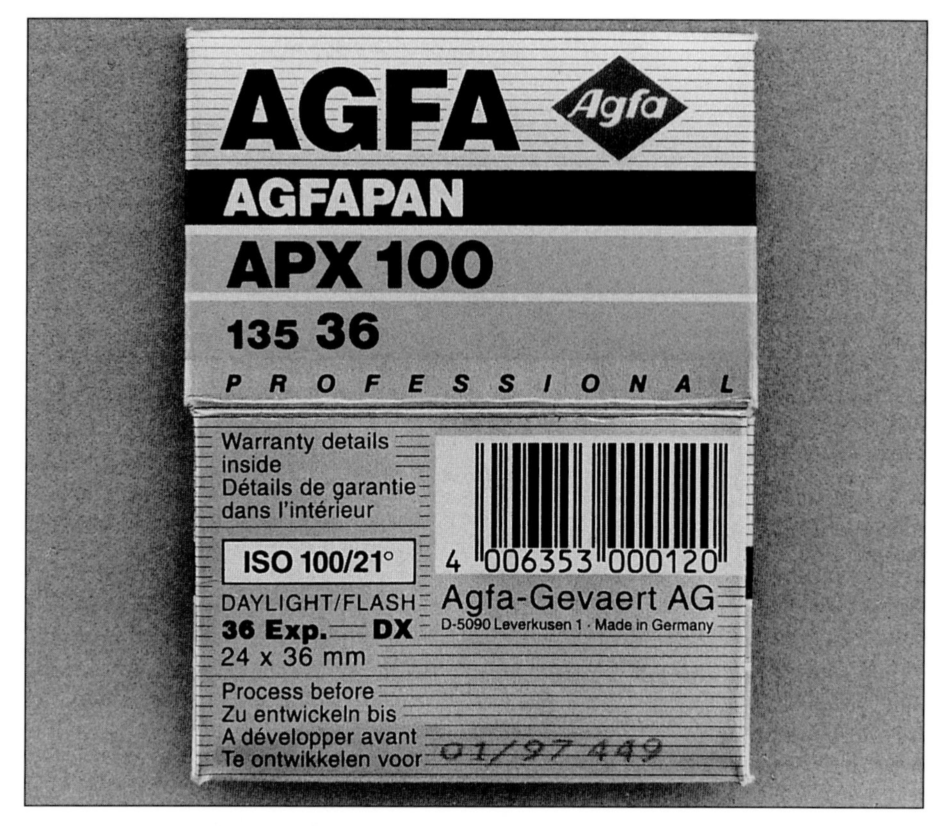

Figure 4.9 Check out the information on this film box: film type, ISO rating, size, number of exposures, process by date and batch number.

4.7 Film faults

The very high standards of quality control employed by manufacturers means that it is rare to encounter a manufacturing film fault. Most faults occur as a result of processing and handling; no control can be exercised over process laboratories but care can be taken when handling or processing film yourself.

Tramlines, scratches down the length of the film, are usually caused by grit in the camera body, the light trap of the cassette or on the rollers of the processing machinery. This fault cannot be rectified so it is a question of prevention and not cure.

Fogging, excess light reaching the film, again can be caused either in camera or during processing. Accidental opening of the camera back is the most likely cause; once occurred it cannot be rectified.

Processing marks can manifest themselves in several different ways, as coloured stains, run marks, circles of lighter or darker density or uneven drying marks. Run and drying marks can be removed but staining and uneven processing cannot be cured.

Scratches and crescent moons are caused by mishandling of the film before, during or after processing and again cannot be rectified. Care when handling the negatives will minimise these problems, most of which are caused by the photographer not the process house.

Thin, clear, negatives or dark slides are due to under exposure in the camera and probably the result of setting the film speed incorrectly. If there are no images at all on the film but the edge numbers show up, then it was loaded incorrectly and never went through the camera.

Dense negatives or thin slides are the result of over exposure and again probably caused by not setting the film speed correctly on the camera. If this turns out not to be the case then one should look for a camera fault, such as a sticking shutter.

Spots and other colour casts are due to out of date or badly stored film where the emulsion has begun to break down. See Chapter 11 on film processing for other faults.

5 Exposure

In simple terms, exposure is the act of pressing the shutter release on the camera and allowing light to fall on the film. In practice it is the result of a number of calculations and operations. The way in which light levels are calculated, the choice of aperture, shutter speed and film all have a direct effect on exposure. Correct exposure is having just the right amount of light reaching the film to give you a negative or transparency of normal density and contrast. It therefore follows that if a film does not receive sufficient light an under exposed image will result; on the other hand one that receives too much light will be over exposed. That is not to say that every image should be given correct exposure; much will depend on artistic interpretation.

5.1 Determining exposure

Correct exposure is a combination of intensity and time,

$$E = I \times T$$

I is the amount of light passing through the aperture and T the length of time for which the shutter is open. The combination selected will depend on what final result is required, changing the aperture will alter the depth of field and require a change in shutter speed. Changing the shutter speed will affect the way in which the subject is recorded, slow speeds blurring the image and high speeds freezing any movement. Once the appropriate combination has been selected any change in either *f*/number or shutter speed will result in a reciprocal change in the other. e.g. shortening the time for which the shutter is open will require an increase in the amount of light passing through the lens, i.e. a larger aperture, in order to maintain correct exposure. Lengthening the time for which the shutter is open will mean a decrease in the amount of light needed, i.e. a smaller aperture, for correct exposure (see Figure 5.1).

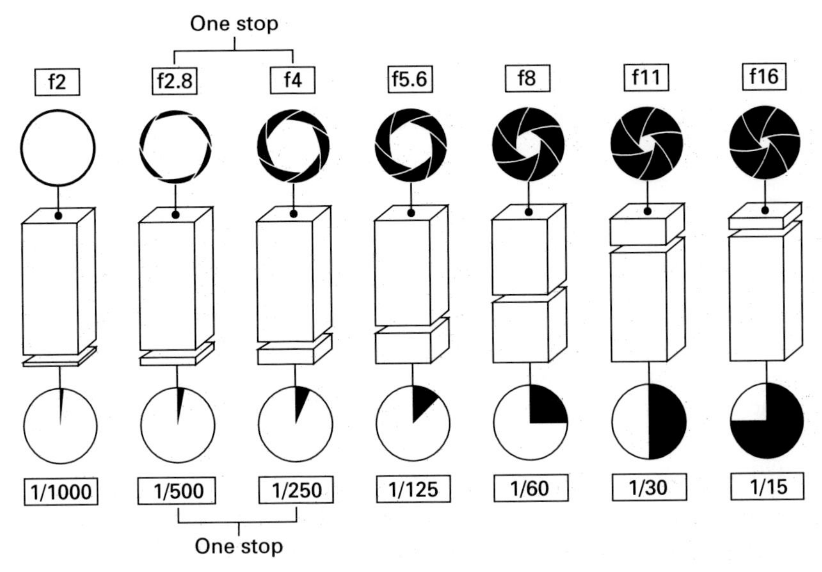

Figure 5.1 Shutter speed/aperture combinations all giving the same effective exposure.

Let us take 1/125 @ *f*/5.6 as our initial exposure and work out the other possibilities.

shortening *T* by	125	@	5.6	requires an increase in
increasing shutter speed	250	@	4	*I* by opening the aperture
by one stop	500	@	2.8	one stop, thereby
				decreasing
(the step between two	1000	@	2	depth of field
shutter speeds is also a				
called a stop, see Chapter 3)	60	@	8	requires a decrease in *I* by
increasing *T* by reducing	30	@	11	closing the aperture one
shutter speed by one stop				stop thereby increasing depth
	15	@	16	of field

As the shutter speed is increased, and *T* reduced, so the *f* number is reduced, making a larger aperture, and *I* increased. Conversely, as the shutter speed is reduced, thereby increasing *T*, so the *f* number is increased, making the aperture smaller, reducing *I*. If either is changed without the corresponding change in the other then incorrect exposure will result. Any of the above combinations will give the same level of exposure as the original setting. Rather than specifying shutter speeds and *f* numbers, exposure levels can be quoted as exposure values (EV).

5.2 Self-test exercise

To prove the above rule set the shutter speed on the camera to 125 and using the through the lens metering system set the *f* number for correct exposure. Now change the shutter speed and see how the exposure indication changes, alter the *f* number until the reading is correct. Having done this alter the *f* number and then change the shutter speed until the exposure reading is once again correct.

5.3 Exposure values

Exposure values were developed in Germany during the 1950s as a substitute for the shutter speed and *f* number combination. EVs can be found on hand held meters and some older camera lenses and range from 1 to 22. Whatever the ISO rating of the film the EV will give a constant exposure, combination of shutter speeds and *f* numbers. An increase of one in EVs equates to a halving of exposure (see Figure 5.2).

The main function of EVs today is to define the range of a light meter, the greater the EV range the more sensitive the meter. On some cameras where the shutter speeds and *f* numbers are on the lens, then an EV scale is also incorporated linking the two together, so that as the EV is changed so the aperture and shutter speeds are changed.

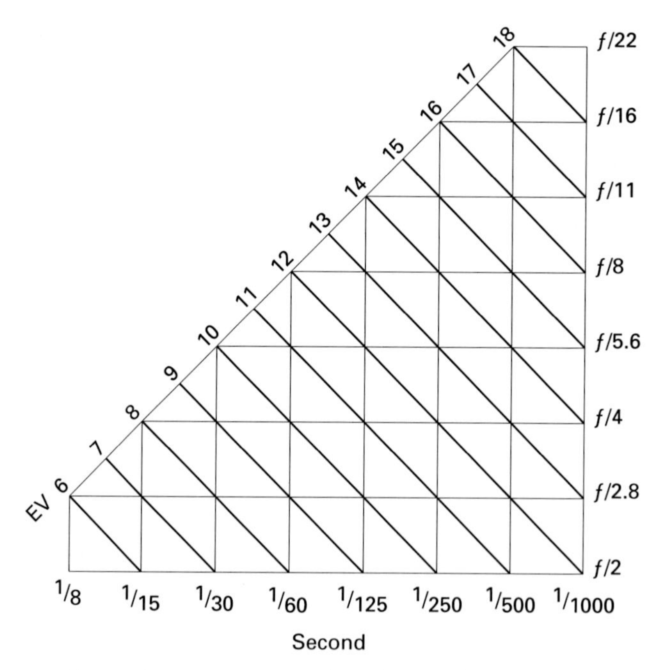

Each value expresses a series of shutter/aperture combinations which will give the same effective exposure

EV11 - 1/125 at *f*/4 1/60 at *f*/5.6 1/30 at *f*/8 etc.

Figure 5.2 Exposure value table.

5.4 Light meters

Obtaining correct exposure is achieved by the use of a light meter either hand held or built into the camera. Measurement of light levels is made in one of two ways, reflected and incident. Reflected light works by reading the amount of light reflected off the subject. This is the method used by the built-in meter in cameras and one of the two options for hand held meters. An average exposure reading is taken from an average subject, one that is mid-way up the brightness scale. When starting out the best method of obtaining a correct reading is to exclude the extreme ends of the brightness range, i.e. sky and very deep shadows. Take a reading pointing the camera or hand held meter at 45° to the ground on grass or tarmac that is well lit, this will give an accurate reading for negative film.

There are a number of ways in which the camera meter will let you know when you have correct exposure, all of which are shown in the viewfinder.

It may be a simple needle which has to be aligned with a central mark, a ring which has to be centred over a needle or a series of small lights showing + 0 –, where 0 is correct exposure, + over exposure and – under exposure. The needles or lights are altered by changing either the shutter speed or the aperture until they indicate correct exposure (see Figure 5.3).

A camera's built-in meter will take a reading in one of several different ways, with the more expensive models giving a choice. Centre weighted average metering takes a reading from the whole of the scene, concentrating on the central portion (see Figure 5.4). This assumes that most amateurs place their subject in the centre of the frame, which of course will not necessarily be the case. This method also includes the very bright areas such as sky and will be inclined to give a false high reading, resulting in under exposure. By using the 45° method described earlier a much more accurate reading can be obtained for negative film, however, the system does work reasonable well for transparency material.

Partial metering again takes the reading from the centre of the scene but this

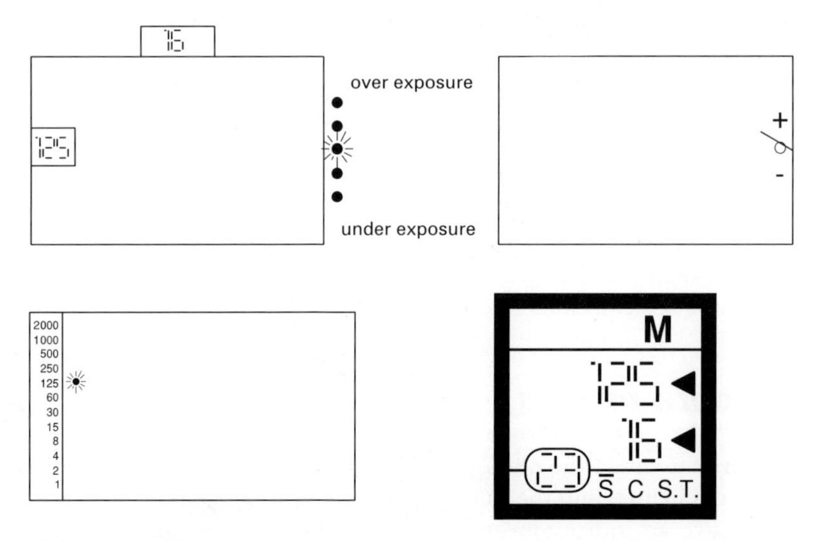

Figure 5.3 Some of the correct exposure indications seen on various cameras.

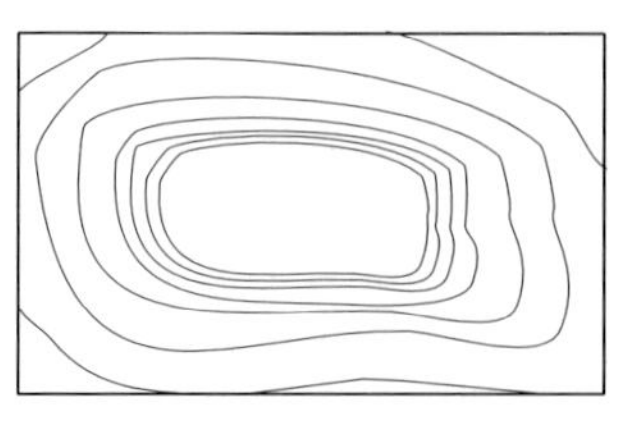

Figure 5.4 Centre weighted metering

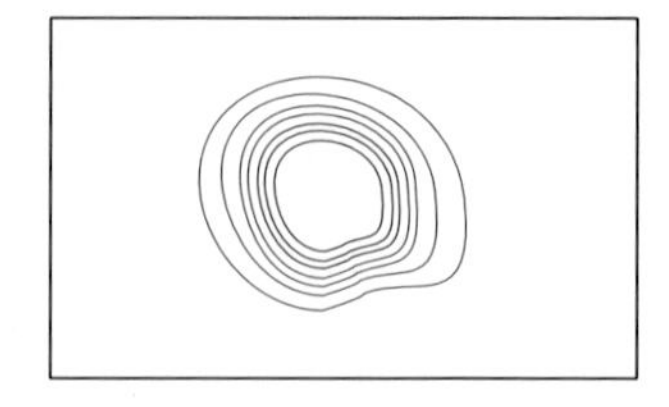

Figure 5.5 Partial metering.

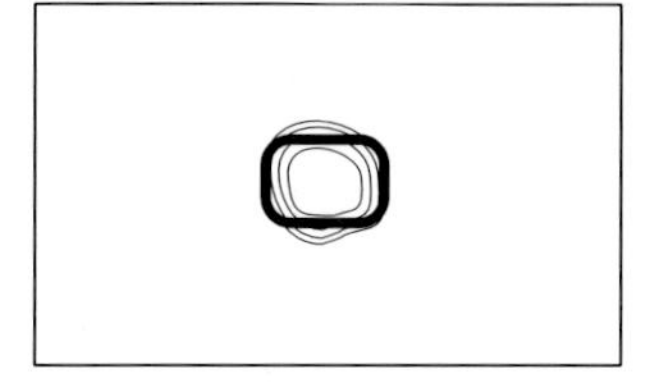

Figure 5.6 Spot metering

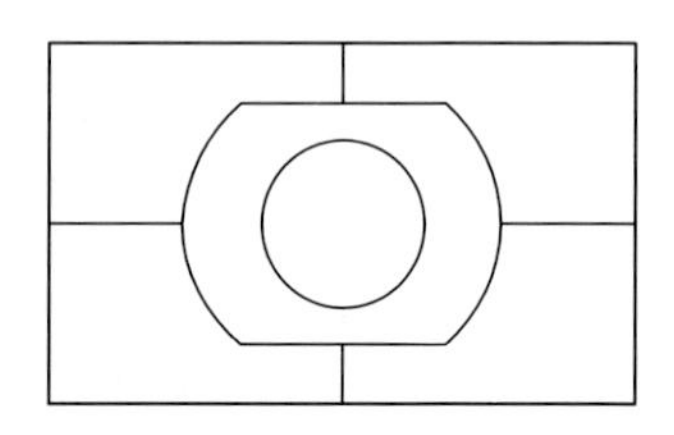

Figure 5.7 Integrated metering

time takes a much smaller area into account, as little as 15% of the frame (see Figure 5.5). This is slightly more accurate than average metering and enables the photographer to choose the area from which to take their reading.

Spot metering, as the name suggests, takes a reading from a very small area usually in the centre of the frame, again giving the photographer the freedom of choice as to where the reading is taken from (see Figure 5.6). On top of the range cameras a spot reading can be taken from one or more positions within the frame, or a number of them combined to give an accurate average.

Integrated metering is a system where the scene is divided up into sections and separate readings taken from each, the camera's computer then works out an exposure taking into account information held in its memory (see Figure 5.7).

On manual cameras the shutter speed and aperture are set by the photographer and the camera cannot change them. On automatic models the chosen exposure will be overridden unless it can be fixed in some way. Many modern cameras enable the photographer to take an exposure reading from a selected part of the scene and then lock the reading in. This is achieved by using the meter lock (ML) or the average exposure lock (AEL) button. Some models will hold the information until the shutter is released, others require the button to be held down while the picture is taken, often requiring a second pair of hands. Automatic cameras come with three basic options for exposure.

5.5 Camera modes

Shutter priority is where the photographer selects the shutter speed according to the needs of the picture and the camera works out the appropriate aperture. Most models will give an indication of the *f* number selected in the viewfinder and therefore, the photographer has an idea of the depth of field likely to be achieved. The camera will also give a warning if light levels are too low for correct exposure, in which case the shutter speed will have to be reduced.

Aperture priority is where the photographer chooses the *f* number according to the depth of field required and the camera will select the shutter speed. The chosen shutter speed will normally appear in the viewfinder but there are one or two models that do not let the photographer know. Once again there will normally be an indication of under exposure, but as there are more shutter speeds than *f* numbers it is less likely to occur. Remember with shutter speeds lower than 1/60 some form of camera support will be required.

In full program mode the camera will select both shutter speed and aperture but very often will not give any indication of either speed or *f* number. The photographer therefore has no idea whether camera shake will be encountered or what depth of field will be achieved. Fortunately most manufacturers have seen the error of their ways and with the digital read out cameras as much information as possible is shown.

5.6 Hand held meters

A hand held meter is essential for large and a lot of medium format cameras as they do not have built-in meters. The main advantage over built-in meters is that they can record much lower light levels, and will very often give exposure times in excess of 15 minutes. Once the shutter speed dial of a camera has been turned to *B* it automatically switches the meter off. Probably the most useful type of hand meter is the averaging one which has a very large sensitive cell, but hand held spot meters are also available. To use them the film speed has to be set on the meter just as it is on the camera. The meter is then pointed at 45° to the ground as described earlier, the reading from the needle is then transferred to the exposure dial and a selection of shutter speeds/apertures is given, any of which will give correct exposure. Readings can be taken from any part of the scene or several readings averaged out (see Figure 5.8). For very accurate exposures a 'grey card' should be used; this is a piece of grey card (halfway on the scale between black and white), that reflects exactly 18% of the light that falls on it.

To obtain a reading from a grey card it should be placed in the scene with the light source illuminating it evenly. The hand held meter should then be placed 25–30cm from it and a reading taken; the same method can be used with the camera by ensuring that the card fills the viewfinder.

The hand held meter is capable of taking another type of exposure reading which is far more accurate than the reflected light method. This is called an 'incident' reading and is taken using a special piece of plastic known as an invercone. The invercone is placed over the sensitive cell and the meter pointed towards the light source from either the camera or subject position. An incident reading and a reflected reading taken from a grey card should be identical. The main thing to remember with hand held meters is that they do not take account of any filters used, loss of light through extension tubes or other accessories.

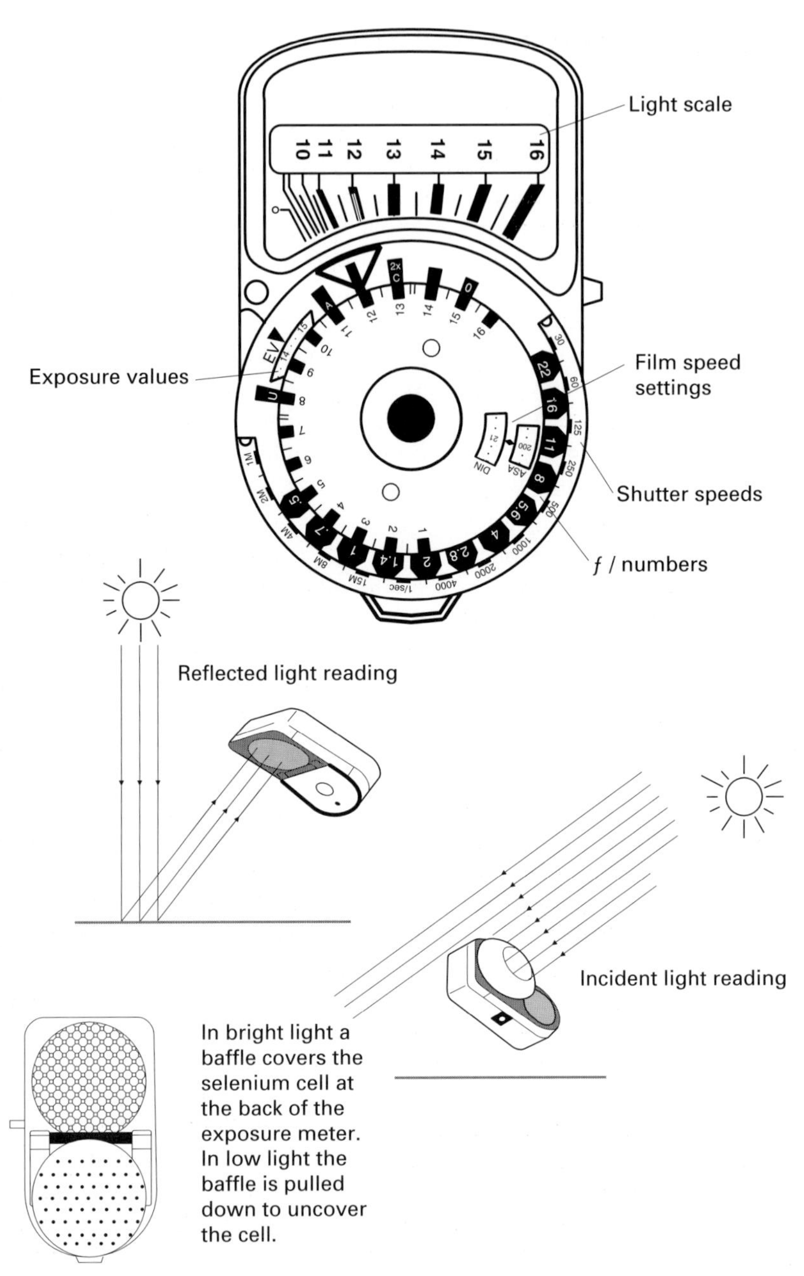

Figure 5.8 The Weston meter is the best known and most widely used of hand held exposure meters.

5.7 Exposure compensation

As mentioned in Chapter 2 on the camera there is an exposure compensation dial, usually situated around the film rewind knob. It will be seen that there is a normal position indicated by a 0 plus two sets of figures, one with a + sign the other with a – sign; occasionally both signs will be +. The + 1 and + 2 increase the exposure by one and two stops respectively, whereas the –1 and –2 or + $^1/_2$ and + $^1/_4$ decrease the exposure by one and two stops respectively. Increase in exposure is likely to be required more often than a decrease and the commonest example is where the subject is backlit, as with shooting into sun or against a window. The auto exposure function on a camera will give a reading for the bright back light and if exposed in this way will result in the background being perfect but the subject being silhouetted (see Figure 5.9a–b). By dialing in + 1 or + 2 the increase in exposure will put detail back into the subject but the background will become over exposed. Conversely, if the subject contains large dark areas it is likely that the metering system will increase exposure to the level required to record detail in these areas and thereby over expose the rest of the scene. By dialing in –1 or –2 the decrease in exposure will render the main scene better but there will be a consequent loss of detail in the shadow area.

If in doubt then one can always resort to 'bracketing'. This is simply taking more shots either side of the recommended exposure, under and over exposing, to ensure getting the right one. For all standard photography it is a waste of time and film, if you are not getting the exposure right then find out what the cause is and rectify it. However there are some occasions where lighting conditions prove difficult and a number of readings give different exposures. With negative film there is no point in under exposing so take one shot at the selected exposure and then another increasing the exposure by one stop, either by decreasing the shutter speed or *f* number. In extreme cases further shots can be made by increasing the exposure by one stop each time. With transparency film the bracketing needs to be towards under exposure and each additional shot should only be changed by half a stop. The reason for the different technique is that to put information on negative stock more exposure is required, whereas transparencies need less.

Recognising the tricky situations comes with experience, but as a guide any scene with sea, snow or sand making up the majority of the shot will fool the camera's metering system into thinking there is a lot more light around than is the case. An increase in exposure will be required to correct this and two stops should be enough. Shots taken into light will also fool the camera so under these circumstances it is best to take a reading looking away from the light and set it manually or by using the meter lock. The camera's meter will indicate over exposure when returning to the original scene but this should be ignored.

Night time photography can be one of the most rewarding types of photography for amateur and professional alike, but determining the correct exposure can prove very difficult (see Figure 5.10). This is particularly true if you are using the camera's metering system, as it is unable to give the long exposure times required. To overcome this requires a little time and concentration but becomes fairly straightforward once it has been mastered. The aperture must be set at the

Figure 5.9a

Figure 5.9b

Figure 5.9a–b Backlit photographs exposed: a for the background, resulting in the subject being silhouetted, and b for the subject, resulting in the background being burnt out.

Figure 5.10 Night shot lit only by the street lamps and using the ground as a camera support.

lowest definitive *f* number, 2, 2.8, but not necessarily the smallest number.

Many lenses have a maximum aperture in between the definitive numbers, such as 1.7, 2.4 etc. but these must be avoided for the purposes of this exercise. Having set the lens a reading is then taken from the highlight areas of the scene, reflected from the subject not direct from the light source. For this hypothetical case we will take it that the shutter speed works out at 1/2 second, with an aperture of *f*/2. Two things are immediately apparent, one a tripod and cable release are going to be required and secondly at *f*/2 there is no depth of field. Taking *f*/16 as the aperture needed to give sufficient depth of field the shutter speed will need to be altered accordingly. For each *f* number we close down, the exposure time needs to be doubled.

	1/2 second	@	*f*/2
becomes	1 second	@	*f*/2.8
	2 seconds	@	*f*/4
	4 seconds	@	*f*/5.6
	8 seconds	@	*f*/8
	16 seconds	@	*f*/11
	32 seconds	@	*f*/16

It can be seen from this chart that quite long exposure times can be worked out using the camera's limited metering system. A hand held meter of course will give all this information without it having to be worked out. Unfortunately things now begin to conspire against one, and if an exposure is made at the calculated time it will be under exposed; this is due to reciprocity failure.

5.8 Reciprocity failure

All films are designed to be used within certain limitations, particularly exposure times, and once these are exceeded the film will not react correctly. Although reciprocity failure occurs at both short and long exposure times, it is impractical to do anything about it until the time exceeds 1 second. Basically it is a failure of the emulsion to respond to the light levels existing at the time, requiring an increase in exposure. With black and white film it is only exposure that is affected and as a simple guide with exposure times up to 10 seconds then double the time, up to 1 minute multiply by three and over that by a further half factor for each minute, so that 5 minutes has to be multiplied by 3 plus 2 equals × 5 and becomes 25 minutes. Going back to the table on p.85 we can see that the 32 seconds exposure will become 1 minute 36 seconds. Alternatively the aperture could be opened by one and a half stops to *f*/8–11, with the consequent loss of depth of field.

The same guidelines can be used for colour negative film but there is the added problem that each of the three layers of emulsion will react differently to the low light levels. This results in a shift in colour balance which will need to be corrected by the use of a filter, thus extending the exposure time and needing a further increase; it very soon becomes a vicious circle. For all practical purposes it is not worth worrying about filtering negative film, as the usual orange/red colour cast is quite acceptable and helps create the right atmosphere. Should the cast be exceptionally heavy then it can be corrected in printing.

Colour transparency film, on the other hand, needs far more accurate exposure calculation and colour correction. Because transparencies are seen using transmitted and not reflected light the increase in exposure to allow for reciprocity failure needs to be much less. Up to 10 seconds requires only a 50% increase 1 second becomes 1½, 10 seconds becomes 15. Up to 30 seconds needs double the exposure, beyond that it is not recommended that slide film is used. It is impossible to give definitive filtrations for colour film as each one will differ in its requirements even though made by the same company. The information leaflet supplied with a film with give recommended filtrations at various exposure times as well as the maximum exposure times. As a guide daylight film will require a blue filter to correct for the artificial light plus a pale red to correct for reciprocity failure. Tungsten colour film will only require the red filter to correct for the lengthened exposure times. Remember neither a built-in meter nor a hand held meter allow for reciprocity failure, but if in doubt about exposure it is safe to double it with negative stock.

With experience the intricacies of exposure will be understood and become less of a minefield, but it does need to be given more thought than a lot of amateurs are prepared to give it. Because of the vast range of light levels confronted at night it may prove impossible to maintain detail in all areas of the image, resulting in something being sacrificed (see Figure 5.11).

Figure 5.11 After allowing for reciprocity failure, an exposure time of $2^1/_2$ minutes was required for this night shot, taken on a freezing cold and wet November night.

Reciprocity failure will also occur when undertaking still life photography using low level tungsten illumination. At close focusing ranges a small aperture will be required to give sufficient depth of field, resulting in longer exposure times, thus requiring a further increase to allow for reciprocity failure.

6 Light

Without light there can be no photography and the quality of that light is probably the single most important factor affecting the image. In the main the light we use for photography is visible so that what the eye sees is what the film will record. However, film is sensitive to light beyond the visible spectrum, particularly in the ultraviolet range, and this will affect the image without us knowing precisely to what extent. The direction and strength of the light will alter the appearance of our subject, both physically and aesthetically. To understand its effect fully we must first understand some basic principles.

6.1 Wavelength

All light travels in straight lines and the direction can only be changed by refraction or reflection. Although light travels in a straight line it does so in a wave motion and the measurement across the peaks of those waves is known as wavelength. The unit of measurement is a nanometre (nm) which is 10^{-9} metre, one thousand millionth of a metre, or one millionth of a millimetre.

The human eye is only sensitive to a small portion of the electromagnetic spectrum, 400–700nm, known as the visible spectrum (see Figures 6.1 and 6.2). Photographic film however is sensitive beyond this range into the ultraviolet, and infra-red film is sensitive beyond the limits at the other end (see Figure 6.1).

6.2 Colour temperature

Colour temperature is only of concern to us when using colour film, as black and white film does not mind what the light source is. All light has a particular colour, what we understand as white light is really a mix of all the colours of the rainbow or visible spectrum. Colour temperature is measured in Kelvins (K) which has its zero at –273°C. To measure colour temperature a black body is heated until it matches the colour of the light source, the material used is of little consequence

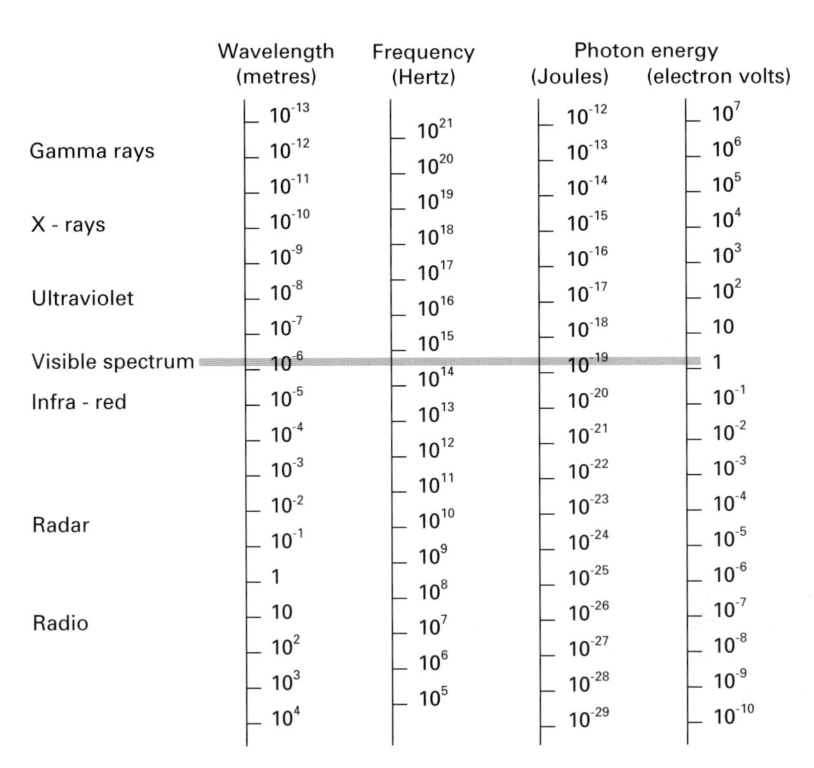

Figure 6.1 The electromagnetic spectrum.

here. We are all aware that when we heat metal it slowly glows red, then through orange and yellow, if we could heat it up sufficiently without it undergoing chemical change it would glow blue. So from this we can see that the lower the colour temperature the 'warmer' the light in terms of redness, the higher the temperature the 'colder' (bluer) the light.

	K
Standard candle	1930
Dawn sunlight	2000
Tungsten filament bulb	2700–2900
Fluorescent light	3000
Photoflood	3400
Daylight fluorescent light	4500
Mean noon sunlight	5400
Photographic daylight	5500
Electronic flash/blue flash bulb	6000
Blue sky	12 000–18 000

The brain is capable of correcting any inbalance in the colour of light to make it look white, but film is incapable of doing this and therefore, must have light of the correct colour in order to record colours accurately. Photographic film is balanced to a particular colour temperature to match the most widely used light source. Daylight film is balanced to 5500K which has been calculated as being

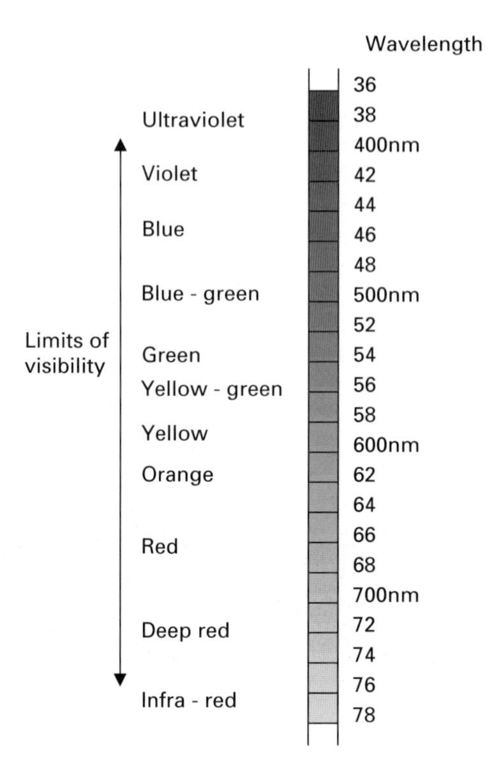

Figure 6.2 The visible spectrum.

average sunlight, as measured at noon in Washington DC. A cloudless bright blue sky will have a colour temperature of between 12 000K and 18 000K producing a heavy blue cast on the film, the reason for those rather rich blue skies in pictures taken abroad. Tungsten film is balanced at 3400K to match a photoflood lamp which used to be the standard photographic light source for studio work; this has now been replaced by electronic flash which has a colour temperature almost the same as daylight. For the professional and dedicated amateur colour temperature meters can be used to measure the colour of the light source and give the filter corrections needed.

It is more important to correct the colour of the light source when using transparency film as there is no room for adjustment in processing. With colour negative stock one can very often get away with using daylight film under artificial lighting conditions and having the colour corrected in the printing stage. When taking photographs under warm lighting conditions the idea is to record that warmth and filtering would only destroy the mood. However, using tungsten film in daylight would be totally unacceptable, giving a very blue result, which can only be corrected by filtration on the camera.

There are many light sources whose wavelengths fall within the visible spectrum and we divide these up into two categories, natural and artificial.

6.3 Daylight (natural light)

Daylight will change throughout the day in intensity, direction and colour. The time of year and one's location in the world will also directly affect its quality. For those of us living in the developed industrial areas of the world the quality of light is usually very poor owing to pollution. In mountainous regions and other areas

Figure 6.3 Bright sunlight creates a light and airy mood in this woodland shot.

with high rainfall the light is always crisper because the pollution is washed out of the air.

Light of course is responsible for creating the mood of a photograph, be it bright and sunny or overcast. Light from the sun in a cloudless sky will be very directional and harsh creating bright highlights and deep shadows. With cumulus cloud in the sky sunlight will be reflected from them and the subsequent result somewhat softer (see Figure 6.3). With a totally overcast sky the light will be very diffused with soft highlights and little in the way of shadows. In the early morning and late evening light has further to travel through the atmosphere and therefore produces much warmer light than at high noon. Typically morning light will take on a yellow hue whilst evening light is much redder. This is due to water and dust particles in the atmosphere scattering the short wavelength light at the blue end of the spectrum and reflecting the longer wavelengths at the red end. It is this same scattering of blue light that makes the sky blue and creates the ultraviolet haze in the distance. No control can be exerted over daylight when taking large scenes but limited control is possible where portraiture or close up work is concerned. Here harsh shadows can be softened with the use of reflectors or fill flash.

The weather will have a direct bearing on the quality of light but this can be exploited to advantage – fog, mist and rain all add an extra dimension to our photographs (see Figure 6.4). Under snow even the most mundane subject can take on a completely new form and produce an interesting photograph. All subjects take on a different form and feeling at night especially if caught at the magic hour, one hour after sunset or one hour before sunrise, when the sky is light but there is no direct sunlight.

Figure 6.4 Mist has obscured the background and created a different mood for this shot.

6.4 Artificial light

The most common form of artificial light is the tungsten filament bulb as used in the average household, having a colour temperature of between 2700K and 2900K. Even when using tungsten balanced film the result will have an orange/yellow cast, but when using daylight film the final image will be very red. Colour correction filters can be used to raise or lower the colour temperature of a light source and thereby correct the colours (see Chapter 9 on filters and accessories).

The photoflood is designed specifically for use with tungsten balanced film and is just a larger version of a normal filament lamp, but very much brighter, usually 250–500 watts. It has a colour temperature of 3400K and therefore is in the orange band of the spectrum. When using daylight balanced film under photofloods the result will be very red and require a blue filter to correct it (see Chapter 9 on filters).

The next most common form of artificial lighting is the fluorescent tube, as found in industrial and office complexes. There are a large variety of these all of which have a different colour temperature, ranging from yellow through to green. Although the eye will pick these up as being almost white, daylight and tungsten film will show a cast. Some film manufacturers have build complementary filter layers into the emulsion of films to counteract these casts, with some success. Fluorescent lights pulse and this can cause an interesting phenomenon where

Figure 6.5 An extended exposure time allowed this photograph to be taken using only the artificial lighting seen in the picture.

several images of the lamp will appear on the film when long exposures are used. Other forms of gas lamps include sodium vapour, the orange street lights which will give everything within the range of illumination an orange cast, and mercury vapour, the bluer street lights.

6.5 Electronic flash

Flash will be dealt with in detail in Chapter 8, but with reference to colour temperature it can be considered to be the same as daylight, although in fact it is slightly bluer with a temperature of 6000K. Flashbulbs are still available though little used these days and they too have a colour temperature of 6000K. Flash can be used to help correct colours where mixed daylight and artificial light is used to illuminate the subject, a very useful technique. The colour of the flash can be changed by placing a filter over the head, this will influence the colour of the subject within the range of the flash, but not beyond. By placing an orange Wratten 85 filter over the flash head the normally 6000K balanced light can be changed to 3400K for use with tungsten colour film.

6.6 Direction

For years the amateur photographer has been told to ensure that the sun is over their left shoulder when taking a photograph. This is understandable when using a simple camera because the lens is not shielded. However, there could not be a

Figure 6.6 A portrait taken using directional flash, with very little modelling or mood.

worse position for the light to come from, producing flat uninteresting pictures. The SLR camera lens can be fitted with a lens hood which shields it from non-image forming light which produces lens flare. Using a lens hood for every shot will improve the colour saturation of the final colour image and the contrast of a black and white one. It will also enable you to use side lighting which produces a much more effective picture showing form and texture in the subject. Photographing people with the sun behind you will result in your subjects squinting, whereas with side lighting they will be much more comfortable (see Figure 6.7 and 6.8). When taking portraits or close ups using side lighting any harsh shadows can be softened using a reflector or fill in flash.

Back lighting is always a difficult situation, causing the photographer problems with exposure. A decision must be made as to whether the background lighting is to be the subject, or whether the subject is between the camera and the light source. In the first instance, such as sunsets, the exposure is made for the light and will produce excellent results. However, in the second instance a decision must be taken to either let the subject go into silhouette or maintain detail within it. For the first example the exposure is taken for the background, in the second, a reading must be taken from the subject thus causing the background to over expose. With automatic cameras the camera will expose for the background unless the backlight compensation is used. Shooting straight into light can cause problems with lens flare; this can be minimised by ensuring that the lens is clean and using a hood.

Flare is often visible in the viewfinder as pink or purple hexagons and can sometimes be eliminated by an adjustment in camera position. Results of flaring will appear as these hexagons or as a general milky appearance to the print or slide.

6.7 Quality

The next consideration is that of the quality of the light, whether it is hard or soft. Directional light from a point source such as the sun will produce hard lighting with very bright highlights and deep shadows. This can be useful to highlight textures if coming from 90° to the subject's surface. Hard lighting is often used in male portraiture to emphasise a weathered face or make the sitter appear tough and strong.

Soft lighting will be omnidirectional, as with an overcast sky, providing softer highlights and shadows. This is the sort of lighting that is likely to prove best for portraiture of women and children, giving a soft 'feminine' feel to the subject (see Figures 6.9 and 6.10).

6.8 Contrast

Contrast is the difference in illumination levels between the brightest and darkest part of the scene (see Figure 6.11). The eye can cope with quite a wide range of brightness levels but film is restricted to a much smaller ratio. If one exposes for the highlights then the shadows become under exposed and very black, losing all

Figure 6.7 Side lighting has shown up the relief detail in this photograph of coins.

Figure 6.8 Here the shadows created by side lighting have helped to highlight the shape and form of the ground.

Figure 6.9 These two illustrations show how the scene changes with lighting. The bright sunshine has made the highlights bright, created shadows and given depth to the photograph. There will inevitably be a slight loss of detail in shadow areas.

Figure 6.10 The same shot, this time under an overcast sky, no shadows and the difference in brightness levels between the covered area and the exterior reduced, allowing more detail to be seen.

Source: ('A' grade GCSE, Melissa Butler Adams).

Figure 6.11 In this photograph of a french horn high contrast lighting accentuates the form and texture of the instrument.

detail. If the other course is taken and exposure made for the shadows then the highlights will over expose and burn out, becoming very white with little or no detail. The only way around the problem is to reduce the brightness range by introducing more light into the darker areas by filling in with flash or using reflectors. Negative film will cope with about three stops difference in brightness between the highlights and shadows, beyond this a compromise will have to be accepted. Because transparency film is viewed by transmitted light it copes with the shadow areas better and therefore accepts a greater contrast range.

Sunlight is very strong and therefore there will not be any fall off in intensity when using side lighting, the same is not true of artificial light sources. Those parts of the subject furthest from the light will suffer from fall off and the eye may not readily pick this up. A simple way of checking is to take an exposure reading at both ends of the subject or, just hold a pencil against the surface and watch the shadow as it is moved from the end nearest the light source to the end furthest away.

Apart from obvious points such as avoiding ugly shadows and ensuring there are catch lights in the eyes of a portrait subject, there are no hard and fast rules to lighting and it is a case of experimenting to find out what suits your needs best. Highly reflective surfaces, such as glass and metal can cause enormous lighting problems and the only successful way of treating small objects is to 'tent' them. Here a tent of thin translucent paper is built around the subject and lit from the outside, with the camera shooting through a hole in one wall.

When using artificial light to illuminate the subject it is always best to start off with a single lamp and gradually build up the lighting until the desired effect is achieved. Simplicity is the key, keep the lighting to the minimum, the more lights used the greater the problems with shadows and reflections. Portrait subjects wearing glasses need extra care to avoid reflections, these are easy to see when using lamps but difficult to anticipate with flash. Tilting the head slightly down will help to minimise the problem – rather like snooker, it is all to do with angles.

6.9 Self-test exercise

To really understand the effect of lighting on the appearance of the subject take an orange and place it on a complementary background. Either take a series of photographs using a small flash gun or spotlight, or just practise with a lamp. Start by placing the light to the side of the subject so that you have one half lit and the other half in shadow. Gradually move the light round to the front of the subject and watch the change in feel and mood as this happens. Having done this, start at the beginning again but this time use a reflector board opposite the light to soften the shadows. Continue to progress by introducing another light at the front and move them around watching the way in which the appearance of the subject changes.

Having understood the effects of frontal lighting move a light behind to illuminate the background throwing the subject into silhouette. Gradually add some front lighting onto the subject until a balance is achieved, this can be checked with your camera meter. Carry this a stage further by putting a light behind the subject but pointing towards the camera, thus creating a rim light.

The important thing to look for at all times is the strength and position of the shadows (see Figure 6.12); ugly prominent shadows will ruin a picture, be they on the subject or background. A lack of shadows will make the image flat and uninteresting, showing little or no relief or texture.

Source: ('A' grade GCSE, Jo Allen).

Figure 6.12 Here harsh lighting has helped to create an interesting shadow pattern behind the main subject.

7 Composition

Is photography an art form, a craft, or a technical science? The answer to this question will depend upon your outlook on life and photography in particular. The only true answer has to be that it is a combination of all three disciplines. The technical side may not concern us too much, as we leave that to the manufacturers of cameras and materials. Many of us will also leave the processing and printing of the final images to someone else. The craft side of photography is the effective use of the camera, its accessories and the understanding of how light affects the subject. Once mastered, it leaves us free to put maximum effort into the artistic side of our photography, probably the most difficult and frustrating part.

Picture structure or composition in photography is as vital an element as it is in art, though there is less control over it. The artist has the option to sketch a scene in rough before committing it to canvas. In this way they can change the relative position of objects to each other, add detail that will enhance the picture, remove unwanted clutter and alter the effect of lighting. If a photographer wants to take a picture at a particular time of day or under special lighting conditions then he must be there at the right time. Adding small objects can be achieved but removal of anything other than light portable objects is out of the question. The only way unwanted clutter can be excluded is to change camera position, which will inevitably alter the composition.

As with other art forms creativity is in the eye of the beholder and every one of us will put a different interpretation upon any given picture. The photographer can set out to be informative, controversial or just creative. How the viewer receives and assesses the information contained within a photograph will depend upon their mood at the time and how receptive they are feeling.

Taking and viewing photographs is a solitary occupation and requires us to open our souls and delve into the depths of our emotions. A photograph taken without feeling will be dead and lifeless and this will be conveyed to the viewer. Communication is the name of the game and if your picture fails to communicate then you have failed in your prime task. The photograph may be technically perfect but lacking that part of ourselves that is required to make it work. The initial idea must be clearly formed in the photographer's mind before the picture is taken, a statement of intent. Failure to do this will result in confused and muddled photographs which will be rejected by the viewer in an instant. The audience must be provoked into thought, even if at the end of the day they do not like what they see.

In this age of mass visual communication the eyes are bombarded with feeble, poor quality images that have dulled the senses and made the vast majority of us less responsive. However, when a high quality image is confronted all the senses are re-activated and the viewer begins to enjoy the experience. A classic case occurred in Britain a few years ago when a new national newspaper was launched with an emphasis on high quality photography, which soon had the other newspapers looking to their laurels. Prior to this the reading public had become used to very inferior photographs illustrating their news stories. The general public are all too willing to accept poor quality photography and this must stem from a lack of education. How often do you accept the process house telling you that the poor images are your fault? All too often, do you ever question it? Probably not.

A photograph is a simple two dimensional image into which we try to put all five senses of sight, sound, smell, touch and taste. When presenting that image we must try and re-evoke those senses to the best of our ability, relying largely on that great human capacity of imagination in the viewer. In a good photograph the viewer should be able to tell you what your emotions were at the time and have a feeling of being there.

The human brain looks for order, pattern and rhythm in a picture and there are certain ways of dividing a format up that are pleasing to the eye. Let us now look at some basic principles which will improve composition.

7.1 Rule of thirds

All the photographer's rules of composition come from art and are well proven. As with all rules they are set out as guidelines and not hard and fast, they should never be bent but can be smashed. The rule of thirds suggests that the frame be divided up into three parts, horizontally or vertically (see Figures 7.1 and 7.2).

This rule can be taken a stage further by dividing the frame into three unequal sections and even different shapes. There is no requirement for the thirds to be of equal size; much will depend upon how the photographer wants to interpret the subject (see Figure 7.3 and 7.4).

Dividing the frame through the middle will separate the image into two individual pictures, causing confusion and conflict. This is one of the commonest faults amongst amateurs, particularly with landscapes; much of the problem caused by the split image focusing in the middle of the viewfinder. It must not be assumed that a picture should never be divided equally because there will always be the occasion when symmetry will produce a stunning photograph (see Figures 7.5 and 7.6).

7.2 Golden means

Taking the standard means of dividing the frame into three vertical and three horizontal sections, the lines intersect at four points known as the 'Golden means'.

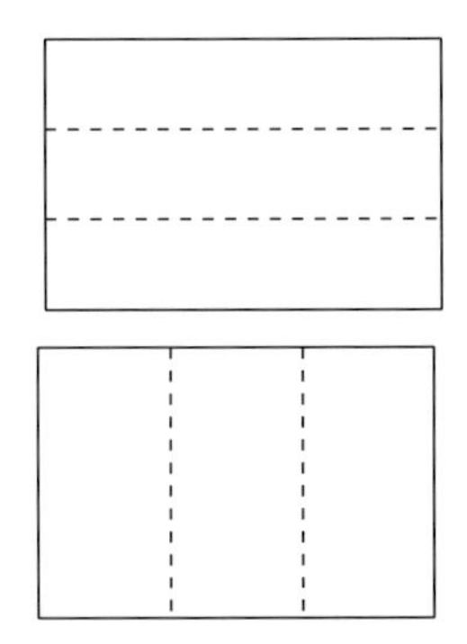

Figure 7.1 The image area divided into thirds horizontally or vertically.

Figure 7.2 This shot can be divided up easily into vertical thirds.

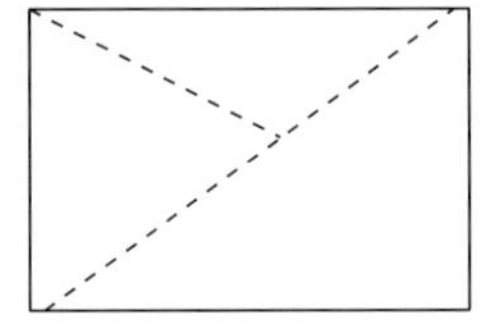

Figure 7.3 The thirds do not have to be equal or of the same shape.

Figure 7.4 This image can be divided up into unequal horizontal thirds.

These four points are very important in picture structure as the positions where a focal point or vanishing point can be placed, the idea being to utilise one or more of these in picture construction. In landscapes one or two points may be used for placing an object on, as a point of focus, and for leading the eye into the distance, whereas in portraiture all four might be brought into play, placing eyes and hands on each of the points (see Figures 7.7 and 7.8).

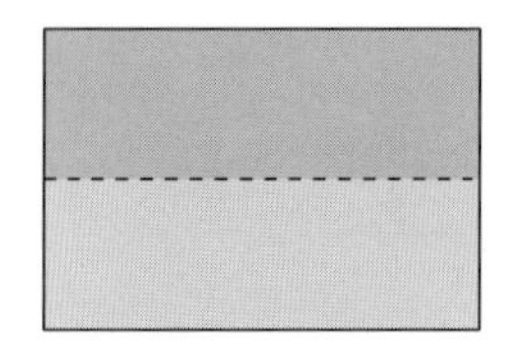

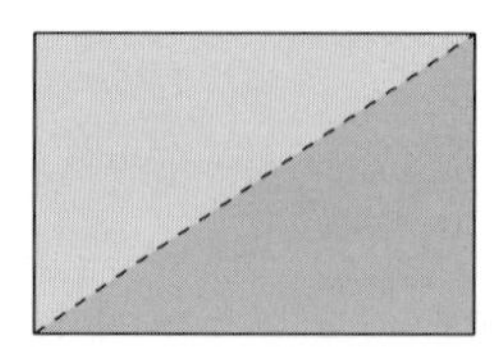

Figure 7.5 Dividing the frame equally will result in poor composition.

Figure 7.6 A landscape with the horizon line dividing the image in two.

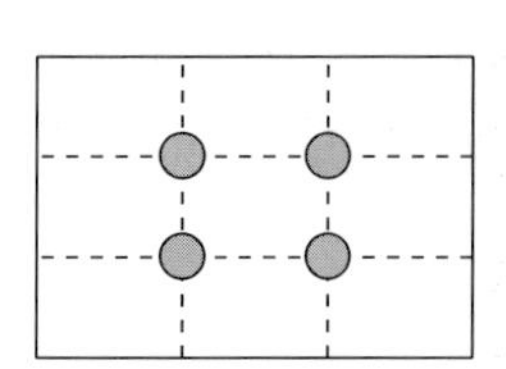

Figure 7.7 The four golden means within the picture area.

Source: ('A' grade GCSE, Sopie Camu)

Figure 7.8 In this composition the hand and face are placed on the golden means.

7.3 Golden section

The Golden section rule states that a line is divided so that the ratio between the shorter and longer parts of the line is the same as the ratio between the longer part and the whole line, that being 8:5 (see Figures 7.9 and 7.10).

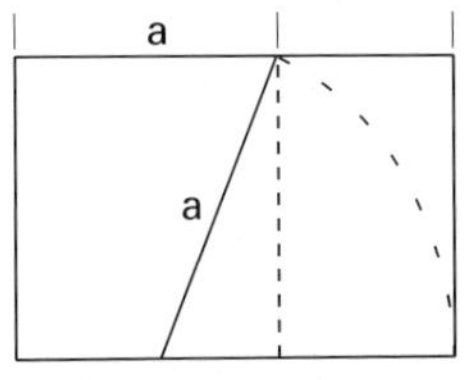

Figure 7.9 The golden section rule.

Source: ('A' grade GCSE, Nicola Kent).

Figure 7.10 The golden section rule can be applied here from the left.

By describing an arc from the division until it bisects a vertical line extended from the horizontal, the basis for a rectangle is produced. This is known as the Golden rectangle, and again has a ratio of 8:5 between the short and long sides. The old box camera format of 6cm × 9cm worked on this principle, that of a ratio of 3:2, and the 35mm film does exactly the same, 36mm × 24mm. It can be seen that although neither format equates exactly to the Golden section rule, they are close enough not to make any significant difference. For those photographers who are using cameras other than 35mm, for instance a square medium format camera, vast improvements in composition can be achieved by taking the Golden rectangle into consideration. This, of course, means that more will appear on film than is required, but this can be cropped out in printing; having said that many a square photograph will work very well.

7.4 Lines

Lines within a photograph help to create the mood or feel of the picture and in so doing affect the emotions of the viewer. Careful planning of the picture structure will ensure that the right feel is transmitted, failure to do this will result in conflict within the frame. The message that the lines send out must support that intended by the photographer. Again no hard and fast rule can be applied, because every picture will consist of more than one element, but simple guidelines can be followed.

Vertical lines create a feeling of strength as in tree trunks, columns, walls and an upright body (see Figures 7.11 and 7.12). Horizontal lines suggest peace and tranquility and an ordered structure as might be found in a landscape shot. Diagonal lines are active and imply movement or action and should be used in all forms of photography involving motion, athletics, water sports, aeroplanes, etc. (see Figure 7.13). Circles and curves, on the other hand, can spark off a range of feelings from high activity, in the form of circular motion, to confusion and conflict.

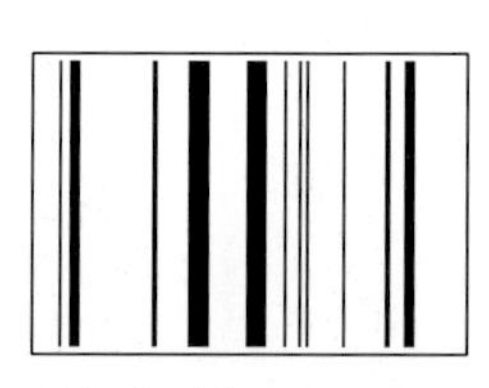

Vertical for strength

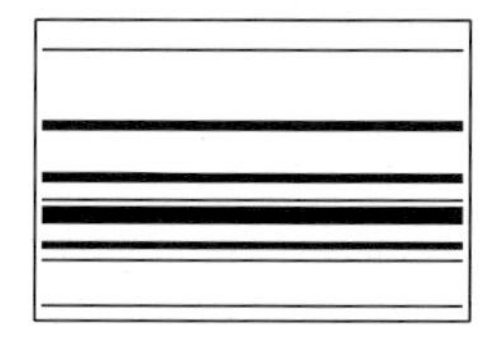

Horizontal lines for tranquility

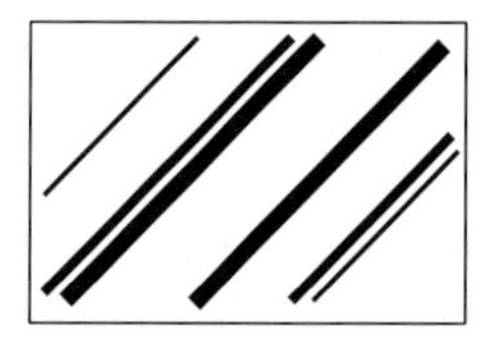

Diagonal for movement

Figure 7.11 Vertical lines for strength, horizontal lines for tranquility and diagonal lines for movement.

Figure 7.12 The vertical lines of this bridge give a feeling of strength.

7.5 Leads

As the name suggests, leads are used to draw the viewer into and around the picture until all the information contained within is assimulated. Various methods of leading the eye through a picture can be utilised depending on the subject matter

Figure 7.13 (above) The diagonal lines of the wings on this aircraft give a sense of movement to the subject, making it appear to be coming round towards the camera.

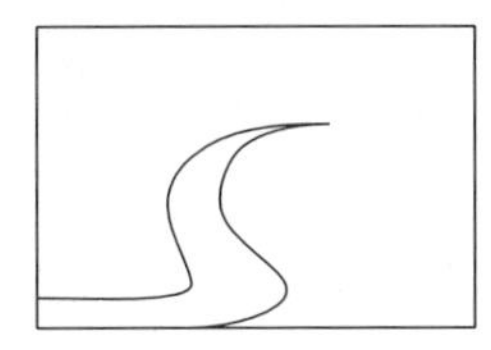

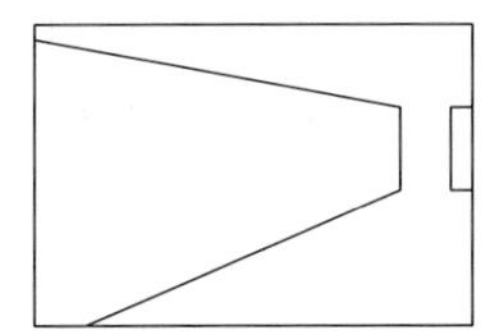

Figure 7.14 Leads are used to draw the eye into the picture.

Figure 7.15 The strong lead lines all take the eye to the top of the mast.

Figure 7.16 Here the leads take the eye across the picture. In both this image and Figure 7.15 the eye is taken into the picture and the information assimulated.

(see Figure 7.14). With landscapes a road, river, fence or hedge line can draw the viewer in from the foreground through the middle distance to a vanishing point on a Golden mean. Once there the viewer has no alternative but to return through the picture, perhaps via a different route, to the foreground. In place of a steady line a series of stepping stones could be used, objects which are not connected but follow on from each other taking the eye through the composition. In close up portraiture an arm or piece of clothing can lead the eye through the picture to the face. Clothing can again be employed for full length portraiture, but props are more likely to provide the leads. Where human form is part of a larger picture then the face or eyes can be utilised to direct the viewer to various parts of that photograph.

In some forms of photography taking the eye through a picture is reduced to a simple lead across, where the eye is taken from one side to the other or from front to back, without winding around the image (see Figure 7.16). This is likely to be the case when photographing subjects such as cars, ships and planes full frame. Most of us will tackle such a subject by photographing it from a three-quarter front angle. The lead is provided by diminishing perspective, the subject becoming smaller the further away from the camera it goes, which in turn gives the picture depth (see Figure 7.17). The same technique is used for photographing street scenes and can be utilised in landscapes, where the foreground consists of an even subject such as crops or sand.

Source: ('A' grade GCSE, Sophie Cranston).

Figure 7.17 The repetitive lines of the arches and doors, plus the diminishing perspective take the eye right to the back of the picture.

7.6 Blocks

Blocking is used as a means of keeping the viewer within the frame of a picture. Here objects can be placed at the edge of a frame when composing the photograph

Figure 7.19 In this shot the blocks are used to blank out a bland sky. The strong leads, in the form of the walls and paving, take the eye towards the gate which must be open to allow the eye to continue up the path and through to the church.

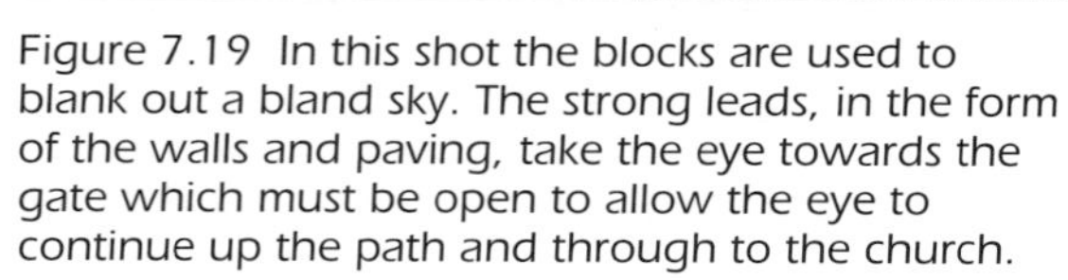

Blocks

Figure 7.18 Blocks used to hold the viewer's attention within the frame.

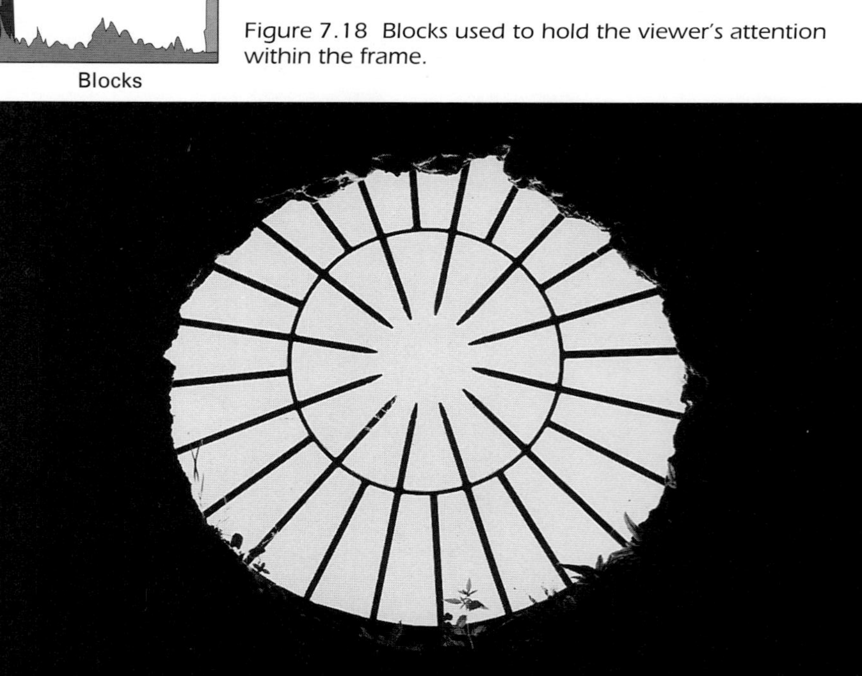

Figure 7.20 The ultimate in blocking where the image is completely framed and in this case is the picture.

Plate 1
Candid photography requires patience and a keen eye to catch the right moment. Being aware of what is going on but at the same time being unobtrusive is essential. This colourful market stall in Paris makes a very pleasing picture.

Plate 2
Another candid photograph, this time catching people relaxing; this is a more difficult shot to take because the subjects are likely to spot the camera and stare at it or move away.

Plate 3
Photographing interiors with ambient light produces the effect that the architect intended. Here a ceiling at the Louvre has been shot on daylight film using the subdued daylight from windows.

Plate 4
Nature will provide ready-made photographs if one is observant; here the retreating sea has created patterns in the sand around the pebbles and shell.

Plate 5
These pigeons add a touch of humour to this study of patterns, the rounded shapes of the birds contrasting with the straight lines of the paving stones.

Plate 6
The 'magic hour' after sunset and before sunrise provides the right exposure balance between natural and artificial lighting.

Plate 7
Colour is an all important ingredient which is often not given sufficient thought. Here the subtle contrast between the wood and the blue paintwork gives impact to this shot.

Plate 8
Here shape, pattern and colour combine to make a very powerful picture.

Plate 9
Being in the right place at the right time is nearly always a matter of luck, however, there are times when determination and hard work will achieve the desired result. Here the positioning of the camera boat was all important to catch the light on the sails.

Plate 10
Night shots require extended exposure times necessitating a stable camera support, ideally a tripod and cable release. This shot of the Eiffel Tower was taken by resting the camera on a wall with an exposure time of/÷¢ second.

Plate 11
Fireworks always make attractive photographs, more so when they are reflected in water. In this shot, taken at Cowes Week, there is the added interest of the lights on boats dancing around on the water.

Plate 12
This photograph of a yacht racing at Cowes has been taken against the light to give the water more life and make the colours on the sails stand out.

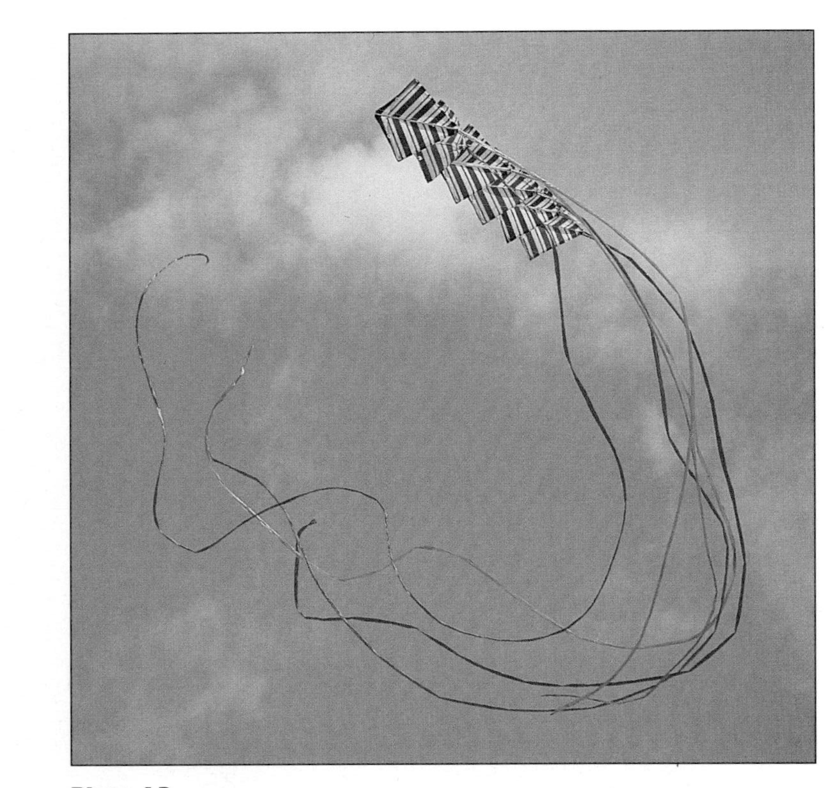

Plate 13
In action photography a sharp eye and quick trigger finger are demanded in order to catch the right moment for exposure. The circular pattern created by the kites and the tails give a strong sense of movement.

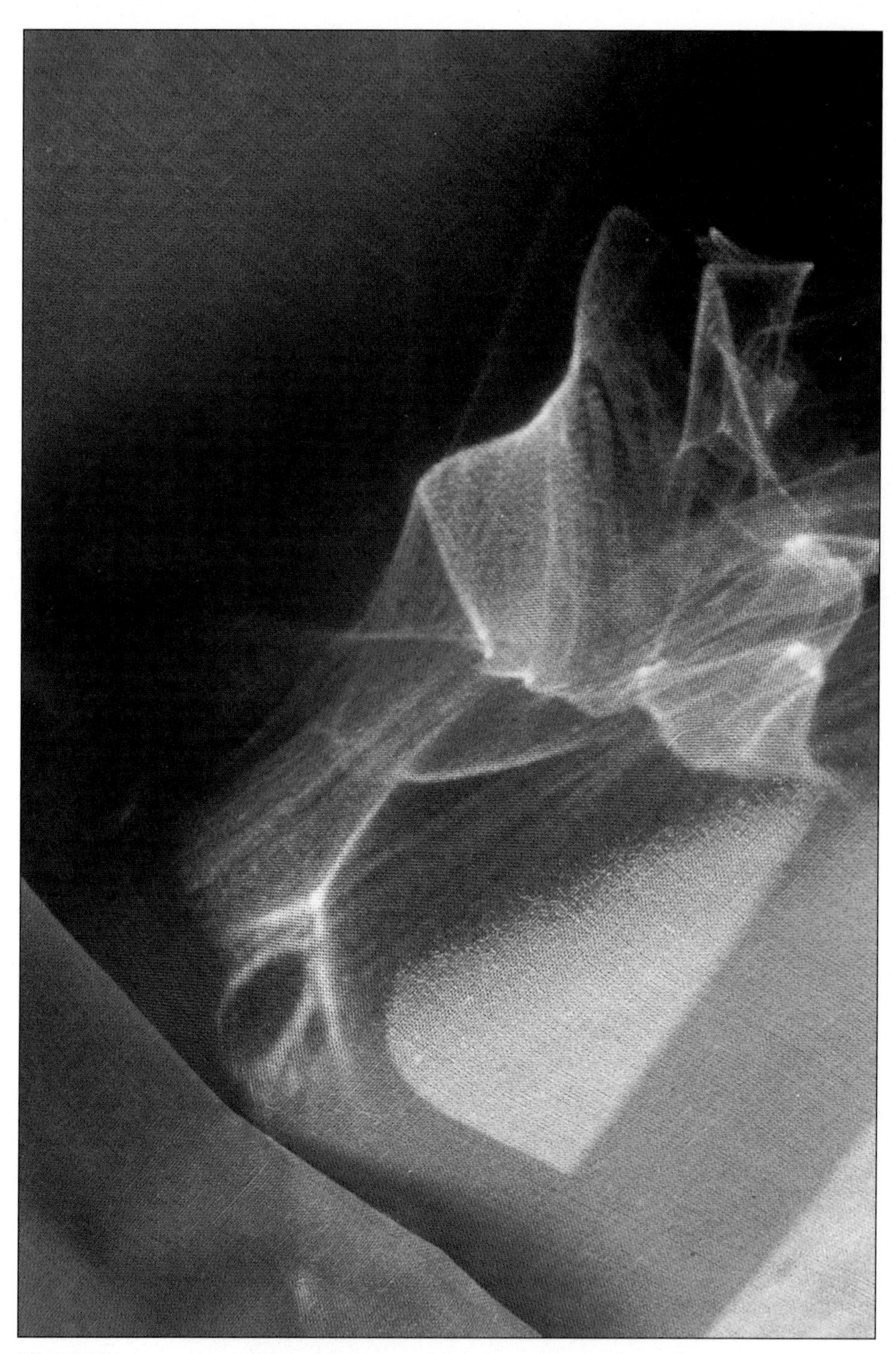

Plate 14
In this unusual shot it is light itself which makes the picture. The shape has been created by sunlight reflecting off metal foil, anything other than a single colour background would have detracted from the main subject.
(Judy Chidlow)

Plate 15
City and Guilds 9231 'Starting Photography' is the base module of the series and is undertaken to a given theme. This frost-covered plant was used in a portfolio entitled 'winter'.
(Frank Oldaker, C&G Starting Photography 'Credit' grade)

Plate 16
Some subjects can be found very readily but others need time and thought to work out, this interesting interpretation was on the theme of reflections.
(Malcolm Morrisen LRPS, C&G Starting Photography, 'Distinction' grade)

Plate 17
This boat and reflection are easier to spot in terms of the theme, in this case its strength lies in the simplicity of the composition. (Malcolm Morrisen LRPS, C&G Starting Photography, 'Distinction' grade)

Plate 18
In this striking sunset shot a tobacco graduated filter was used for the sky and fill flash for the foreground.

Plate 19
Contra-jour can produce very appealing photographs, this seascape is ideal for the City and Guilds Landscape Photography module.

Plate 20
Good framing holds the viewer's interest within the picture; here the tree and its shadow act as blocks around three sides.

Plate 21
Effective lighting is essential for landscape work; here dappled sunlight has created interest in the lawn and water.

to prevent the eye leaving – trees, buildings or any fairly solid object can be used as a block (see Figure 7.18). Blocks will tend to be introduced when the leads of a picture are weak, they may appear on both or on just one side. To extend this further shadows can be used as blocks at the bottom of the frame and overhanging leaves at the top. This latter point is very useful for blocking out a bland and uninteresting sky on an overcast day (see Figure 7.19). Using the framework of a doorway or arch makes very effective use of total blocking, or framing, especially when silhouetted (see Figure 7.20)

7.7 Patterns

Pattern plays a vital part in all photographs, whether it be irregular or defined and repetitive. In many cases the pattern can support or enhance the message contained within the photograph, at the extreme it will become the message. This style of photography we know as abstract, the relationship between different or similar shapes.

Most of us will at some time or another be attracted to a scene where regular shapes dominate, a skyline of skyscrapers, a row of bollards and so forth. Very often an abstract photograph will contain regular patterns not one of which is whole, either cut off at the photograph's edge or through objects overlying each other. Although it may seem that the eye risks being drawn out of the picture, in fact the eye is attracted by the similarities (see Figure 7.21).

Abstraction can be found in almost any subject but to find it the photographer

Figure 7.21 Regular patterns are an important part of composition; here the curves of the balloons repeat and reflect each other.

will have to look very closely. The most successful pictures of this type come from photographing small areas of a larger object. It is in this style of photography that pure symmetry is likely to work most successfully.

7.8 Colour

As the vast majority of photographers start off in colour before progressing onto black and white, consideration must be given to the effect of colour on composition. The way in which colour is represented can have a major impact on the picture, it can be intense or weak and this we know as colour saturation. The greater the saturation, the greater the impact on the eye, and the more striking the picture may appear. However, muted colours can be just as effective, especially when concentrating on shades of a single colour. Contrast can be introduced by using complementary colours in a picture, such as blue and yellow. Other colours are very aggressive and demand attention, red is by far the most dominant. Even a small amount of red in a photograph will attract the eye, so care must be taken in the combination of colours used. As may be deduced from nature the most pleasing colour to the eye is green, giving a sense of freedom and health. Oranges and yellows give a feeling of warmth, whilst blues introduce coldness.

The interplay of colours can be the subject of the photograph with no identifiable objects appearing. When undertaking this sort of photography it is but a short step to impressionist abstraction (see the Plates section between pp.000 and 000).

7.9 Shape

Another important consideration for all photographs is that of shape. For most cameras the choice is that of landscape (horizontal) or portrait (vertical). The message behind a picture can be changed simply by changing the format. A portrait format will give emphasis to vertical lines, increasing the feeling of strength, whereas a landscape format will accentuate the horizontal lines and sense of calmness (see Figure 7.22a–b). The square picture of the medium format cameras tends to be neutral and gives the advantage of being able to be printed either way. The shape of an image and the positioning of the subject within the frame takes on greater importance when it is to be reproduced in print form. Consideration must be given to where the picture will appear and how much page space is likely to be allocated. Sufficient unimportant sky or foreground must be left for any overprinting, particularly for banners on front covers.

7.10 Background

One thing that all amateurs and professionals have fallen foul of at some time is not being aware of the background. Busy and cluttered backgrounds will detract from the subject and make the picture difficult to look at (see Figure 7.23). With portraiture it is the object growing out of the head that catches the photographer

Figure 7.22a

Figure 7.22b

Figure 7.22a–b Here the same view is treated both horizontally and vertically; one can see that there is a change of emphasis with the change in shape of the frame. By accentuating the vertical lines the portrait framing has a much stronger feel to it than the more peaceful horizontal one.

Figure 7.23 Messy cluttered backgrounds ruin a picture, distracting the eye away from the subject.

Figure 7.24 This unusual movement shot has the subject stationary with a moving train passing in front, creating the blur.

out. The reason for this and the cure is very simple, we are so concerned with getting the subject right that the background tends to be forgotten; take time to study the background and surrounding areas either before or during setting up. If a cluttered background is unavoidable then it should be put sufficiently out of focus so as not to intrude.

7.11 Movement

Movement can be captured in one of two ways, frozen or blurred. In the first instance high shutter speeds are required in order to stop any movement in the subject, capturing an instant in the continuous action. Whilst making for an interesting picture, frozen shots are often lifeless. A more interesting way of depicting them is to keep the subject sharp and blurring the background, known as panning. Here the subject is followed by the camera and the exposure made during the panning action, the shutter speed does not have to be very fast, 1/60 second is quite adequate. The third option is to use a long exposure time and let the subject blur against a sharp background, it will depend very much upon personal choice and the message that is being put across, see Chapter 14 on disciplines for more detail.

7.12 Scale

Very often one needs to put across the enormity or minuteness of the subject, which may not be immediately obvious, and to do this some form of scale needs to be introduced. We are not talking about rulers, but objects with which everyone can associate readily (see Figure 7.25). Perhaps the first choice might be a person, but one may not wish to include human interest, so another familiar object has to be found. With landscapes it could be buildings, animals or perhaps vehicles; trees do not always work because they vary so much in size. At the other end of the scale when undertaking macro photography then a small everyday object such as a coin can be introduced. Wherever possible the scale object should be part of the composition, but of course this may not always be achieved. One very important point to remember when using people or vehicles to scale a scene, they will immediately date the photograph and this needs to be avoided if the pictures are to be sold.

7.13 Colour or black and white

Most of the above guidelines apply to both colour and black and white photography, but there is a further point to consider. For the vast majority of people starting out on photography colour is going to be the obvious choice, after all we see in colour and all the high street process houses are geared up for colour. At some stage, though, there will be a desire to try one's hand at black and white. It is very important to remember, right from the start, that a completely different approach

Figure 7.25 'All out and push': Here the people not only give an indication of size but also add the important element of humour.

is required to that used with colour. An awareness of tonal ranges and how colour translates into tones of grey needs to be acquired and this can only come with practice. It has to be remembered that blues and yellows record as light tones and reds as dark tones. Without colour it follows that the composition must be very much stronger, with more emphasis on light, shade and pattern (see Figure 7.26).

7.14 Self-test exercise

Look out some of your favourite photographs and analyse them, bearing in mind the rules of composition. The most pleasing pictures will be those to which some of the various rules can be applied, although there may not have been any conscious act in applying them at the time of taking.

Take a good colour photograph, one that has impact and obeys the rules of composition, make a black and white photocopy of it and do a critical analysis of the two prints and see if the photograph works in black and white. Failure to translate from colour to black and white will be due to weak composition and/or a rendering of different colours into similar grey tones. From this exercise it can be seen that one should not try to take both colour and black and white photographs on the same occasion, it will inevitably result in poor images in both mediums.

Figure 7.26 Simplicity is the key to good black and white photography: here the subject matter has been kept to a minimum and printed in high contrast.

8 Flash

Long gone are the days of the flash bulb and the fiddle of having to change a hot bulb every time one took a picture. Even the multi shot flash cube has gone, to be replaced by small electronic flash units.

The flashgun is probably the most useful accessory that the photographer can have in their kit. Flashguns come in a variety of powers and sizes to suit all needs, most fitting onto the hot shoe of the camera. For most people the flash is only used indoors as the main source of illumination, but there are a lot more uses to which it can be put.

A large number of modern compact cameras have a flash built-in with a sensor that will automatically switch it on in low light conditions. This accounts for a lot of the frustration at sports meetings when spectators are asked not to use flash-light; they have no control over whether the flash comes on and their only alternative is not to take pictures.

All small flash guns are powered by batteries which will give between 40 and 60 flashes depending on the power setting. On the larger guns rechargable ni-cad units are used, giving around 60 flashes per charge with a life of approximately 10 000 flashes.

8.1 Guide numbers

To indicate the power output of a flash the manufacturers give them guide numbers or GNs. There are two systems in operation at present, the metric and the imperial. Both are based on ISO 100 film at a distance of 3m/10ft. To work out the power of a flash unit the guide number is divided by 3 or 10. i.e. GN24 ÷3 gives an aperture of *f*/8 at 3m, the imperial equivalent is GN80 ÷ 10 to give the same aperture at 10ft. The imperial system is being phased out to leave the metric as standard. The correct *f* number for any given distance can be worked out using the guide number. Having focused on the subject, read off the distance from the lens and then divide the GN by that distance, i.e. with a subject at 6m the aperture will be 24 ÷ 6 = *f*/4, for ISO 100 film. When using any film other than

ISO 100 the result will be different. The smaller the GN the less power the flash will have. For most practical purposes a GN of 24 is quite sufficient, the more powerful guns tend to be used off camera and are bulky, heavy and expensive.

8.2 Setting up

With cameras whose shutters are in the lens, the flash will work at all speeds but the 35mm SLR has a focal plane shutter, and this must clear the whole of the film area before the flash fires. For the majority of 35mm SLR cameras the shutter speed is between 1/60 and 1/125 second, but as technology advances these speeds are increasing. If the shutter speed is set too fast then the shutter blades will cover part of the film and a black area on the print will result. This may be along the bottom or down the side of the image, depending on the direction of travel of the shutter blades.

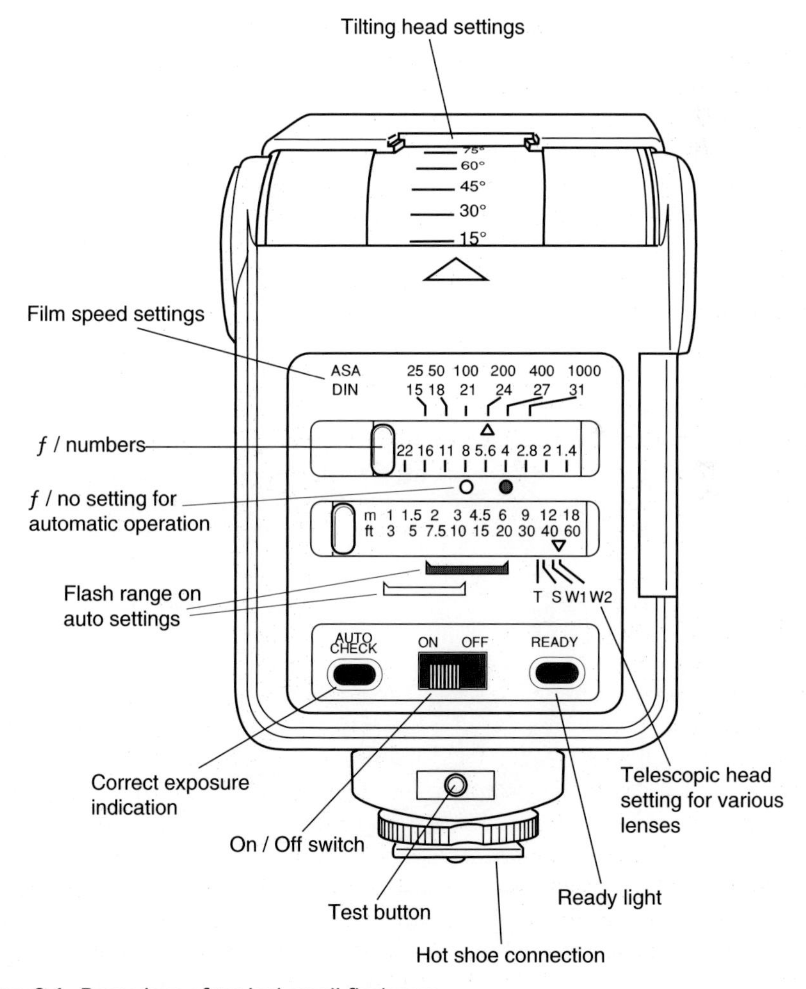

Figure 8.1 Rear view of typical small flashgun.

So, the first step is to ensure that your camera shutter speed is set to the flash synchronisation speed or slower, usually picked out in red, with a lightning symbol or X alongside. Next place the flashgun onto the hot shoe of the camera and dial in the film sensitivity on the flashgun, just as one does on a camera (see Figure 8.1), failure to do this will result in under or over exposure. Some smaller flash guns are totally manual, so in order to work out the *f* number required the camera must first be focused on the subject and the camera to subject distance read off the lens. This is then transferred to a table on the flashgun and cross referenced with the film ISO to give an *f* number, which must then be set on the lens. Those units with an auto sensor must first be set to one of the auto settings, usually a switch on the front of the unit. By looking at the table on the rear of the unit an *f* number will be given and this must be set on the lens; the table will also advise on the maximum camera to subject distance. A small sensor at the front of the unit reads the light reflected back from the subject and will automatically switch the flash off when it has achieved correct exposure. As long as your subject is within the flash range, correct exposure will always be achieved regardless of the camera subject distance, saving a lot of fussing around changing apertures. A number of auto units will have a green check light which will illuminate when the correct amount of light has been received by the sensor. A manual test button will enable

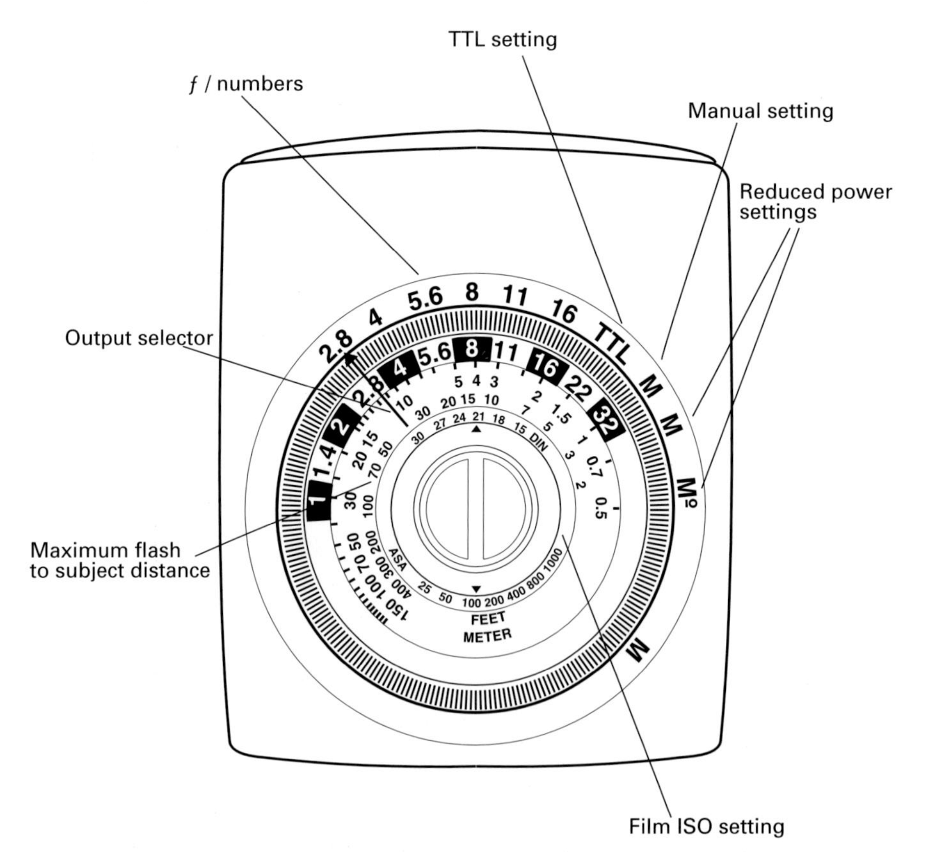

Figure 8.2 The power output of the larger flashguns can be selected.

the photographer to check that the setting is correct before taking any photographs by firing the flash and making sure the check light illuminates.

Many flashguns have a telescopic head which enables the angle of flash to match the angle of view of the lens in use. *T* will normally give a narrow angle of light for use with long focal length lenses, *N* is for use with a standard lens and *W* for wide angle lenses. A diffuser can be added to the front of the flash head for use with extra wide angle lenses. A series of coloured diffusers will often come with the flash, red, green, blue and orange are normal. All they do is to inject colour into the subject within the flash range and are somewhat gimmicky; the orange one, however, is quite useful for changing the colour temperature of the flash for use with tungsten film. See Chapter 9 on filters for colour back filters for flashguns.

Larger flash units enable the photographer to choose a variety of *f* number settings and as long as the same aperture is set on the lens and the subject is within the flash range, correct exposure will result (see Figure 8.2). These tend to be the hammerhead variety that are attached to the camera via a flash bracket (see Figure 8.3). The synchronisation is by a lead which plugs into the flash synchronisation socket on the front of the camera. Unfortunately many modern cameras do not have a synchronisation socket and so an adaptor has to be fitted to the hot shoe to provide the connection.

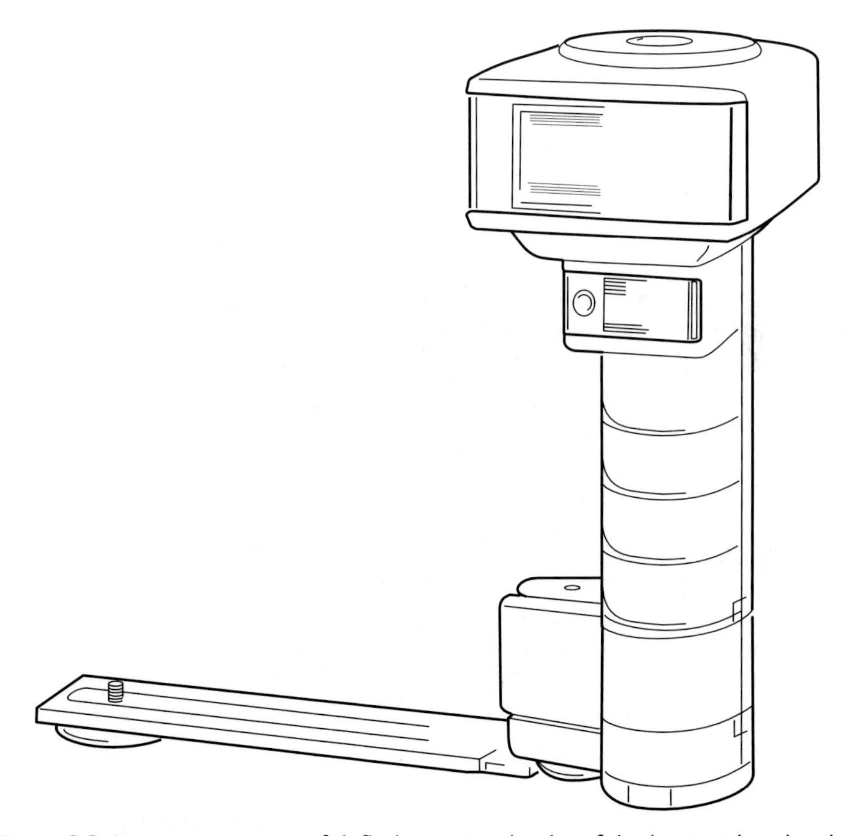

Figure 8.3 Larger, more powerful, flashguns tend to be of the hammerhead variety and used off camera.

8.3 Dedication

Dedicated flashguns are those designed to be used with a specific make and model of camera, usually automatic. Fully automatic cameras with through the lens (TTL) metering can use a dedicated flash unit where everything is worked out for you. As soon as the flash is fitted to the hot shoe the shutter speed is set at the synchronisation speed, the aperture is set by the camera and when sufficient light has reached the sensors the camera will switch the flash off. Many dedicated flash units allow daylight fill to be achieved by being run at half or quarter power.

8.4 Red eye

The biggest problem with any flash unit mounted on top of the camera is that of red eye, caused by the flash being reflected off the retina of the eye. To overcome this the sitter's eyes could look away from the lens, or the flash bounced off a ceiling or reflector board. Some flash units use a strobing effect, a series of low power flashes, to prepare the eye for the main flash. This does not eliminate red eye but does reduce it significantly by making the pupil contract. Another alternative is to take the flash off the camera and fire it from one side; this of course, will require a synchronisation lead.

8.5 Bounce flash

Another big problem with on camera flashguns is that of large black shadows falling on the background behind the subject; bouncing the flash is the easiest way around this. Bounce flash is simply directing the light onto the subject via another surface, either a reflector board, ceiling or umbrella (see Figure 8.4). This increases the size of the light source, spreading and softening the light. This can be achieved with simple flashguns by removing them from the hot shoe and directing them by hand; this will require a synchronisation lead connection. Synchronisation leads are available for most flashguns and come with male and female hot shoe connections; some will even maintain dedication and enable you to use the higher shutter speeds and TTL metering. Some experimentation will be required to work out the power setting as the sensor will give an incorrect reading. The more expensive flashguns will have a tilting head to enable the light to be directed upwards at the ceiling or reflector; beware though, if the surface is coloured it will put a cast into your picture. The sensors on these units remain facing the subject and will therefore give correct exposure, as long as the flash to subject distance is the same as the camera to subject distance. Others will have detachable sensors that can be left on the camera remaining connected to the gun by a lead; correct exposure is thus assured. A further refinement is a rotating head which enables the flash head to point backwards whilst the sensor remains facing the subject. These are ideal for use with reflector boards and umbrellas.

Flashguns designed for portrait work and having a tilting head will very often also have a second, smaller, flash head underneath the main one. This is because

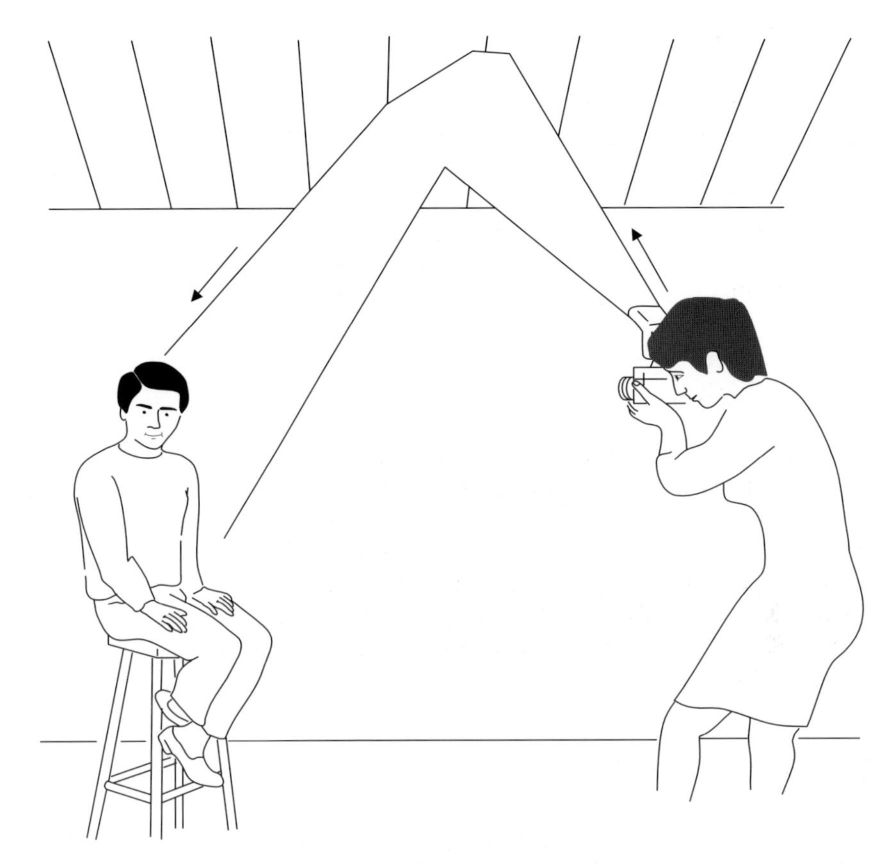

Figure 8.4 Using bounce flash off a ceiling.

bouncing a flash off the ceiling will create shadows under the eyes and chin; this small flash will put in sufficient light to kill these shadows (see Figure 8.5). The smaller flash can be switched off when not required but cannot be used independently.

8.6 Fill flash

Fill flash is the technique of using flash to illuminate shadow areas when taking photographs in daylight. Again the shutter must be set at flash synchronisation speed and then a normal daylight exposure reading taken. Having assertained the *f* number the flash must be set to fire at two stops less than the daylight aperture. Taking an example of 1/60 at *f*/11 as the correct daylight exposure the flash must be set to fire at *f*/5.6. This will lighten the shadow areas within the range of the flash and prevent harsh shadows from the flash light forming (see Figure 8.6). Should you be unable to set the exact *f* number when using the automatic settings on the flashgun then use the nearest one below that required. i.e. *f*/4. This will still put enough light into the scene to lift the shadows and improve the picture.

Setting the flash at the same aperture as the daylight reading will result in an

Source: ('A' grade GCSE, Emily Wills).

Figure 8.5 Softer lighting results from use of bounce flash.

Figure 8.6 Fill flash used in daylight to soften shadow areas, particularly on the face so that the eyes can be seen.

artificial glow to the picture as well as extra shadows. The only time this may work is at dusk where the flash becomes the main illumination and daylight the fill. The same technique can be used indoors on long exposure times, again ensuring that the flash is firing at a lower level of illumination to the ambient light. The only time that the flash illumination will equal the existing light levels is when taking photographs against the light from a window; here the idea is to balance the exposure outside the window with the flash illumination inside. A further use of the technique is to correct the colour balance when shooting daylight film under tungsten lighting conditions. This will correct the colours within the range of the flash with only the areas beyond the flash taking up a colour cast from the artificial lighting. If using tungsten balanced film indoors, flash can still be used by placing a sheet of Wratten 85 (orange) gelatine over the flash head, changing the colour temperature of the light as mentioned on p.93.

8.7 Multiple flash

Eventually the day will come when you will want to use more than one flashgun when photographing your subject, thereby improving the lighting. Today this is a very simple operation using 'slave units'. These are photo-sensitive cells fitted to the secondary flashguns either to the hot shoe connector or to their synchronisation lead. When the main flash fires the slaves are trigged and fire the other units instantly; a test is recommended as some slaves do not see light coming from behind. Larger studio flash units already have this facility built in.

8.8 Close up

With the flashgun fitted to the hot shoe on the camera one will encounter the problem of parallax error, just as with viewfinder cameras. Here though it is the flash that is not illuminating the area being photographed. The closer to your subject you get the more pronounced the problem will become. To overcome this the flash should be taken off the camera and placed to one side with reflector boards to fill in from the other side. There will come a point where the camera is so close to the subject that it is physically impossible to get the flash into position. A rethink is therefore required and the answer comes in the form of a ring flash. This is a circular flashgun that screws onto the lens of the camera and is thereby illuminating the subject from all sides. Exposure has to be worked out carefully as these units are not automatic, it all depends on camera to subject distance and the power of the flash. The other drawback is that they tend to be very expensive and unless one intends to do a great deal of close up work, something of a luxury.

Figure 8.7 A flashgun was fired manually a number of times in order to illuminate dark corners in the roof and corn.

Source: ('A' grade GCSE, Nicola Kent).

Figure 8.8 Flash was used here to recreate the lighting effect of the candle.

8.9 Flash for effect

A lot of fun can be had from using a flashgun, it is not solely for illumination in low light conditions (see Figure 8.8). When photographing a moving subject and used in conjunction with a slow shutter speed, it can give a solid crisp image combined with a blur, created by the slow shutter speed, thus giving an illusion of

Figure 8.9 Multiple flashes fired manually with the camera shutter open on brief, were used to create this photograph.

movement. Multiple imaging can be created by photographing a subject against a black background and firing the flash manually. To achieve this the camera is put on a tripod, the *f* number is set on the lens according to the flash setting and the shutter left open on brief, the flash is fired manually each time the subject changes position giving a series of images of the same person on a single frame (see Figure 8.9).

8.10 Studio flash

Moving away from the small camera mounted flash units, the next step forward is studio flash equipment. These units are quite large in comparison to the camera flashes, but small enough to be easily portable. They all come with modelling lights, a tungsten bulb that is used for achieving the correct lighting before taking the pictures with the flash. Each unit comes with a telescopic stand and there are a variety of accessories, such as diffusers, umbrellas, soft boxes (a tent like structure that fits onto the flash head, giving a very soft overall light), and snoots (a tapering tube that concentrates the light into a spot). The camera connection is made via a flash synchronisation lead, so the camera must have a synchronisation socket or an adaptor fitted. Slave sensors are usually built in, enabling more than one unit to be used without the need for leads all over the place. Although the studio flash set up is quite expensive, it is far more flexible than smaller units and gives greater control over the lighting. If one is going to do a lot of portraiture or still life work, then these units are a must (see Figure 8.10).

Figure 8.10 Studio flash gives much more control over lighting, enabling important features to be brought out in the subject.

Flash is a very under used accessory and after a little practice should prove indispensable for all types of photography. The small units take up very little room in the camera bag and are well worth the extra weight.

9 Filters and accessories

Camera filters are something of a double edged sword – they can improve a good photograph or completely ruin it. Filters will not make a poor photograph great, but with careful use they can make a good photograph better. There are a large number of filters on the market, creating all sorts of effects, the vast majority of which can be ignored by the average photographer. However, there are a handful of essential filters that should be part of every camera kit. All filters should be given careful consideration before use, a filter used just for the sake of it will never produce a good picture. Basically there are three categories of filter to be considered, contrast, correction and effect. Many can be used with both colour and black and white film, whilst others are for use with just one medium.

There are a number of options open to you when buying filters, screw on or system - (a holder which screws onto the lens into which the filters are slotted), glass or plastic. Screw on filters tend to be the highest quality, being a fine gelatine sandwiched between two optical flats (high quality, perfectly flat glass). Filter systems tend to be organic glass, a polymer by-product of the oil refining process, and of poorer quality. All filters have a density and this is defined by using filter factors, the exposure must be increased by this factor to obtain correct exposure.

9.1 Filter factors

All filters have a filter factor, but those below 1½ can be ignored as far as average photography is concerned. Although the table below is correct for practical purposes, exposure needs to be increased further and this is shown by the second set of figures. Some filter manufacturers use + as a guide, i.e. + 3 means an increase of 3 stops, whereas a filter factor of × 3 means an increase of only 1½ stops.

Practice shows that as the filter factor increases, so an increase over the suggested exposure must be made, otherwise under exposure will result. If using through the lens metering, under exposure may occur because of the sensitivity of the photo cell, so an increase in exposure is again to be recommended.

Factor	Suggested-increase	Recommended-increase
1	no increase	no increase
$1^1/_2$	$^1/_2$ stop increase	$^1/_2$ stop increase
2	1 stop increase	1 stop increase
3	$1^1/_2$ stop increase	$1^1/_2$ stop increase
4	2 stop increase	2 stop increase
6	$2^1/_2$ stop increase	3 stop increase
8	3 stop increase	4 stop increase

9.2 Contrast filters

As the name suggests, contrast filters are used to improve the colour or tonal separation in a picture. The first of these to consider is the ultra-violet series for cutting down haze. The earth's atmosphere scatters blue light to a greater extent than red or green, which is why the sky is blue. UV light is affected to an even greater degree causing the blue haze so apparent in the distance on landscapes. To combat this many modern multi-coated lenses have a UV filter element built in which negates the use of a separate filter. However, many people will fit a low value UV filter as protection for the front element of the lens. The danger here is that if a cheap filter is fitted it will degrade the final image, so fit the best that you can afford. The weakest of UV is the Wratten 1A or skylight filter which has a very slight pink tinge to it, others in the series include pale yellows and reds. UV scatter is much less of a problem the higher up you go and the thinner the atmosphere becomes.

In black and white photography contrast can be improved by the use of coloured filters. The first thing to appreciate is that a filter will lighten its own colour and darken the complementary colour on the final print (see Figure 9.1). Black and white film has its maximum sensitivity in the blue band of the spectrum and therefore blue objects will tend to come out very light. This becomes very apparent in pictures which include the sky, resulting in a light grey area lacking details. Clouds can be enhanced by fitting a filter of opposite colour to blue, in this case yellow or pale orange. A red filter will have a much more marked effect and produce a very dark dramatic sky (see Figure 9.2a–c).

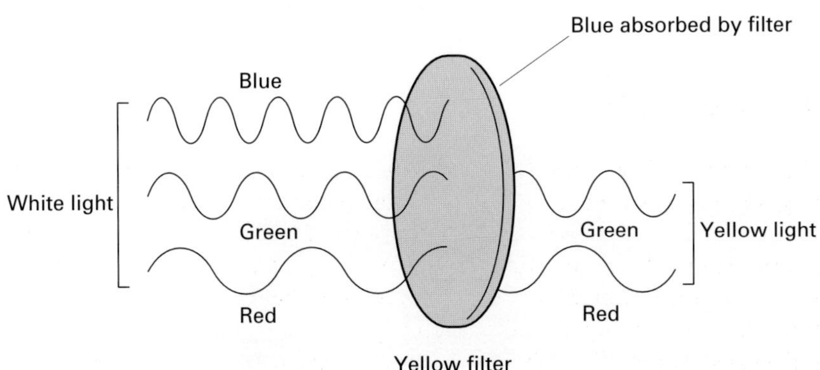

Figure 9.1 A coloured filter will only allow light of its own colour to pass through. In this case a yellow filter passes red and green light (which makes yellow) and blocks out the blue light.

Figure 9.2a

Figure 9.2b

Figure 9.2c

Figure 9.2a–c Three shots of the same scene taken a without filtration, b with yellow filter and finally c with a red filter. Note how the tones of other colours change when a filter is introduced.

Yellow-green and green filters are used to lighten dark foliage in landscape photography and at the same time darken the sky. Reds will normally record quite dark on black and white film but by using a red filter, a great wealth of detail can be brought out. This is particularly useful when photographing wood to bring out the grain.

Also included in the contrast bracket is the polariser, the most expensive, but also the most useful filter. As will be remembered from Chapter 1 on photographic history it was Edwin Land that produced the first polarising lens familiar to most of us through Polaroid sunglasses. Light travels in wave motions in all planes and the polariser acts rather like a venetian blind by allowing those rays in the same plane to pass through, those at 90° are blocked and others are partially blocked. By this method reflections are cut down and the contrast and colour saturation increased. To achieve this the filter is rotated and the effect is visible through the viewfinder; the image will darken and there is a loss of around two stops of light when using the polariser. The other job of the polariser is that of cutting out reflections in non-metallic surfaces such as glass and water. The best results are achieved at an angle of approximately 40° to the surface and one can choose to eliminate the reflections totally, or just partially (see Figure 9.3a–b).

Exposure calculation with through the lens metering systems can prove difficult when using a polarising filter, so two types are available, linear and circular. Check with your camera manual which type you require or ask your friendly dealer to help by testing both on your camera.

9.3 Correction filters

This category of filter is for use primarily with colour film and they are therefore known as colour correction (CC) filters. As we have already seen there are two types of colour film, one for daylight and one for artificial light. Most amateurs only use daylight film and when taking photographs under artificial lighting conditions do not consider the use of a filter. The orange-red cast resulting is acceptable if not too strong. When using negative film and having prints made the colour shift can be corrected, or at least lessened in printing. With slide film there is no opportunity to correct the bias during processing and so it becomes more important to correct at the taking stage. The range of filters used to correct this colour cast are the blue 80 series consisting of 80, 80A, 80B and 80C, the letters denoting an increase in density. The filter factor will recommend an increase in exposure of up to two stops, depending on which one is used. Finding the most acceptable filter will entail shooting test exposures and viewing these under controlled lighting conditions. To add to the problem with transparencies, the processing laboratory may inject a constant colour bias as a result of their chemicals or working methods.

The likelihood of the amateur using tungsten balanced film is fairly remote, but if the case does arise and shooting under daylight conditions becomes necessary, then one of the orange/amber 85 series filters will be needed. Without it the result will be an unacceptable blue cast to the final print or slide. It will be nearly impossible to remove this bias in printing from negative film.

Figure 9.3a

Figure 9.3b

Figure 9.3a–b Using a polarising filter can cut down reflections in glass and water. These two shots (a without filter, b with polariser) show how the polarising filter has cut out the flare on the glass in the roof and allowed the framework of the building to be seen.

There are weaker orange filters which can be used in daylight with daylight film to inject some warmth into the picture. These are the 81 series and they will brighten up an overcast day and take out the blue from shadow areas, they are particularly useful when taking photographs in the snow. In portraiture they will give a suntanned appearance to the subject whether taken outdoors or in the studio.

The largest range of colour correction filters come in the three primary and three complementary colours, red, green, blue, cyan, magenta and yellow. Densities range from CC05 to CC50 and can be used in combination with each other. Again these would be used mainly with transparency film. To discover what filters are required in any given situation a test would have to be carried out. Film must be shot under various conditions without any filtration and the results viewed on a corrected light box. Place the filters over the slide in turn until the correct colour balance is achieved. Then take further exposures using the corrected filtration in front of the camera lens; follow this by a further two shots using one of each of the adjacent values, higher and lower. Everything being equal the best result will be either the chosen or lower value filter.

Apart from correcting colour casts the CC filter will also be needed to correct a shift in the emulsion sensitivity when using extended exposure times. We have already seen the need to increase exposure times to allow for reciprocity failure; as the time increases so will the correction filter requirement. Most CC filters only require an exposure increase of $\frac{1}{3}$-$\frac{1}{2}$ a stop until the high values are used. When using more than one filter and the higher values, test exposures will be needed as the camera metering system may not always give a correct reading.

Although not strictly correction filters this is probably the best place to mention Neutral Density (ND) filters. As their name suggests they have no colour only density. They are used to cut down the intensity of available light, thus giving greater control over shutter speeds and depth of field. An occasion may arise when using high speed film you run out of shutter speed/aperture options and the only way of avoiding over exposure is to use an ND filter. The range of NDs available start at ND0.1 which has a factor of 1.25 requiring an increase in exposure of $\frac{1}{3}$ stop, the highest is ND4 with a factor of 10 000 needing 13 stops increase in exposure. As with all filters they will degrade the image, the cheaper ones even putting in a colour cast.

9.4 Effect filters

The final category of filters are those which produce visual effects, such as starburst, graduates, diffractors and fogs. Although the effects are perfectly visible through the viewfinder, they are the most difficult to use successfully. The temptation is to use them on every picture taken, whereas in truth, they should be used very infrequently.

Starbursts create between two and sixteen radiant arms from any point light sources in the picture (see Figure 9.4). This works well with just a few small points but can overwhelm the image if there are too many of them or they are too big. Another problem to watch out for is the fact that the 'stars' increase in size with the aperture, the smaller the *f* number the bigger the starburst. Contrast and sharpness will also be reduced at wider apertures, so careful thought must be given to choice of *f* number. A similar effect can be achieved without the filter by closing the iris diaphragm down to the minimum aperture.

Cosmic diffraction filters are similar to starburst but have the added effect of breaking the white light into the three primary colours. Most photographs taken with this filter are a waste of film but, very occasionally, it can work. They are more likely to be used in advertising photography to liven up an otherwise mundane shot, but they are no substitutes for good composition and lighting.

Probably the most useful range of effect filters are the graduates, coloured filters that fade to clear from top to bottom (see Figure 9.5). These are used to introduce some colour or tone into the sky, very useful on overcast grey days. Again there is a wide range of colours available and careful consideration must be given to their choice. The idea is to darken the sky without affecting the foreground, hence the clear lower half. Care must be taken in lining the horizon up and this should be done with the depth of field preview button in operation. Of course anything that breaks into the sky will take on the colour of the filter. The blues and greys will darken a sky without affecting the colour whereas the tobaccos, yellows and reds can introduce startling effects into the sky. An exposure reading should be taken without the filter in place and locked into the camera, otherwise over exposure will occur.

If you use any coloured effect filters in your photography it is as well to mention this to your processor; they may well spend a lot of time trying to remove them for you!

Beyond the true filters are a number of other special effect devices such as multiple image prisms which repeat the image several times within the frame. Speed prisms create the effect of movement by stretching part of the image. Then there are double exposure masks and various other shapes that can be put in front of the lens. All of these have a very limited application and are really only gimmicks.

9.5 Colour back filters

These filters are specifically designed for use with small flashguns and again must be given very careful consideration before use. Two filters are involved, one for the flash and one for the camera. A filter is placed over the flash head, say yellow, and its complementary over the camera lens, in this case blue. The yellow and blue filters cancel each other out so that the background, beyond the flash range, takes on a blue colour cast due to the filter on the camera lens. The through the lens metering system on the camera will take care of the increase in exposure needed for the filter on the lens, and the sensor on the flash will increase the light output to allow for the filter over the head. If using a flashgun without a sensor then the distance between flash and subject must be reduced to allow for the reduction in light output due to the filter; halving the distance increases light levels by one stop. There are other combinations such as red and cyan or green and magenta. They can be quite effective in some portraiture or for creating a specific mood, but are not everyone's choice. As mentioned in Chapter 8 on flash, a colour filter

Figure 9.4 Starburst filters can be overpowering unless used with care; if the sun had come out further the starburst would have overpowered the shot, here it is just right.

Figure 9.5 A grey graduated filter was used on this shot to reduce the brightness of the sky.

can be placed over the flash head alone, thus colouring up the area within its range and leaving the background to record normally.

9.6 Homemade filters

The use of filters is not confined to those commercially produced and a lot of fun can be had from designing and making one's own filters. Small pieces of good quality glass can be worked on with vaseline and translucent paints, or pieces of coloured cellophane and plastic film can be used. At the extreme, photographs reminiscent of Turner's later paintings can be achieved. These techniques are ideal for use in the City & Guilds module on constructed images.

9.7 Tripods

Apart from being out of focus or suffering from subject movement, unsharp images can be a result of camera movement. Now we are not talking about very obvious camera shake, but a slight wavering of the camera caused by its weight or length of lens. The slightest movement when using a telephoto lens can cause real problems with sharpness. The answer is to support the camera in some way thus removing it from our hands, the most common method being the use of a tripod (see Figure 9.6).

Besides providing a stable platform for the camera, tripods also force the photographer to take more time over setting up the picture. They allow slow shutter speeds to be used in conjunction with small apertures for maximum depth of field, and give the photographer the option of using very slow film for maximum image quality. Tripods come in a variety of sizes to suit all needs and pockets. As the name suggests all tripods have three legs which usually have telescopic triple extensions. The more stable models have stays between the legs and a central column giving added rigidity. Further height can be obtained by use of the central extension, but as this is only a single column it is not very stable and should only be used as a last resort.

The first considerations when selecting a tripod must be that of maximum height and weight. There is no point in buying a tripod that extends above eye level, you do not want to carry a set of steps as well. Most modern tripods designed for SLR cameras are made of aluminium and are fairly light, but you must decide how long you are likely to have to carry it. Even the lightest of tripods can become a burden after a couple of hours.

Two types of head are available, ball and socket, which is controlled by a single lever and the more difficult to use, and pan and tilt, which is controlled by one or two levers and much easier to operate. At the bottom of the range is the small table-top version, about 6 ins high, for shooting still life photographs. Then come a variety of sizes to suit all weights of camera and size of photographer. Some more expensive models have the facility to fix the camera upside down on the bottom of the central column, ideal for getting down to photograph plants, etc. Other spe-

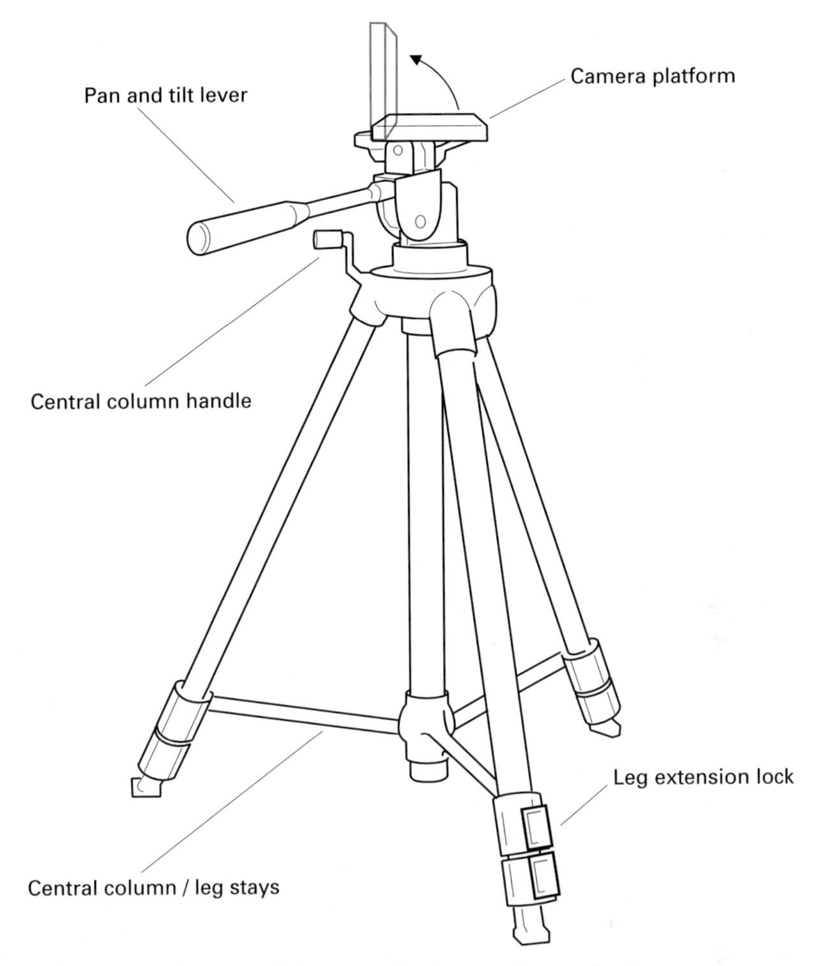

Figure 9.6 A tripod with stays between the legs and central column.

cialist tripods exist where one leg can be swung through 180° to rest on a wall or tree, useful on very uneven ground.

9.8 Cable release

Having fitted the camera to the tripod it should not be touched by hand during exposure, and to achieve this a cable release is required. The cheapest type will screw into the shutter release button and come in a selection of lengths. A locking version is preferable for those very long exposures in low light conditions, look for the ones with a locking ring rather than a thumb screw. Several coverings are available from plaited metal, with or without a plastic overcoat, to black fabric ones. Personally, I find the fabric covered ones last much longer, as the metal plaiting tends to break apart with use. Much longer versions, using an airball and long tube to activate the release, are very useful in the studio to allow the photographer to get close to the subject, particularly children. Increasingly, cameras do not have a threaded hole in the shutter release button, and a special electronic release has to be purchased, costing ten times as much. However, there is a small device on the market that can be fitted over the release button of some cameras enabling a standard cable release to be used. If the picture being taken is inanimate, and the actual moment of exposure is not important, then the self-timer mechanism can be used as an alternative.

For those wishing to undertake natural history photography then investment in a remote release system will be worthwhile. These are similar to the infra-red devices used for televisions and can operate the camera at a distance. More sophisticated devices are available where the subject will break a beam and trigger the camera, taking its own photograph. Both these systems would be used in conjunction with motor wind so that the camera can be left for a period of time.

9.9 Monopods

The monopod is like a single leg from a tripod with the same triple extension, but a fixed camera platform. These are designed to steady the camera and take the weight of a long lens off the photographer's neck. They prove much more convenient to use in a crowded situation or where rapid movement of the camera is required.

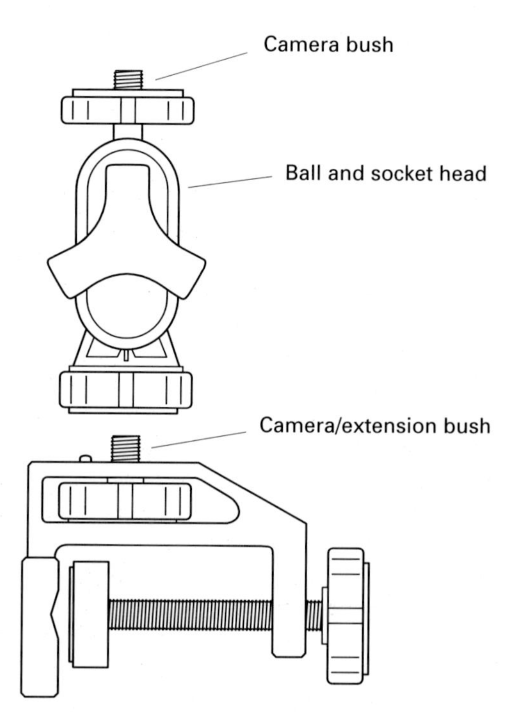

Figure 9.7 A 'G' clamp is just one of the many small camera supports available.

9.10 Pocket supports

This range of camera supports include the bean bag which will mould itself around the camera whilst supporting it on a wall or other suitable surface. The 'G' clamp can be clamped to a table or something similar to support the camera and has a ball and socket head for adjustment (see Figure 9.7). Some will also have legs which can be screwed in, turning it into a small tripod, and a screw fitting for gate posts or other wooden structures.

9.11 Grips

Pistol grips and rifle grips are very useful for steadying the camera particularly for action photography and when using long lenses. Again there are a number on the market and it is a case of trying them out in the shop before buying.

9.12 Levels

There is nothing worse in a photograph than having an horizon line that slopes or a building that is falling over. To help overcome this problem many tripods will have a built in spirit level as an aid to getting the camera perfectly level. Where the tripod does not have one fitted then a separate level can be bought to fit onto the accessory shoe of the camera, or one can use a builder's line level.

9.13 Camera bags

Once the photographer owns more than just the basic camera and lens, thought must be given as to how the equipment is to be transported. There are a wide variety of camera bags on the market from fabric covered cardboard to aluminium. The main problem with most of them is that they scream 'camera equipment' to a potential thief, particularly the aluminium variety. On the other hand the canvas bags do tend to look more like a fisherman's tackle bag. Never purchase anything that is too large for the equipment to be carried, although there is a case for buying with future expansion in mind, and remember it has to be carried around on the shoulder. Therefore, look for one where the carrying strap has a wide shoulder pad to spread the weight, the bag should also have a handle as an alternative to give the neck a rest. The interior needs moveable partitions or foam that can be cut to hold each item separately. Avoid bags that have camera manufacturers' names plastered all over them, this is a give away as to the contents. Likewise avoid putting stickers all over the outside of the bag, it needs to remain as inconspicuous as possible. The bag should also be waterproof, or at least showerproof, and have sufficient padding to give the maximum protection to the equipment against knocks. There should be room for sufficient film for your needs, although this could be carried in a film belt. The choice will very much be dictated by cost and available funds, but like a lens one should purchase the best that can be afforded.

9.14 Odds and ends

Other small essential items that are a must include a camera cleaning kit with a blower brush, a spare camera battery, notepad and pen for recording location and other specific information. For some of the City & Guilds modules technical information such as shutter speed and aperture will be required for the portfolio. It is also a good idea to carry a film retriever, in case one needs to change film and the leader is wound right in, and a light tight black changing bag to put the camera in should there be any problems with film jamming or tearing.

10 The darkroom

Once you have mastered the art and technique of taking photographs there will come a time when you will be dissatisfied with the prints produced for you by your processor, or there may be a desire to move into black and white photography. The darkroom is where the miracle of photography takes place, turning an invisible image into a visible one. If you intend to move into processing and printing (black and white or colour) then a permanent darkroom will be essential. Some people make do by temporarily converting a spare bedroom or the bathroom. Neither situation is ideal because of the dust factor, carpets and bedclothes produce an inordinate amount of dust which is not conducive to photography. However, for a large number of us there may be no alternative and we have to make the most of it. The first consideration must be that of making the room light tight by blanking out windows and the gaps around the door. Black boards fitted into the window recesses are essential for working during daylight hours, but you may get away with heavy curtains when working at night. The gaps around the door could be dealt with using another curtain or sealing with black tape. To test the effectiveness of your blackout sit in the room for about five minutes with the lights out, you should then be able to see any light leaks quite readily. Converting part of the loft space is another solution, the major drawback to that being that it is likely to be very cold and damp in winter and very hot in summer.

Decoration is not of overriding importance, the old myth of the walls needing to be black should be dispelled here and now, it seems to be perpetuated by architects and decorators who are not photographers. A light colour will help reflect the light around the room, cream or beige are ideal. If more than one enlarger is to be set up then a black division between them will help prevent light spillage from one to the other. Vinyl flooring will help keep the dust down and can be cleaned easily in the event of a chemical spillage. Running water in the darkroom is an advantage but not essential, films and prints can be taken to the bathroom or kitchen for washing. A light trap to enable people to walk in and out of the darkroom without interfering with the work going on is an ideal, but impractical for most of us.

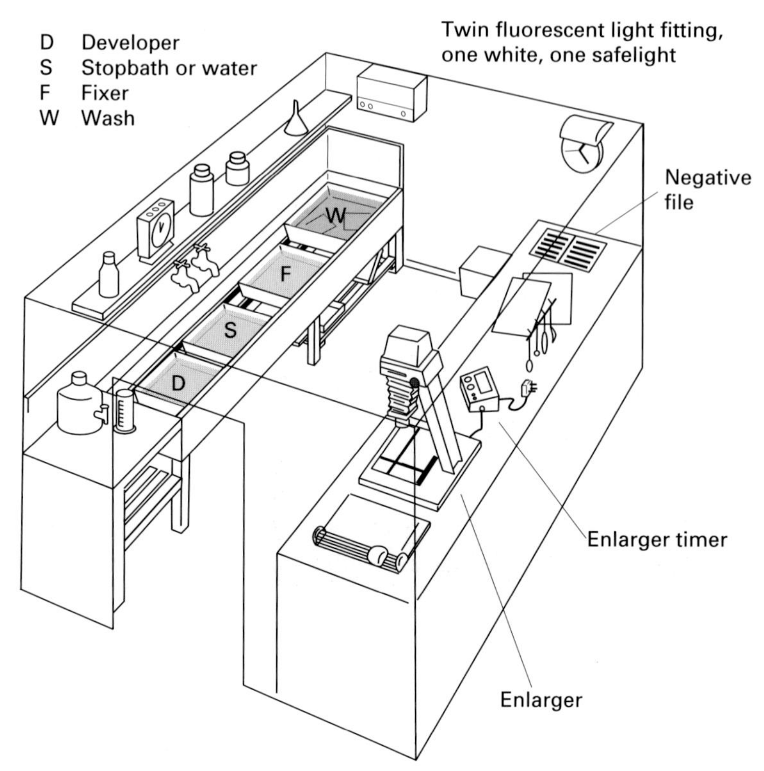

Figure 10.1 The ideal layout of a darkroom, a luxury for most people.

10.1 Setting up

The essential thing to remember is to keep the wet and dry processes completely separate, ideally on opposite sides of the room. The sink, processing and chemical storage should be on the wet bench where there is no electricity, film loading, printing and post-printing activities should be undertaken on the dry bench where there will be an electric supply (see Figure 10.1). Ideally all electrical equipment that is likely to be touched with damp hands, such as lights, should be operated by pull cords. A supply of fresh air is useful along with a means of removing the stale air, especially over the chemical trays. Ensure that there is no carry over of chemicals to the dry bench, handling film or paper with contaminated hands will ruin it, so make sure they are clean and dry - cleanliness must come before godliness in photography. There is no substitute for methodical working such as laying out the processing trays so as to work towards the sink, developer, stop, fix and wash. Careful labelling of bottles used to store diluted or part used chemicals with contents and date is essential: if in doubt throw it out.

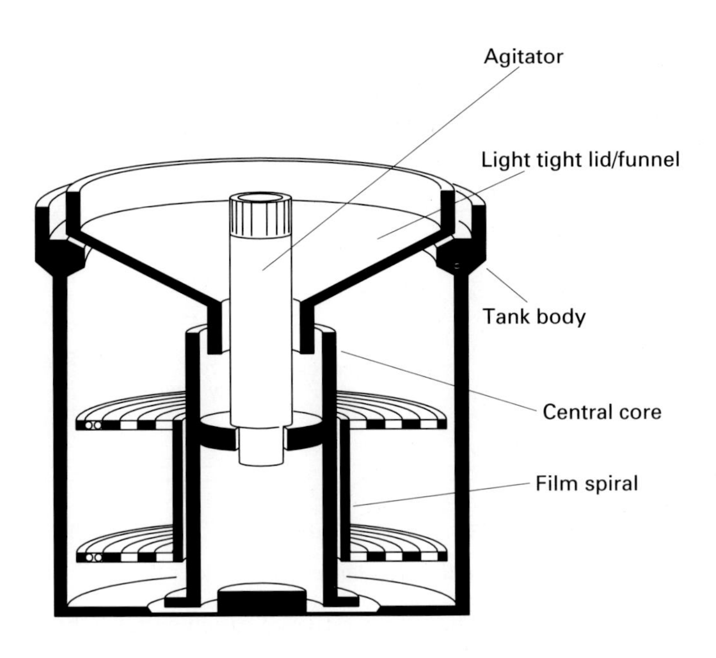

Figure 10.2 Cross-section of a daylight film processing tank.

10.2 Equipment

The amateur is perfectly capable of processing and printing both black and white and colour film and some of the City & Guilds modules are aimed at those wishing to undertake this. However, commercial colour processing is acceptable for the GCSE exam and most of the City and Guilds modules. Starting with film processing, the first piece of equipment that you will need is a daylight processing tank (see Figure 10.2). These tanks enable the film to be processed in normal room lighting once the film has been loaded in total darkness. A film retriever or cassette opener are needed to remove the film from the cassette along with a pair of scissors. A small piece of hose will be required to fit between the tap and the tank for washing, there are proprietary ones available.

Once processed the film will need printing and this is done using an enlarger. Basic 35mm black and white enlargers are very reasonable in cost and of course there is always the chance of picking up secondhand equipment. Alternatively a more expensive colour enlarger could be purchased as a future investment. Two types are commonly available, the condenser and the diffuser enlarger (see Figure 10.3). The condenser is usually fitted with an opal bulb and gives a much harder light and better contrast; care needs to be taken to ensure that the bulb is adjust-

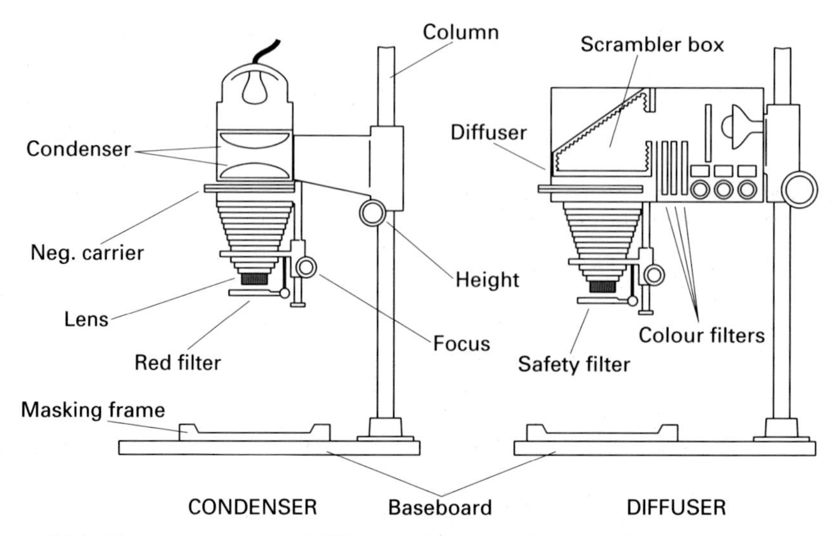

Figure 10.3 The condenser and diffuser enlarger (with colour head).

ed to give even illumination. The diffuser gives a much softer light and is more forgiving of scratches on negatives. With both types look for one that is capable of being swivelled about its vertical axis to help in correcting converging verticals. This facility will also enable the image to be projected onto a wall allowing a greater degree of enlargement than would be possible at the maximum height of the column.

It is always best to go for a glassless negative carrier as this will remove the problem of Newton's rings (a series of rings created when two smooth surfaces touch) forming between the negative and glass holder. The focal length of the lens should match the standard lens for the film format wherever possible, i.e. 50mm for 35mm film. On some enlargers it will also be necessary to match the condenser to the film size. If you intend to use a multi-contrast black and white printing system, then there should also be a filter drawer above the negative holder, or a colour printing head.

A set of multi-contrast printing filters and an adjustable printing easel will also be required. To start with it is unlikely that you will want to print larger than 25mm × 20mm so an easel of that size is adequate. It pays to make contact prints of all your negatives, thus giving a quick reference of everything on film, and for this you will need a contact printing frame. The next requirements are a couple of graduated measuring beakers for mixing chemicals and a thermometer, choose a digital or a blue spirit thermometer as they are easier to see under red light conditions. A set of developing trays for black and white prints, or a processing drum for colour will be needed, the trays usually come in sets of three and different colours. A pair of tongs for handling the prints in the various chemicals will prevent any problems with skin irritation. The chemicals are not dangerous but anyone with sensitive skin should take sensible precautions to avoid contact with them, a pair of thin disposable gloves will do the job. Concertina bottles for keeping diluted chemicals in are useful, as might be a focus finder for checking the focus of negatives under the enlarger. A good clock, with a large sweep second hand, for both film and print process timing, darkroom timers are available, although expensive. For the timing of print exposures the same clock could be used, or an electronic timer fitted to the power supply of the enlarger, alternatively you could count elephants, the actual unit of time is irrelevant so long as it is consistent. Finally, you just need a red safelight or two for black and white work, depending on the size of your darkroom; colour printing is best done in total darkness, although a very dark green safelight can be used.

The drying of both film and modern papers can be done naturally by hanging them from a line in a dust free atmosphere. Drying cabinets for film and paper are expensive and not really worthwhile unless you are putting a lot of material through. Squeegees for removing excess water are acceptable if used with care on prints, but film tongs are not to be recommended as permanent damage may occur; instead try gently running your fingers down the length of the film. If the darkroom is not heated, or kept at a low temperature then an electric dishwarmer will maintain chemical temperatures.

If money is not a problem then there are proprietary portable darkrooms on the market, looking rather like a portaloo. One may find that the local camera club has a permanent darkroom, or that a local secondary school or college has one that it is prepared to hire out. Some people do find that they have a problem with the confined space and low light levels that exist in the darkroom, but once you have experienced processing and printing for yourself there will be no turning back.

11 Film processing

Home processing of both colour and black and white film is perfectly possible for the amateur given reasonable working conditions, the main difference being that time, temperature and agitation control with colour is much more critical. However, colour processing and printing would require a book on its own to do it justice so we will concentrate here on the slightly easier black and white. It pays to become proficient in black and white before moving onto colour, as all of the skills learned will be taken forward.

11.1 Film processing

To make life easier you should try and retain the leader of 35mm film (the tongue used to load the film into the camera) when rewinding after exposure. With modern motor rewind cameras, the leader is taken inside the cassette and you will need a film retriever to get it back out. The leader must be cut off before processing so that the film is full width, but do not discard it, it will be needed later. Next, round the corners off to ease the passage of the film through the spiral ensuring that it is perfectly dry. The first 75mm or so of film have been fogged when loading the camera, this can be pulled out of the cassette and fed onto the spiral in room lighting with the emulsion (lighter side) facing inwards, once caught by the bearings the film will not fall out. The central core should now be placed in the spiral from the right if you are right handed, or the left if you are left handed. The reason for this is that should you choose to agitate by rotation, then it ensures that the direction of rotation pushes the film into the spiral, and that it will not unwind during processing (see Figure 11.1).

Make sure that all parts of the tank and a pair of scissors are placed so that they can be found easily in the dark. The lights should now be turned out and the rest of the procedure done in total darkness. If a light tight room is not available then this procedure can be carried out in a black changing bag. Holding the spiral firmly at the film entry points the film is pulled out of the cassette (about 30cm at a time), and one side of the spiral moved back and forth so that the film is

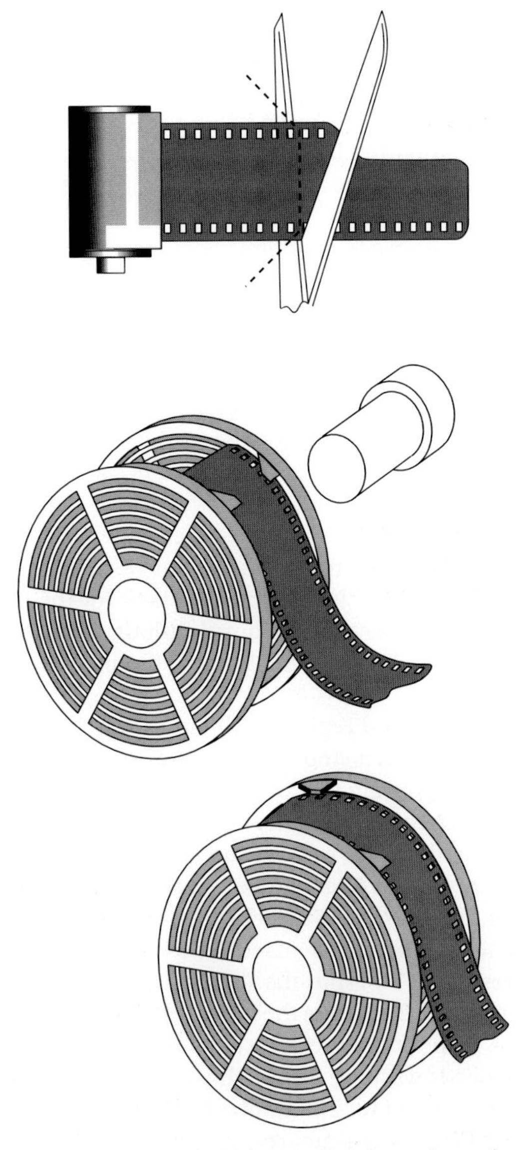

Figure 11.1 Starting a film on the spiral in room lighting prior to loading in total darkness.

`transported in. Continue the procedure until you come to the end of the film when the cassette should be cut off, a further three or four winds will take the tail of the film into the spiral. The spiral and core must now be placed inside the tank, ensuring that the base of the core goes to the bottom of the tank and the lid put on. The tank is now light tight and the remaining steps can be done in room lighting.

With 120 roll film the whole process must be carried out in total darkness. The film comes on a spool with a paper backing and this has to be spooled off until the beginning of the film is found. The end is loose and has to be fed into the spiral with the greatest of care; once started, the technique is the same as for 35mm. When loading is complete the film is cut or torn from the paper backing and wound well into the spiral.

It is recommended that a trial run be made using an old film before committing yourself to the dark, particularly for roll film, as it is much thinner and can easily be kinked. Carry out the procedure above with your eyes closed and then check to see how you have done.

There are many ways of processing film, none of which are wrong, the following method is one that has worked for me over the past thirty years. All stages are carried out at 20° Centigrade with the exception of the final wash. First pour in plain water as a pre-rinse and put the rubber lid on, agitate by inverting the whole tank, leaving to stand for a couple of minutes, this softens the emulsion and removes the anti-halation backing enabling the developer to work more efficiently. When poured away the water may have a colour to it, this is nothing to worry about, it is the dissolved film backing. Make up the developer according to the manufacturer's instructions whilst the pre-rinse stands, type and dilution is personal preference, but to start with a one shot liquid concentrate is easier. Set the timer for the required time and pour pre-rinse away, pour developer into tank and start clock, agitate film by continuously inverting the tank for the first minute. A gentle but sharp tap of the tank on the bench will dislodge any air bubbles. Leave to stand for 45 seconds and then agitate for 15 seconds, and repeat this every minute until the time is up.

Pour the developer away and replace with either stop bath or plain water for a couple of minutes. The use of a stop bath is not essential but it will prevent possible dichroic fog. After pouring the stop bath or water away the film has to be fixed; again a liquid concentrate is easier, diluted for use with film. This is poured into the tank and agitated for one minute and then left to stand for the remainder of the time (5–10 minutes). As fixer can be re-used it should be poured back into a storage bottle, and this is where the leader of your film comes back into the system. The state of the fixer should be checked each time before use, this is done by putting the leader of the film into the solution and timing how long it takes to clear. If this happens within 2 minutes the fixer is okay; if, however, the film remains milky in appearance then the fix is exhausted, and fresh should be made up.

Finally your film needs washing thoroughly to get rid of all the chemicals; this is carried out in running water for 20 minutes. Insufficient washing will cause your film to degrade over a period of time, resulting in the loss of the images. For full archival quality, films must be fixed and washed properly; they may not seem important now but they soon become historical documents. After washing, a couple of drops of wetting agent should be added to the water in the tank, and the film allowed to soak for a few minutes. This helps the water run off smoothly and reduce the chance of drying marks, where impurities in the water are left as a residue on the back of the film. It is almost impossible to avoid drying marks completely, especially in hard water areas, but they can be removed when the film is dry by the use of a soft cloth. Drying can be carried out in a dust free atmosphere by hanging the film up and putting a weight on the bottom, or by using a drying cabinet. Some people advocate the use of a hair dryer; all that does is disturb the air and blow dust onto the film.

The processing of colour film takes much the same line to start with by loading into a processing tank. The difference between developing colour negatives and black and white is that there are more chemical stages and working temperature is higher. Maintaining developer temperature at around 38°C is the most critical part of the operation, the tolerance is less than 0.25°C. Any variation in temperature during processing will result in a shift in colour balance of the negative. All other stages have a reasonable temperature tolerance of around 15°C, but for optimum results all stages, including washing, should be carried out at the same temperature. All colour negative films use the C41 process and there are a number of processing kits on the market. It is not recommended that the processing times be altered in any way as a shift in colour balance will result.

Colour transparency film needs greater temperature control at all stages of processing. There are two developer baths and both of these have to be maintained within ± 0.3°C and there is a tolerance of only 6°C for the other baths. All transparencies can be processed in E6 compatible chemicals and these can be purchased as kits from various sources. There are more stages in transparency processing than colour negative, the most important of which is the reversal bath, where the basic black and white negative image is reversed before colour development takes place. Times for each stage will vary according to the particular kit in use, as will the number of stages. Once washed, colour film and chromogenic black and white, i.e. Ilford XP2, will have an opalescent look to them until completely dry.

Should disaster strike and the film come out blank, then there are two possibilities as to the cause. Firstly, check the rebate numbers along the edge of the film, if they are a good density and readable then the film has been processed correctly, just not exposed. This is most likely finger trouble at the camera loading stage, resulting in the film not being transported through. If on the other hand the film is totally blank, with no rebate numbers, then the film has been fixed before development. On the other side of the equation, if the film comes out black then it has been fogged most likely when being loaded into the processing tank.

11.2 Developers

Film and print developers consist of four main ingredients the commonest of which are listed below.

Developing agent: Turns the exposed silver halides into black metallic silver:

Metol (M)
Phenidone (P)
Hydroquinone (Q)

These are usually used in conjunction with each other producing MQ or PQ developers. Metol and Phenidone are not used together but can be used on their own as can Hydroquinone.

Accelerator or alkali: Speeds up the action of the developing agent:

Sodium carbonate
Potassium carbonate
Borax

Restrainer: Prevents the unexposed silver halides from being developed:

Potassium Bromide
Benzotriazole

Restrainers also help prevent chemical fogging during extended development time or higher temperatures.

Preservative: Prevents oxidation of the developer and chemical staining:

Sodium sulphite
Potassium metabisulphite

The same constituents are used for both film and paper developers, and there are a few on the market, known as universal, which can be used for both. Once opened black and white developers have a shelf life of around 3–6 months undiluted, whereas colour chemicals will last only around 2 months.

11.3 Stop baths

Acid stop baths are used to stop development but not fix the image; such a bath also neutralises the developer in the emulsion and prevents contamination of the fixer, commonly it is a 1% solution of acetic acid. Alternatively, a rinse bath can be used; this will not stop development, only slow it down by diluting the developer, but it will help extend the life of the fixer.

11.4 Fixers

Two types of fixer are available, both of which make the developed silver image permanent and insensitive to light and dissolve the unexposed silver halides. Common constituents of an acid fixer are sodium thiosulphate and potassium metabisulphite. The acid hardener fixer has chrome alum as a hardening agent, and prevents excess take up of water by the emulsion during washing. In its most severe form a swollen emulsion will distort the image, however, most modern emulsions have a hardener built in.

11.5 Washing

The importance of washing cannot be over emphasised, especially if the negatives or prints are of historical importance. All the chemical residues must be removed from the emulsion to prevent staining and eventual loss of image. Running water is the best method, with fresh water entering the tank or tray at the bottom forcing contaminated water out of the top. With small film tanks this is achieved easily by the use of a hose fitted between the tap and tank. Water is forced to the bottom by the central core, flows over the film and exits around the lid. Removing all the thiosulphates from prints is extremely difficult and washing aids, or hypo eliminators, are designed to help; the washing time however, should not be reduced.

11.6 Drying

As already mentioned film can be dried naturally by hanging it up in a dust free atmosphere; however, drying cabinets whilst they may be expensive do ensure that warm filtered air is passed over the film. The film is very vulnerable at this stage and great care must be taken in handling. A film clip should be placed at one end to hang it up and a weight on the bottom to prevent it curling up. At room temperature the film will take 2 hours to dry thoroughly, but only about 20 minutes in a drying cabinet. Do not be tempted to speed up the process by using excessive heat as the emulsion may twist and buckle.

11.7 Compensation development

Having mastered the basic technique of film processing, the next step is to look at ways of correcting exposure mistakes by means of altered development. If a film has been accidentally under-exposed, usually by incorrect setting of the film speed on the camera, then normal development will result in a thin negative with little or no shadow detail. A negative of more normal density can be achieved by increasing the development time, although this will result in an increase in both contrast and grain size. Known as 'pushing', the time is increased by 25% for each stop under exposed, i.e. an ISO 100 film being exposed as an ISO 200. This will work well up to a maximum of two stops for most films, but some of the more sensitive films, such as Tri-X and HP5 Plus, can be pushed by three or even four stops. These films also lend themselves to the technique because of their lower contrast. It is also usual to use a special compensation developer, particularly for the higher ISO rated films.

Looking at the opposite situation, a film may be accidentally over exposed, and therefore if developed normally will produce a thick negative of high contrast. Reducing the development time will reduce the density and contrast of the image, as well as grain size. Known as 'pulling', the best results are achieved by using a fine grain developer and reducing development time by 25% per stop over exposure, to a maximum of two stops. Most developers will carry instruction sheets giving an idea of dilutions and times for both pushing and pulling.

Adjusting development by changing the time is just one method of controlling density and contrast, the other is to change the temperature. Again most developers will give an indication of how to do this, but the rule is, increase temperature–reduce time, and vice versa. Success in any of these areas will be a result of trials until the desired effect is achieved.

11.8 Faults

Most negative faults are avoidable, but very few are curable, so the maxim must be prevention. It will not hurt to go over the common faults again, plus some less common ones. A thin negative lacking detail, but where the rebate numbers are well defined, is the result of under exposure. If both the image and rebate numbers are weak then the film has been under developed. Where the image is dense and the rebate numbers well defined then the film has been over exposed, if both image and numbers are blocking in, then that is the result of over development. A completely clear film without image or rebate numbers has been fixed before development. Uneven density across the negative will result from uneven agitation during development.

Reticulation is a problem that will, hopefully, occur very rarely and is caused by plunging the film into a very hot or cold solution, usually from the fix to wash water. The appearance is that of a large irregular pattern over the emulsion, rather like crazing on an oil painting. Other faults are the result of rough handling before or after processing. Crescent shaped marks are caused by kinking the film during the loading or unloading of the spiral. Parallel scratch lines can be caused by dust or grit in the camera, in the velvet light trap of the cassette or by pulling the negative through the carrier in the enlarger.

Finger-marks are the result of incorrect handling and usually permanent, although they can sometimes be removed by carefully re-washing. Run marks from the sprocket holes of the negative are the result of too much agitation during development. Clear areas on the image indicate that the film was touching whilst wound on the spiral, and developer was unable to reach the emulsion. Small clear circles on the film are the result of air bubbles trapped on the emulsion during processing. An overall grey look to the images and rebates is a result of low level fogging during loading into the tank.

11.9 Self-test exercise

Over a period of time, develop correctly exposed black and white films in a series of different developers, keeping temperature and agitation consistent. From these negatives make 5 × 7in or 10 × 8in enlargements for comparison of grain and sharpness, this will help in establishing the best combination of film/developer for your needs. One drawback that will be encountered is that developers made by the major film manufacturers will not always include times for other makes of film. For such occasions develop a test film for the same time as an equivalent ISO that is listed, analyse the negatives and adjust times for the next film accordingly, remembering to keep detailed notes.

12 Printing

The photographic print is the two dimensional end product into which all the emotions of a five dimensional world have to be squeezed. All too often people take a great deal of care and trouble in taking a photograph, only to accept rather inferior prints. Once embarked on your own processing and printing the real enjoyment of photography begins, if you really get bitten you may find yourself spending more time in the darkroom than taking pictures.

12.1 Printing paper

Before moving onto printing methods we must look at printing paper and the choice available. Taking black and white first, rather like film, printing paper is just a base coated with a light-sensitive emulsion, but only responds to blue and

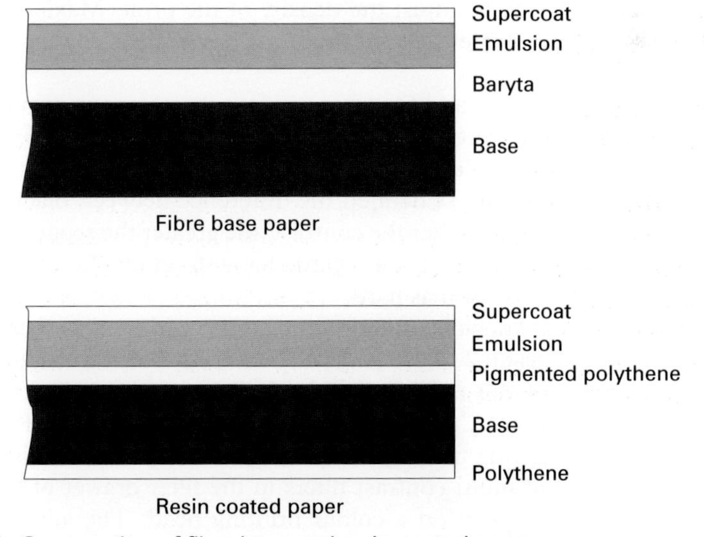

Figure 12.1 Cross-section of fibre base and resin coated paper.

green light, therefore it can be handled quite safely under a red safelight. Two types are available, the traditional fibre base paper and the modern resin coated variety, the main difference being that resin coated paper has a plastic coat around the paper base (see Figure 12.1). Within both types there is also a variety of tints to the paper base, from a bright white through to soft browns. The choice of base tint will make a considerable difference to the final print.

There is also a difference in processing technique as described below. First though the chemicals must be made up and put into the appropriate dishes; as with film chemicals, it is best to use the liquid concentrates. Use the white or grey dish for developer and stop bath and the red dish for fixer, the idea being red for danger. As with film the chemical temperatures should be 20°C ± 2°.

	Resin coated	*Fibre base*
Development time	1½ minutes, maximum 2 minutes	minimum 2 minutes
Rinse or stop bath	30 seconds	30 seconds
Fixer	4 minutes	10 minutes
Wash	4 minutes	20 minutes
Drying	naturally or in RC dryer	with heat under pressure

The print must be put into each of the chemicals as quickly as possible, and when developing the tray must be agitated continuously to prevent uneven development, a gentle rocking from side to side is sufficient. You cannot over fix or over wash prints within reason, so these times are guides; however the development times are much more crucial and consistent timing is important. Leaving prints in the developer for an extended period of time in the hope that they might go darker will only result in chemical fogging, a patchy greying of the white areas. Resin coated paper must be in the developer for at least 1 minute in order to achieve a good black, but no longer than 2 minutes. Working to 1½ minutes gives a little leeway either side to adjust the density of the print. Maximum black on fibre base paper is not achieved until the print has been in the developer for 2 minutes.

Within both resin coated and fibre base papers there are two ways of altering contrast, how black and white the image will be. The first is graded paper where a packet of paper has a single grade ranging from 0 to 5. The lower the number the lower the contrast, the less defined the difference between black and white. The higher the number the higher the contrast, the greater the separation between black and white. Grades 0 and 1 are regarded as soft, grade 2 is considered normal and grades 3–5 are known as hard.

The other system is known as multi-contrast or multi-grade, where the paper comes as a nominal grade 2. To change the contrast a series of filters are used to alter the colour of the enlarging light, yellow produces soft grades and magenta the hard grades. A much wider range of grades is available from 00 to 5 in half grade steps, giving much greater control over contrast. This is achieved either by using a set of multi-contrast filters in the filter drawer of the enlarger, or by dialling in the colours on a colour printing head. The advantage of the multi-contrast system is that you only need to purchase one packet of paper to

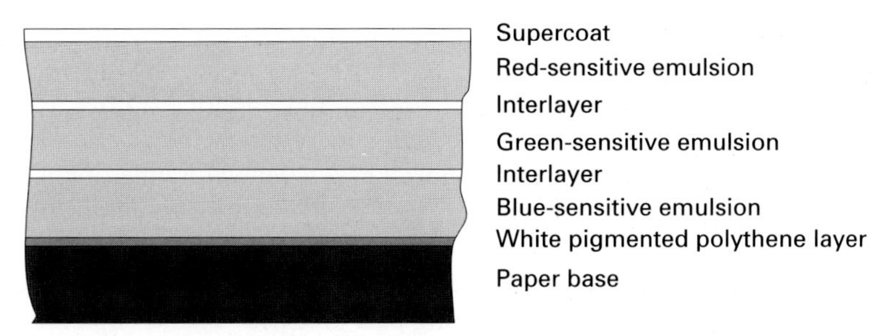

Figure 12.2 Cross-section of colour printing paper.

achieve all the grades, as against one packet for every grade needed in the graded range. It also enables you to change the grade within a single print, something to consider as you become more experienced. A word of warning with multi-contrast papers, there are a number of cheaper brands on the market which do not give good results above grade 3. The reason being that in order to produce a lower priced product the quantity of silver in the emulsion is reduced and this prevents a good black being achieved.

Beyond grades, both types of paper come in various surfaces, glossy, semi-matt and matt, each manufacturer will produce a number of different surfaces within the matt and semi-matt range. Fibre base paper also comes in two 'weights' (thickness), single and double, whereas resin coated is all medium weight. The main advantage of fibre base paper is that it has a much longer life and tends to be of superior quality and favoured for exhibition work.

With colour printing paper, only resin coated is available, and like colour film consists of three emulsion layers, each sensitive to one of the primary colours with filter interlayers (see Figure 12.2). Being panchromatic in sensitivity, the paper has to be handled in complete darkness or under a very dark amber/green safelight. Paper surfaces are restricted to just the three basic types and there is no facility for varying the contrast. Every pack of colour paper will vary in characteristics and colour balance, and therefore, the manufacturers print recommended filtrations for each batch. From this it can be seen that colour printing is much more limited than black and white. Processing of the colour print is best done in a light tight drum or tank under very strict temperature control. 32°C ± 0.3°C. Liquid concentrate kits are readily available and each comes with comprehensive instructions.

Colour developer	3.5 minutes
Bleach-fix	1.5 minutes
Wash	3.5 minutes
Drying	naturally or with RC dryer

New chemistry is constantly being introduced and the fastest available at present produces a print in just 4 minutes.

Once the decision is made to try colour printing then a good book on the subject is essential. The actual process is not a lot different to black and white printing, but some extra items of equipment will be required.

12.2 Safelights

There are a number of safelights on the market suitable for printing from small beehive types to fluorescent tubes. A red light is required for black and white resin coated paper and can also be used for fibre base, a yellow/orange one is suitable for fibre base paper but not resin coated. As already mentioned colour printing is normally undertaken in total darkness.

To test the safety of your darkroom safelight, take a piece of printing paper and lay it down 1m from the safelight, covering part of it with a solid object. Leave for 5 minutes and then develop it in the normal way; if the shape of the object cannot be discerned then the level of lighting is all right, if there is a greying of the exposed area, the light level is too high and the safelight must be moved further away or a lower wattage bulb used.

12.3 Photograms

Photograms should be the first exercise undertaken in the darkroom, as it helps to establish working techniques. Set the enlarger so that the light covers at least a 25mm × 20mm area on the baseboard, close the aperture down to *f*/8 and put

Figure 12.3 This photogram was created using plant material laid straight onto printing paper and exposed under an enlarger.

the red safety filter over the lens. Place a sheet of black and white printing paper, emulsion (shinier side) uppermost, on the baseboard and lay a few related objects on it so that they create an interesting pattern. Remove the red filter and expose the paper for about 10 seconds and process in the normal way. The result is a reversed silhouette with white shapes on a black background, similar to the photogenic drawings made by Fox Talbot. Flowers, leaves and grasses work very well, giving some grey tones through the thinner parts (see Figure 12.3). Cut glass will refract the light passing through it, creating some intricate shapes and patterns on the paper around the object. To appreciate this fully the exposure time will have to be reduced giving a grey, rather than black background.

12.4 Contact prints

Having got your negatives, the next stage is to produce a positive from each; this is achieved in the first instance by making a contact sheet, a series of prints the same size as the negative, made by placing the negatives 'in contact' with photographic paper (see Figure 12.4). The roll of film is first cut into short lengths of between four and six images for 35mm, and three to five for roll film, count the total number of images on your film and divide it up accordingly. Extreme care

Figure 12.4 A contact print giving an indication of pictures on a film at a glance, with space for technical information and date.

should be taken in handling the negatives, holding them by the rebates only, finger-marks are impossible to remove. The negatives are placed in the lid of the contact frame with the back or shiny side to the glass, this will ensure that your prints come out the right way round. A sheet of 25mm × 20mm printing paper is placed on the base, emulsion uppermost, and the lid closed. With the red safety filter in place over the lens, the enlarger is set high enough on the column so that the light covers the frame, and the aperture set to *f*/8. With the contact frame in place, move the safety filter and make a test strip of set exposure times. This is achieved by covering up all but a small part of the frame with a piece of card, and exposing for say 2 or 3 seconds; the card is then moved 25mm and a second exposure made and so on until the whole piece of paper has been exposed. This is then developed for the required time in print developer, rinsed and fixed. Once fixed the sheet can be viewed in normal lighting, what one has is a series of exposures each one darker than the previous one, and from this the best exposure time chosen. Another sheet of paper is placed in the contact frame and this time the whole thing given the required exposure time. Once processed and dry you have a complete set of miniature prints from which the selection for enlargement can be made. Not all the images will be perfect due to the variation in density of individual negatives, but as your camera exposure technique improves, so will the consistency of your negatives.

12.5 Enlarging

Having chosen an image to enlarge, the appropriate strip of negative is placed in the carrier of the enlarger. To ensure that the image comes out the right way round the shiny side (back) must face uppermost. Another check is that the rebate numbers are reading correctly when the image is projected. Any dust on the negative must now be removed by gentle use of a blower brush, remember to clean both top and bottom of the negative. Every speck of dust on the negative will look like a golf ball on the print. Next ensure that the enlarger lens is clean and free from finger-marks, using a soft cloth and proprietary lens cleaner for the purpose. Set the printing easel to the size required, remembering to allow for a border of 5mm all the way around. The enlarger is then moved up or down the column until the image is the right size, once the correct image size is achieved, make a note of the magnification from the figures on the enlarger column.

Focusing can be done either by eye or with the aid of a focus finder, if you have a colour head on the enlarger, dial in some cyan as this will make focusing a lot easier. Cyan is a mix of blue and green light, and as the eye has its peak sensitivity in the green area, it helps brighten the image under the red light. Once everything is focused and set, a test strip has to be made to ascertain the required exposure and grade of contrast. If using a multi-contrast paper, then place a grade 2 filter in the drawer or dial in the appropriate filtration on a colour head. Avoid doing test strips without any filtration in place, as exposure times will change dramatically with a filter. The lens aperture setting will depend upon the density of the negative, but always try and work around *f*/8 or *f*/11. A piece of printing paper is then placed in the easel, grade 2 if using graded paper, emulsion uppermost.

Figure 12.5 A test strip of 2 second exposure steps from the right, for ascertaining correct exposure for the print.

Figure 12.6 The final print exposed for 12 seconds.

Make a habit of closing the paper box every time a sheet is removed, this will prevent fogging of the whole packet. A series of exposures must now be given to a set time, perhaps 3 or 5 second steps. Try to ensure that the brightest and darkest areas of the scene appear in each section of the strip. The first exposure is made with the paper uncovered, and then each successive exposure made after covering up 25mm of paper at a time. The same procedure applies to making a colour print in the first instance. The print is then developed for a precise time according to the developer you are using. Failure to do this makes the whole process of producing a test strip a waste of time. If using multi-contrast paper always use the recommended developer for optimum results; whilst graded papers can be processed in multi contrast developer the reverse does not give good results. Once fixed the print can be viewed in normal lighting and the correct exposure ascertained, the contrast can also be checked at this stage and an adjustment made if necessary (see Figure 12.5). When making a colour print a test strip must now be made for filtration, increasing the exposure times to allow for the filter factor, the appropriate filtration is selected and any adjustment made to exposure. A whole print can now be made by giving another sheet of paper the selected exposure (see Figure 12.6). A word of warning here, with multi-contrast black and white if the grade of paper is changed the exposure chosen may not be right, in spite of what the manufacturers tell us. If there is a jump of more than one grade then a new test strip will be required, and of course if using graded paper, the sensitivity of the emulsions between different grades and boxes will vary. Trying to guess exposures will only result in the wasting of a lot of paper and time, there is no substitute for methodical working. This new print is developed for exactly the same time as the test strip and, everything else being equal, should be spot on. Fixing and washing should follow to the times suggested earlier. If washing a number of resin coated prints together beware of skate marks on the emulsion. The corners of the prints do not soften, and when they are swirling around in the wash, scratching of the emulsion may occur; this is not a problem with fibre base paper. The best method of washing prints is a cascade system, where the paper spends time in each of the different levels (see Figure 12.7).

12.6 Drying

Resin coated prints can be dried by hanging from a line with pegs, taking around 30 minutes, fibre base prints however, are best dried with heat and under pressure. Special flat bed driers with an internal heating element and canvas cover to hold the prints flat are available for this purpose. Some printers advocate hanging them from a line back to back or even letting them dry naturally on a flat bed; however, there is a risk of curling if this is done.

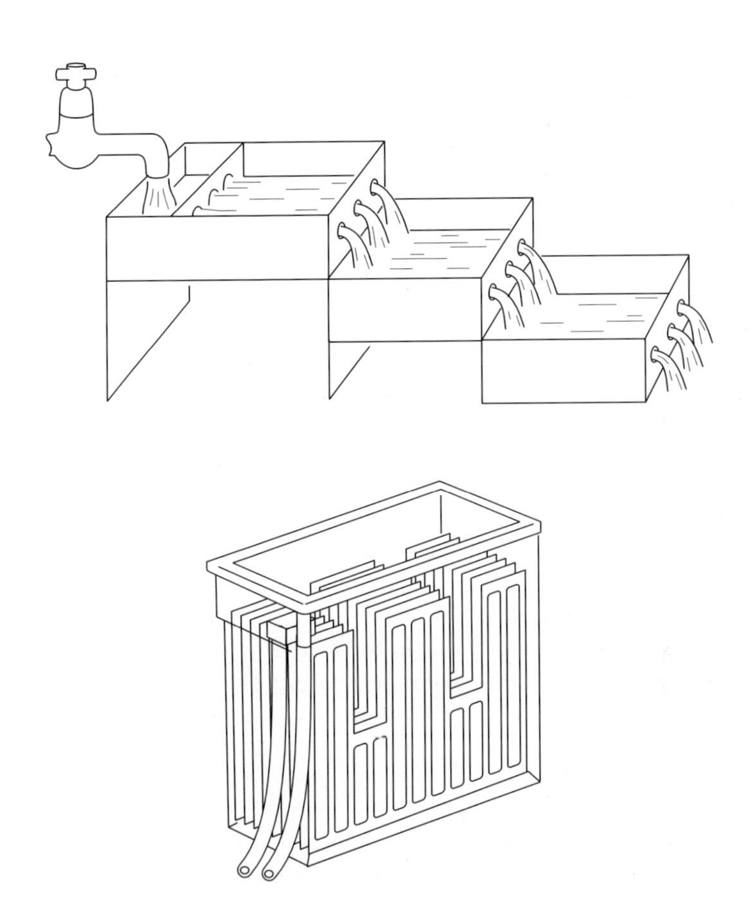

Figure 12.7 A cascade washing system and proprietary print washer.

12.7 Self-test exercise

To get a good appreciation of how a change in grade of paper affects the image, make a series of prints from the same negative on each of the six grades or a representative selection. Take a correctly exposed and processed negative of normal contrast range and using the technique described above make your prints. Laid side by side these prints will show just how marked the difference between the soft and hard grades of paper is. Compare Figure 12.8a-c.

12.8 Printing control

From time to time when making enlargements there will be a need to give small areas of the print more or less exposure. This is due to the film's inability to cope

Figure 12.8a

Figure 12.8b

Figure 12.8c

Figure 12.8a–c Three prints from the same negative using grade 1, 3 and 5 paper; notice the increase in contrast and consequent loss of detail in the highlights and shadow areas.

Figure 12.9a

Figure 12.9b

Figure 12.9a–b A straight print a and one where the highlight areas have been given a little more exposure b, 'burnt in', to show the detail in the container and wing.

Figure 12.10a

Figure 12.10b

Figure 12.10a–b In the straight print a detail is lost in the girl's jumper, reducing exposure in that area; in b 'dodging', has allowed detail to be retained.

with vast differences in brightness range of the subject. The following techniques can be used in both colour and black and white printing.

When a small area needs extra exposure to make it darker, it is called 'burning in', and this can be achieved by shaping your hands or cutting a piece of card to the shape required (see Figure 12.9a-b). After giving the whole print the correct initial exposure the masks are placed in position between the lens and the paper. The extra time is then given, ensuring that the mask is kept moving gently during exposure, this will give a soft unnoticeable edge between the two areas. If the mask is placed immediately on top of the paper and not moved a sharp edge will occur. The actual amount of extra exposure can be ascertained from the test strip.

'Dodging' or holding back, is exactly the opposite of burning in where a small area needs less exposure than the rest of the print (see Figure 12.10a-b). Whilst it may be possible to achieve results using your hands it is easier to cut out card shapes and stick them on the end of a piece of thin wire. The actual time for which these areas are held back can be worked out from the test strip. As a general rule one should aim not to dodge or burn in for more than 50% of the overall exposure time. As with burning in the masks should be kept on the move during exposure to ensure a soft edge between different areas, and also to make sure that the wire does not leave a light line.

12.9 Trouble shooting

Many problems will be encountered during the early stages of printing and all are avoidable with a little extra care and thought. A badly under exposed negative will never give a satisfactory print, as the information has not been recorded on film, and is really only fit for the waste bin. An over exposed negative, on the other hand, has the information on film, and a print should be possible with extended exposure time. The same is true of under and over developed negatives.

Most print faults can be avoided by clean and careful working methods. Dust is your biggest enemy and will manifest itself as white spots or hair shapes on the final print and this is by far the most difficult problem to cure totally. As negatives get hot in the enlarger they build up a static charge which attracts dust; blowing with an anti-static aerosol will help reduce the problem. There will always be small white spots on the print and these can be removed by retouching after drying.

Uneven development, particularly with resin coated papers, can be cured by ensuring that the paper enters the developer quickly and is agitated continuously. Another problem that can occur due to heat in the enlarger is the image going out of focus, in a glassless carrier the negative will buckle as it gets hot, so sharpness should be checked between each print. A double image is caused by the enlarger being knocked during exposure. With resin coated papers staining may occur through prolonged handling with fingers, a pink mark will appear where the print was held. Using tongs will overcome this but care will be needed not to scratch the print surface or mix developer tongs with those used for fixer.

All these problems will cause a great deal of frustration in the early days, but as you become more proficient so the occurrence of such problems will reduce.

Methodical working methods and patience are prime virtues in photography, and will bring their own reward.

12.10 Self-test exercise

Take an over exposed negative and make a print from it on a soft grade of paper, 1 or $1^{1}/_{2}$, an acceptable result can be obtained. A satisfactory print will never be obtained from an under exposed negative, as all the information has not been recorded, showing that over exposure is preferable to under exposure for negatives.

12.11 Special effects

Once the basic skills of printing have been mastered it is time to move onto what can arguably be called the most interesting part of photography, that of image derivation. Here the basic continuous tone negative is transformed into a derived image, which may bear no resemblance to the original. A few of the techniques are very simple and effective whereas others demand a lot more work to achieve results. Whilst some of these techniques can be applied to colour they are beyond the scope of the GCSE and City & Guilds syllabus.

One of the easiest derived image techniques to start off with is known variously as Sabattier Effect, Pseudo Solarisation or Solarisation (see Figure 12.11). The Sabattier effect refers to a phenomenon that occurs only with negatives, pseudo solarisation suggests that it is not real and tends to be used by amateurs to describe this technique. Solarisation is caused by the print receiving a massive exposure to light, typically 1000 times more than would be usual. That essentially is what happens to the print when being derived in this way. The first step is to make a test strip to ascertain correct exposure for the print, the print is then made in the usual way and placed in the developer. Part way through development, between half and three quarters the way through, a white light is flashed on momentarily and the print allowed to continue developing. The effect is that the black areas of the print remain black, the white areas also turn black, leaving a white line between the two, known as the Mackie Line. The amount of reversal exposure and the stage of development at which it is given, will have a direct bearing on the final result. Using this method it is very difficult, if not impossible, to repeat exactly, there is however, a method which is somewhat more accurate. For this second technique the print is developed for the full time and placed in a tray of water, the light is then switched on for an instant and the print returned to the developer for another minute or so. This second method is obviously more controllable and the result easier to repeat. The same technique can be used in colour printing but the results are very unpredictable and can provide some spectacular images.

Lith transfer is where the continuous tone negative is contact printed onto a piece of high contrast lith film, see Chapter 4 on film. This produces a high contrast positive image, from which a contact negative has to be made on another

Source: (Distinction City & Guilds, Image Derivation module, Alison Marchetti).

Figure 12.11 Solarisation can produce some spectacular images.

Figure 12.12 Lith transfer produces very simple graphic images, eliminating all grey tones.

piece of lith film, resulting in the suppression of the grey tones (see Figure 12.12). The process can be carried out under normal safelight conditions in the darkroom as lith film is orthochromatic. The film is developed in its own special developer, which comes as a two bath concentrate and has to be diluted before being mixed together. Once the negative has been washed and dried it can be printed in the normal way, producing a very high contrast graphic image. It is even more important that the original composition is simple for this type of work, as fine detail will tend to disappear in the transfer process.

By placing the original continuous tone negative and the lith positive together slightly out of register, a technique known as 'bas relief' can be achieved on a print. The effect is of an out of focus photograph which appears to be the result of the enlarger being knocked during exposure. Alternatively, the lith negative and positive can be placed together, slightly out of register, to produce something resembling a line drawing when printed (see Figure 12.13).

There are a number of ways in which the original image can be manipulated, the only restriction being the limits of one's imagination.

Figure 12.13 This picture has been created by sandwiching a lith negative and lith positive together just out of register and printing, giving a line drawing effect.

13 Finishing and presentation

Having moved on from the happy snapshot to the more serious levels of photography required for GCSE and City & Guilds, thought must be given as to what to do with all the pictures. Doubtless in the past the vast majority of photographs have remained in the wallet provided by the process house and tucked away in a drawer somewhere. Perhaps lately they have found their way into a flip album with the odd one or two being put into small frames. The negatives have probably fallen out of the wallet and are floating around loose in the bottom of that drawer, being irrevocably damaged. It is incredible that some people even throw the negatives away as being of no further use. As mentioned before, in a few years, and it is surprising how quickly time goes by, all photographs become historic documents of interest to a far greater audience than might be thought at first. Do not assume that because they are of no further interest to you that the same goes for others.

It is therefore in your, and your descendants', interest to look after both the negatives and the prints as best you can. Let us deal with the negatives first, after all they are the original material from which endless reproductions can be made.

13.1 Negative filing

There are a number of manufacturers that make negative storage envelopes and sheets, but they vary in quality quite considerably. Some of the plastic variety contain chemicals which attack the emulsion of the film, so one should look for an inert archive quality type. The most popular type are the sheets that fit into a ring binder, each one holding six strips of six negatives, i.e. a 36 exposure film. Paper envelopes holding just a single strip of six negatives are available for those preferring to file their films in small filing cabinet drawers. A data sheet is provided for the file sheet to record subject matter and date, although this is insufficient to record full details. An index card recording system can work for both the sheets and individual filing envelopes, allowing much more information to be recorded. The modern alternative is to put the records on computer with a cross referencing system. Each individual negative should be numbered rather than being listed as a number of a sheet. Storage conditions must be right to prevent a deterioration of the image, a constant temperature and humidity must be maintained as far as possible. The emulsion will break down if the film is subjected to extremes of cold, heat or humidity. With colour film the effects will be noticeable much sooner because the dyes will begin to break down, and there will be a shift in colour balance.

13.2 Print storage

Probably the easiest and most convenient way to store prints is in an album, again there are numerous types on the market from which to choose. The modern plastic envelope variety need to be chosen with care as, like the negative files, the chemicals used in manufacture can have a detrimental effect on the print. The self-adhesive variety which allow you to move the prints around also allow others to remove them, eventually the adhesive dries out so that the prints will not stick or are stuck for good. There is a return to the traditional album with paper or card pages and tissue interleaves, and these are ideal, keeping the pictures separated. Alternatively, if one takes a lot of photographs it might pay to make up your own somewhat larger album. Card cut to size and holes punched for a large post binder can be obtained from your local printer, paper is very heavy so bear this in mind when planning a large album. A major advantage of the paper page is that information can be written alongside the photograph. Everyone has suffered from a boring slide show of holiday snaps and fallen asleep, at least with an album the viewer can look through at their own pace and put it down after a while.

Having chosen the album to suit your needs the question of adhesive arises. There are always the traditional photo corners which do not damage the prints and allow them to be removed, unfortunately by others as well. Most glues will stick the print in permanently, but some will stain the photograph after a period of time. Spray adhesives are becoming more popular and there is a wide variety available, some of which dry out after a while allowing the print to part company with the page. Whatever method is decided upon, the adhesive should be used sparingly.

Do not be afraid to trim excess areas off your prints, there is no need to keep them the same size or shape that they were originally printed. The beauty of prints is that it gives one a second opportunity to improve the composition. To do this make yourself a pair of card letter 'L' shapes approximately 20cm by 13cm and 5cm wide, placed opposite each other they are moved over the print until the best composition is achieved, the print is then marked lightly and trimmed accordingly. Layout of the page is also important and does not want to be repetitive and boring, so vary the size and position of prints on each page (see Figure 13.1). There should be a sense of continuity between prints such as subject matter, location and so on. This cohesion is of vital importance in the City & Guilds exams and to a lesser extent in the GCSE. A series of images without a tangible link will not make a good portfolio or exam submission.

Figure 13.1 Make the layout of your photo album page more interesting.

13.3 Enlargements

For both the GCSE and the City & Guilds exams, enlargements will be required and these must be presented in a way that sets off the print to best advantage. The occasion will also arise when an enlargement is wanted for framing for the home.

Starting with basics, the first thing to ensure is that the print is cropped to give the best possible composition, and that all the sides are square. Several options are open for mounting the print from flush mounting without borders to highly sophisticated aperture mounting. In the GCSE up to eight prints are mounted on a single sheet of card and thought must be given as to their layout and relationship. With City & Guilds, single prints are presented either on mounting board or within a portfolio, but even here the print must be displayed to the best advantage.

With flush mounting the print is just stuck on top of the board and the whole thing trimmed up to the correct size afterwards. This is the best way of dealing with prints that are going to be framed without a border. Unfortunately photographic paper sizes have changed slightly in recent years, particularly for 35mm negatives, but the frame manufacturers have not followed suit so there is a discrepancy in some sizes, of course the frames can always be made to order. Another form of surface mounting is to leave a border around the print, the actual size of this will depend on the size of print. The borders around the top and sides should be equal but the one at the bottom slightly wider to give some weight to the finished product. As a guide a 25cm × 20cm print will need 4–5cm at the top and sides and 5–6cm at the bottom. Many photographers will state that black or white board is best for mounting photographs, especially black and white. Nothing could

Plate 22
The term 'landscape photography' needs to be redefined to include more intimate studies such as this picture of oil and algae on the surface of water.
(Judy Chidlow, C&G Landscape Photography, 'Distinction' grade)

Plate 23
In the City and Guilds Photographing Buildings module students need to stretch the imagination in order to come up with effective images. This reflection of a stained glass window on a church aisle is just such an example.
(Lin Jury, C&G Photographing Buildings, 'Distinction' grade)

Plate 24

Plate 25

Plates 24 and 25

In these two photographs from the same portfolio the window has been used to take the viewer from outside the building to inside. Once inside the clever use of the mirrors and frame give added depth to the photograph and there is repetition in the shapes of the pictures.

(Judy Chidlow, C&G Photographing Buildings, 'Distinction' grade)

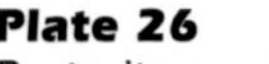

Plate 26
Portraiture will be a natural progression once the student has gained confidence in their ability. Strong sidelighting, a dark background and a masculine pose make this a very effective portrait.
(John Pascoe LRPS, C&G Portraiture, 'Distinction' grade)

Plate 27
This unusual portrait was part of a portfolio with the theme of 'eyes'; in such a photograph it is important that the eyes are pin sharp.
(Malcolm Morrisen LRPS, C&G Portraiture, 'Distinction' grade)

Plate 28
This portrait tells the viewer something about the sitter with the help of the props. Again the dark background helps to concentrate the eye on the subject. (Frank Oldaker, C&G Portraiture, 'Distinction' grade)

Plate 29
The texture created by using ISO3200 film has given an extra dimension to this moonlight portrait. Notice that the subject takes up very little of the picture. (Frank Oldaker, C&G Portraiture, 'Distinction' grade)

Plate 30
The trunks of the tree make a very effective frame for this outdoor portrait. The subdued natural colours complement the more dominant colours of the clothes. (John Pascoe LRPS, C&G Portraiture, 'Distinction' grade)

Plate 31
Everyday objects found around the home can produce very good still life photographs. The ball of oasis reflects the round base of the lamp and the wire cutters lead the eye into the picture. The dark background concentrates the eye on the circle of light. This was shot on daylight film using the tungsten lamp and a 80 blue filter fitted over the lens.
(John Pascoe LRPS, C&G Still Life Photography, 'Distinction' grade)

◀Plate 32
Another shot from a still life portfolio, this time using real flowers, was taken using studio flash.
(Frank Oldaker, C&G Still Life Photography, 'Distinction' grade)

▼Plate 33
Action photography can be treated in several ways; here the movement has been frozen by the use of a high shutter speed.

Plate 34
In this shot a slower shutter speed was used to show the spray but still fast enough to stop the aircraft's motion.

Plate 35
This whiskey bottle has the appearance of being moved by the walking stick; in fact, it is a series of exposures combined with camera movement, with a final flash exposure to give a clear outline of the bottle.
(John Pascoe LRPS, C&G Action and Movement Photography, 'Distinction' grade)

Plate 36

Plate 36 and 37

These two examples of close up photography show how once again everyday objects can make effective photographs. The shower mat was lit by a red light with a green light showing through the drainage hole. Sidelighting on the coins shows up the wording and milling to good effect. (John Pascoe LRPS, C&G Close Up Photography, 'Distinction' grade)

Plate 37

Plate 38
This photograph of pencil shavings shows how imagination can turn waste material into an effective picture; the theme of this portfolio was 'creative art'. (Malcolm Morrisen LRPS, C&G Close Up Photography, 'Distinction' grade)

Plate 39
Beyond close up there is Macro photography. This coin is shown 12 times life size, the detail being highlighted with a low blue light.
(John Pascoe LRPS, C&G Macro Photography, 'Distinction' grade)

Plate 40
This Macro shot is of a very small area of corrugated iron, the patterns are caused by corrosion, easily missed without a keen eye.
(Judy Chidlow)

Plate 41
The City and Guilds Art of Colour Photography demands that the students use their imagination to the full. This shot of lozenges was part of a portfolio with the theme 'red', and inspired by traffic lights, the white background reflecting the light through the sweets.
(John Pascoe LRPS, G&G Art of Colour Photography, 'Distinction' grade)

Plate 42

This stunning photograph was part of the same City and Guilds Art of Colour Photography portfolio as Plate 41. A long exposure time and zoom lens stopped at each of four settings was used to create the effect. The bursts of colour come from using a cosmic diffraction filter.
(John Pascoe LRPS, C&G Art of Colour Photography, 'Distinction' grade)

Plate 43
Probably the most difficult City and Guilds module to undertake is Natural History. This shot of Fly Agaric fungi uses close up techniques and controlled depth of field to make the subject stand out from the background.
(Phil McLean ARPS)

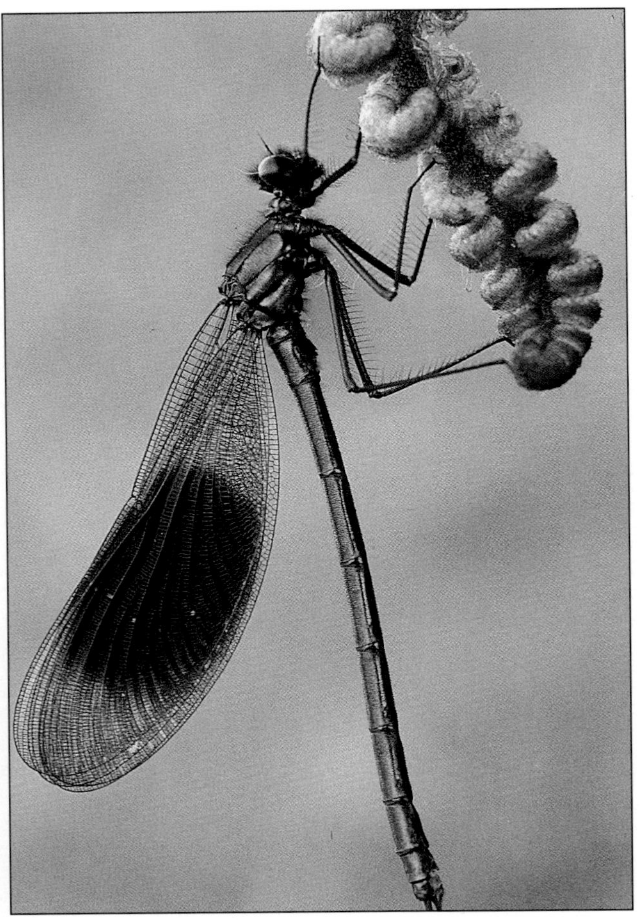

Plate 44
Macro techniques and backlighting were used to take this excellent photograph of a Banded Agrion Damselfly, the shallow depth of field makes the subject stand well away from the background.
(Phil McLean ARPS)

Plate 45

This superb photograph of a harvest mouse on hazel catkins was taken under controlled studio conditions. This is the sort of photography that requires a great deal of patience and a licence.
(Phil McLean ARPS)

be further from the truth or more boring (black/white board tends to clash with black and white prints). Coloured card is ideal for both colour and black and white, the only criteria being that it sets the print off well and does not distract.

Aperture mounting really does set a print off well but requires more time and effort to achieve a good result. First a decision must be taken as to the finished size of the mount, and the print surface mounted on a slightly larger piece of board. It is important that the print is mounted on board and not thin card, as this will just buckle and look awful, and just taping a print to the back of an aperture will look even worse. For the best results the print must be firmly affixed over the whole surface and this can be achieved with a spray adhesive or mounting tissue. Professionals prefer to use mounting tissue but this requires a mounting press which is quite expensive and bulky. The sheets of glue are placed on the back of the print and tacked in place using an iron, the print and tissue are then trimmed to size and tacked in place on the mount. The print and mount are then placed in the heated mounting press with a sheet of silicon release paper over the top. The press is then screwed down tightly and left for a few minutes to allow the glue to melt. On removal from the press the print must be rubbed down to remove air bubbles and assure good adhesion. For very large exhibition prints it may be best to turn to heavy duty wallpaper paste for fixing the print to the mount. A second board of the desired colour then has an aperture cut in it of the required size; it is best to use a rebate cutter for really professional results. Again when cutting to size a slightly wider border at the bottom gives the picture balance. There is no reason to make the aperture rectangular, it could be round, oval or even a totally individual shape.

With both flush and aperture mounting, a keyline drawn around the print will set it off very nicely. Keylining consists of a line drawn at an equal distance around the print with perhaps a wider border at the bottom or even split and overlapped. Again these do not have to be black, any complementary or contrasting colour pen may be used. If drawn with an overlap to one side a space is left for a title or signature.

13.4 Framing

The choice of frames for photographs depends on a number of factors and should be approached from a completely different direction. Thought must first be given as to where they are going to be hung and the surrounding decor. The frame and mount should reflect this and complement the room decoration, all too often frames are bought without any consideration for their eventual surroundings. Modern aluminium frames will not sit well with a classical decor, and conversely ornate gold frames will not go with modern furniture and decoration. The mount now must also suit the frame as well as setting off the print to best advantage. The glass in the frame rarely receives much thought, but if the picture is to be hung near a window or under a light, then non-reflective glass makes viewing much easier. Mounting the print onto card, either flush or in an aperture will overcome the problem of frame sizes not quite suiting the print as mentioned earlier.

13.5 Slide storage

The storage of slides is perhaps more important than that of negatives, although both should be treated with the utmost care. Any scratches or blemishes, such as finger-prints, will show up very clearly when the slide is projected. For projection the slide will need to be put in some form of mount, many will be returned from processing in card or plastic mounts. However, some films are not process paid when you buy them and these will normally be returned as a roll or in strips after processing. The choice of mount is then left to the photographer, either glass or glassless. The advantages and disadvantages have to be weighed up before the choice is made, but at the end of the day it comes down to personal preference. Glass will obviously protect the slide better, but Newton's Rings are likely to be experienced when projecting, also if the slide is mounted with any degree of dampness it will have a detrimental effect on the emulsion. Slide mounts come in two halves of which one is usually white, the slide is placed in the mount so that it is the correct way round when viewed from the white side. For projecting, a spot needs to be put in the bottom left corner of the mount, when placed in the projector, this spot goes at the top right, i.e. so that the slide is in upside down. There is enough space on the white face of the mount to put a reference number or a limited amount of information.

To ensure the maximum life for your slides they need to be kept out of direct daylight and away from harmful fumes. Proprietary slide storage boxes and cases are available from a number of sources holding up to 400 slides with very little space for detailed information. Alternatively, there are hanging file storage wallets, these are transparent wallets holding 24 slides which come with a dust cover and hanging bar for standard filing cabinets. A third way of storing the slides is to use the projector trays, some of which come with lids to minimise dust levels. As with negative filing it is probably better to store detailed information on computer or use a card index filing system. Consideration must be given to storage conditions, ideally constant temperature and humidity, not the loft or cold damp spare bedroom. A small bag of silica gel placed inside the slide box will help minimise dampness, but remember to dry them out from time to time. Taking these simple precautions will prevent fungal growth on the emulsion and the breakdown of the dyes.

Presentation of your slide show must be given a great deal of thought, a very high criteria for the selection of pictures must be adhered to. Nothing but the best will do, correctly exposed and composed images only, and do not be tempted to repeat the subject. Make sure the sequence is snappy to maintain interest, do not dwell on any one picture for more than a few seconds, 10 to 15 seconds at most. Make your commentary short and interesting, better still prepare a script and inject a few humorous comments. Above all keep the presentation reasonably short, no more than half an hour, otherwise your guests will be dropping off to sleep. Ensure your slides are clean, there is nothing worse than hairs dancing on the screen. Make sure that the projector is level and square to the screen, otherwise distortion will result.

13.6 Retouching

Once the print is mounted but before it is framed, any white spots need to be removed. These spots are caused by dust on the negative during printing, or possibly dust laying on the surface of the paper. Retouching, or spotting, is carried out using a fine brush, size 0 or 00, and retouching medium. There are proprietary makes for both black and white and colour prints on the market in the form of liquids and pastes.

The idea is to fill in the white spots with a series of dots which match the background tone using an almost dry brush. For black and white prints it is probably easier to use a black medium and dilute this with water in a small pallet until the correct tone is achieved. The brush is then dried off by rolling on a piece of paper before applying to the print. Using a stippling action, the grain of the film can be imitated and the offending spots disappear. It is much easier to work on matt and semi-matt surfaces as the medium tends to role off the shiny surface of glossy paper. By using a water based medium any mistakes can be removed by re-washing the print. When working with colour prints one has to match the colour and the shade, but the technique is just the same as for black and white.

Black spots caused by holes in the negative are much more difficult to deal with. On fibre base paper it is a case of knifing the offending spot until it matches the background tone. With resin coated paper this technique tends to remove great lumps of emulsion, so it is preferable to use a very weak solution of iodine bleach, and using a small brush apply carefully until the spot is removed. It is unlikely that the background tone can be matched by bleaching and the resultant white area will have to be retouched.

A slightly simpler method of retouching can be used on matt surface papers by using a soft pencil, 2B or 3B are most suitable. A stippling action is still required to simulate the grain texture of the film but one might find it easier for larger areas.

13.7 Toning

Toning is a way of changing the colour of a black and white print, and is usually carried out after the normal developing and fixing process. Most toners come in kit form and provide a range of colours from gold through sepia (brown) to reds, blues and greens. The most common toners consist of a bleach bath and a toning bath, but some have a second bleach bath whilst others, such as blue, are a single bath.

It is advisable to carry out the procedure immediately after processing the print as this ensures the best possible results. If the print is dried and then toned it will almost certainly have picked up grease on the surface and this will prevent both the bleach and the toner from working properly. The method is very simple and can be carried out in room lighting, requiring two trays for the chemicals and running water for rinsing. The chemicals come in concentrate form and need diluting to working strength; as the bleach tends to contain a ferricyanide solution it is as well to wear gloves.

Once the print has had sufficient washing after fixing, it is drained and then placed in the bleach, the image will gradually disappear until only a faint image remains. The print is then washed for a few minutes until all the yellow dye has cleared before placing into the toner. The image will gradually reappear and is left until the desired effect is achieved, the process can be stopped at any time by placing in the wash. The finished print is washed thoroughly and dried in the normal way. It must be stated that with the bleach/tone method the print will never come back to the full density of the original black and white image, there will be about 10% loss. On the other hand the single bath toners will darken the image slightly, so it is as well to start off with a lighter print.

There are more sophisticated toners on the market which enable the image to be toned in sections and even produce a solarised effect. A great deal of fun can be had from experimenting with toners and dyes, even to the extent of using vegetable dyes from the kitchen cupboard. For partial toning one will need a bottle of masking fluid, which is painted onto the areas that are not going to be toned; when dry, it peels off readily with the help of some sticky tape.

As one can see there is a lot more to presentation than merely sticking a print on a piece of paper. Beware though, as with filters, there is a danger of overdoing the effects, so moderation and appropriate use are the guidelines.

14 Disciplines

Photography can be divided up into a number of clearly defined disciplines, each of which require a slightly different approach. Inevitably there will be a certain amount of overlap but for practical purposes each should be treated as a separate subject. The City & Guilds 9231 series of exams enable the photographer to concentrate on a single subject such as portraiture, landscape, buildings, still life, etc. and produce a selection of well thought out and related images. Each of the modules must be undertaken on a theme, the topic itself is not sufficient. So for instance with still life the theme could be a colour or related objects, being made of the same material or having a similar use. Within buildings the theme could be a construction material, type of building or the work of a single architect. In portraiture the theme might be gender, race or even eyes. This thematic approach must be carried through the modules with a coherence that is equally strong and self-evident.

It is advisable that all students undertake the base module 'Starting Photography', regardless of their current abilities, before embarking on any of the other modules. This will ensure that their basic knowledge is up to date and introduce them to the methods of producing a portfolio, bearing in mind that most people will have long since left education behind them. The subject choice for this module should avoid themes that have their own module, such as buildings and portraiture. Keep the choice simple and something to which one has easy access, do not be tempted to undertake a one off event, that is asking for trouble. The portfolio must consist of at least eight images, with technical information in respect of shutter speed, aperture and film stock, to be recorded alongside each picture.

14.1 Portraiture

For the vast majority of photographers portraits, of one kind or another, will be the first venture into the realms of more serious photography. For those undertaking exams or wanting to exhibit with the local photographic club, perhaps a definition of the subject will not go amiss. Portraiture does not have to be formal

Source: ('A' grade GCSE, Sarah Faber).

Figure 14.1 A very strong and sinister mood has been created in this formal 'black' portrait by using 'low key lighting'.

head and shoulder shots of people, nor need it be of faces at all, though of course it can be both. Hands, feet, or any other part of the anatomy can produce a very successful portrait, as long as it says something about the sitter (see Figure 14.1). Where the face forms a substantial part of the picture then ensure that the eyes are sharp. The important thing is that the photograph puts something of the

Source: ('A' grade GCSE, Emily Wills).

Figure 14.2 A very strong mood has been created in this formal portrait of a young woman, careful lighting has prevented flare on the glass and maintained the reflection.

personality of the subject across, revealing a part of their soul, the very thing that many peoples have against photography. Dress must complement the sitter and be typical of their style, the inclusion of props will often help in putting information across to the viewer (see Figure 14.2).

Your first priority must be to become acquainted with your subject and relax them as much as possible by being relaxed yourself and engaging them in light conversation. Nothing could be worse than a stifled self-conscious atmosphere with strained conversation. If you are using friends or relations as models you will find that they are liable to be less patient and cooperative than a professional model. Portraiture demands that the photographer concentrates on the model but remember to watch the background for those obtrusive objects which may protrude from your subject's head.

With adults it is usually best to set the camera up on a tripod with a long cable release or air release. Fit a long focal length lens which will flatter the subject by condensing perspective, a 100mm to 135mm lens is most suitable for 35mm cameras. A large aperture, small *f*/no. will reduce the depth of field, particularly with a longer focal length lens, throwing the background out of focus. A maximum of *f*/5.6 should be used unless one is working very close in when *f*/8 or *f*/11 might be better. Once the camera is set up try and get your model as animated as possible, make the experience enjoyable to obtain that extra sparkle in the eyes. Work from in front of the camera as much as possible so that you do not come across as hiding away, leaving your subject alone. Of course there will be times when you will want more freedom to move around and select different viewpoints for your shots. On these occasions it is even more important to keep up the communication, remember the model is looking into bright light and may not always be able to see you. A lot of sitters will find placing their hands difficult and be ill at ease with

Figure 14.3 Here the man is being used as a prop for the girls and somewhere to place their hands. A number of messages are being emitted by the photograph: (1) he is only incidental to the shot, (2) the girls are being protective towards him, (3) his arms across the girls show he is protecting them–it all depends on your viewpoint.

Figure 14.4 Supporting information from the background and objects around the subject are very important. This informal outdoor portrait contains a lot of information about the subject–his jolly character, country bumkin appearance, age and infirmity. The aircraft in the background is a very important piece of supporting information as he is also a pilot.

them. Should hands be included in the shot then they must be relaxed or better still given something to do, perhaps holding one of those props (see Figure 14.3).

A distinction should be drawn between formal and informal portraiture. It is understood that formal portraiture is where the photographer is in total control of the model, lighting and situation. The model would normally be dressed up for

Figure 14.5 Giving children something to play with can produce different and rewarding pictures.

the occasion; one point to remember is that make-up needs to be slightly heavier than it would usually be worn. The actual photographs do not have to be taken in a studio nor does the model have to be stiff and serious. Informal portraiture on the other hand tends to be taken in a much freer environment with the subject sometimes not knowing that the picture is being taken. These would normally be taken out of doors, though flash pictures taken inside should not be ruled out. If the subject is unaware of the photograph being taken then one is crossing into the realms of candid work. Patience and timing are of prime importance to catch the right moment on film (see Figure 14.4).

Children are always going to cause problems, even for the more experienced photographer. The best way of dealing with them is to play the game and make the session fun for the child. This means allowing the subject free rein to do whatever they want and watching the situation for the good shots. Speed of operation is essential, so being familiar with the equipment is vital. The resultant pictures from this sort of session will inevitably be informal portraits. Formal portraiture of children is much harder and demands a great deal of hard work on the part of the photographer. Time will be limited as the attention span of a youngster will only run to a few minutes. It is essential that a parent or older brother or sister is there to help keep the little ones amused. On the odd occasion the presence of family members will only exacerbate the situation. Children will exhaust you but the results are reward enough (see Figure 14.5).

In all portraiture, whether of adults or children, make the session as short as possible by being fully prepared before the subjects arrive. Hanging around while lights are set up and the camera sorted out will lead to the models becoming bored. Finish the session on a high note after a series of good shots, do not let it run down as both photographer and model become tired, that will only lead to disappointment on both sides.

The workbook for the City & Guilds module should contain preparatory work including a study of other portrait photographer's work, sketches or photographs of lighting layouts and as always an evaluation of the finished work.

14.2 Landscapes

To most people landscapes are large panoramas of countryside and sky; whilst this is true, the term 'landscape' should be redefined. The dictionary describes a landscape as 'a wide view or vista of natural scenery', this is a very narrow and confining definition. Anything from a vista down to an intimate scene of a couple of square metres is perfectly acceptable as a landscape photograph. Seascapes and skyscapes also come under the umbrella of the term 'landscape', as does man-made scenery such as townscapes, urban parks and gardens and miniature landscapes found in the average garden. Around the base of every tree lies a miniature landscape of wild flowers and mosses with textures provided by bark and rock.

Textures are a vital ingredient in landscape photography and are provided by everything from the soil to the sky. (see Figure 14.6). It follows, therefore, that to make the most of these textures the light must be right and an understanding of

Figure 14.6 A traditional landscape of rolling hillsides still obeys the rules of composition.

Figure 14.7 Landscapes can include buildings; this late evening shot shows a reduced brightness range and accentuates the textures in both natural and man made materials.

Figure 14.8 Maximum depth of field is usually required for good landscapes to ensure that both foreground and background are sharp.

the change brought about by it is essential. To highlight textures and bring out the best in a scene it is preferable to photograph in the morning or late afternoon (see Figure 14.7). The height of the day during summer produces too harsh a light with a brightness range that the film cannot cope with, so it is best to confine oneself to either end of the day. Apart from reducing the brightness range, the colour of light will also change, producing a variety of effects.

It is unlikely that good landscapes will result from just wandering around with a camera and chancing to luck. Reconnaissance is essential, visiting a location at different times of the day to see the effect of lighting. There will always be an element of luck involved as with all photography, being in the right place at the right time can produce some good results. Producing that really superb landscape photograph, however, will often be the result of hours or even weeks of frustration waiting for the right conditions. As far as equipment is concerned a tripod is the first essential; this will not only help to ensure sharp pictures but also make one take time in setting up and check levels and composition much more carefully. A standard or wide angle lens is the most useful, but do not rule out the long lens. Maximum depth of field will be required so a small aperture, large *f*/no. must be set on the lens. This is where the depth of field scale comes into its own because one does not focus for landscapes, infinity is set against one side of the scale with the other side giving the closest distance which will be sharp (see Figure 14.8). Focus can be checked with the depth of field preview, if the camera does not have either of these facilities it might be an idea to change it.

Landscape photography can be approached from either a traditional 'straight' viewpoint or from the more visually striking abstract angle. Everyone is familiar with the postcards of yesterday, straightforward record shots of a location, but

Figure 14.9 Simple abstract compositions work just as well as complex pictures.

Figure 14.10 The sky plays a very important role in the construction of landscape photographs.

today there is a distinct move to the more atmospheric interpretation (see Figure 14.9). As with all forms of photography, simplicity is the strength, try to keep the images simple and uncluttered, too much information will lead to confusion. With the wide vista particular attention needs to be paid to detail, as it can all too easily be missed in the overall picture. At the other end of the scale landscapes can become an abstract pattern, either natural or man made (see colour plates between pp.000–000).

The sky may play a vital role in the picture and therefore it pays to watch how the clouds are affecting the landscape, a cloud overhead could cast a shadow over the ground in the middle distance or background (see Figure 14.10). Consider how much of the sky is required in the photograph; with dramatic cloud formations one might want to make more of the sky than if it is just bright blue. It is more likely to be the sky that catches the eye when viewing a landscape than the detail on the ground. Vast tracts of water will prove boring unless there is something of interest in the foreground; to avoid this lower the camera angle and minimise the expanse. Above all do not be overawed by the scene and remember to compose the picture correctly, including some foreground detail to add interest and lead the eye into the picture. If shooting in black and white it will be essential to fit a yellow or orange filter to enhance the cloud detail, but a red filter will make for a very dramatic sky and a green one will help to lighten the darker shades and give more detail in the foliage.

The workbook for the City & Guilds Module should contain examples of research and experimentation plus a study of both a landscape painter and photographer. The works of artists may seem irrelevant, but one will be surprised just how much knowledge, pleasure and inspiration can be gained from this study.

Source: ('A' grade GCSE, Katherine Herald).

Figure 14.11 Converging verticals can be used to advantage in picture structure.

14.3 Buildings

Architecture is probably one of the most difficult disciplines of photography in which to achieve success. Some of the most photogenic buildings are crammed into tight areas within town and are almost impossible to photograph, even with wide angle lenses. However, for both the GCSE and the City & Guilds the

Figure 14.12 The very strong vertical lines and long sweeps of this bridge make for a striking picture.

building does not have to be shown in its entirety. With anything other than a technical camera, converging verticals are a fact of life and will not lose marks, in fact they can be used to great effect (see Figure 14.11).

As with landscapes the term 'building' needs redefining to include civil engineering such as bridges, follies, architectural detail and street furniture where applicable (see Figure 14.12). Again light will play an important part in the photography of buildings, particularly where texture and form are of primary consideration. One major problem in cities is that some buildings never receive sunlight, or they have ugly shadows from other buildings falling on them. It is probably best to abandon these and look for alternatives, there is no point in wasting film on something which will only prove disappointing. There is however, one way of

Figure 14.13 The question of environment must be considered; this is the Sacre Coeur as most Parisians would probably see it.

Figure 14.14a

Figure 14.14b

Figure 14.14a–b Two photographs of the same building, one a straight record shot the other a more intimate view; the sweeping lines of the steps and vertical lines of the columns make for a more interesting picture.

shooting these buildings successfully, and that is to wait until dusk when they will be lit internally and possibly, even floodlit. To be successful at architectural photography one needs to be interested in the subject, be prepared to spend time studying the building and wait until the lighting conditions are at their best. Try and understand what the architect was trying to say, if anything, in the design of the structure. Is the building purely functional or has consideration been given to the environmental questions? Is the design in keeping with older architectural styles in the neighbourhood, or does it clash? (see Figure 14.13). Has the structure been built using traditional local materials or modern ones? Does it function efficiently for those working or living in it? All these and more are questions which must be answered in the photographic interpretation of any structure. This comes under the heading of research and planning and carries marks in both examinations.

The last thing in the world that is needed is a straight record shot taken from square on, this does nothing for the building or your photography. With a modern structure that makes use of strong symmetrical lines try and emphasise these graphic qualities in the photograph. Old buildings that have stood for centuries are obviously well built, try and show this strength by using vertical lines in the picture (see Figure 14.14a-b). Another consideration should be that of location, a building's environment is often as important as the structure itself; here a long

Figure 14.15 This interior shot has been taken using the available artificial lighting plus some fill flash to brighten the seating area.

shot where the building takes up very little of the image area will establish this. Where the building is used by people on a regular basis for a specific purpose, then the inclusion of those people is part of the supporting information; they also give scale to the scene.

A requirement of the City & Guilds, Photographing Buildings module is that interiors should be included and these can present some real problems for the amateur. The main thing to remember is, show the building as the architect intended. Churches and old structures built before the days of electrical illumination should be photographed using natural light only. This is best done on an overcast day or late in the day to reduce the brightness range so that the windows do not burn out. If the exterior view, through a window, is to form an integral part of the shot then interior light levels need to be balanced to match the exterior. Alternatively, exposure readings should be taken from a number of areas and averaged; this will result in a compromised exposure which should produce satisfactory results. The use of a tripod is essential, not just for the long exposure times, but to ensure that

Figure 14.16 This interior was shot using the very limited articial light and fill flash to help brighten up the floor area.

Figure 14.17a

Figure 14.17b

Figure 14.17a–b These two shots show how the feel of a photograph can be changed by an adjustment in camera position. One is light and open and the other more claustrophobic and intimidating.

everything is square and upright. Do not forget to allow for reciprocity failure once the exposure times exceed 1 second. It may be necessary to use a little fill flash in some of the darker corners or the roof space, just to put some detail into the shadows (see Figures 14.15 and 14.16).

When photographing modern interiors which have been designed to be lit throughout the day, the problem of colour casts can be a very serious one when using colour film. Nearly all office and public buildings are lit with fluorescent tubes which can vary greatly in colour; whilst this can be overcome to some extent by using a magenta filter, it is not wholly satisfactory. It will pay to shoot interiors on negative film where there is scope for adjustment at the printing stage. Flash could be used to correct the colour balance of everything within its range, but a cast will still be picked up outside that range which could detract from the overall effect. The art of painting with light appears to have almost disappeared from photography, but is a highly successful means of illuminating a difficult interior. It involves washing the scene with a high power tungsten light, with the camera shutter open on *B*, when using tungsten colour film. When using daylight film a flashgun can be used, fired several times in different directions on manual, again with the shutter open on brief. Of course with black and white film no such problems arise as the scene can be washed with tungsten or flash, or a mix of both. There is no easy way to learn this technique and as each situation will be different it is a case of practice makes perfect.

With both the GCSE and the City & Guilds, there will need to be ample evidence of research into the particular period or style of architecture covered by the portfolio. The amount of effort put into this side will depend very much upon how interested one becomes in the subject, just remember that marks are weighted towards final images, not research material.

14.4 Action and movement

Photographs capture an instant in time and therefore it is impossible to show objects moving, we can only suggest movement by allowing the subject to blur or by the use of diagonal lines in composition. There are two ways of creating the illusion of movement with blur, one is to have the camera in a fixed position, possibly on a tripod, and allow the subject to blur by using a slow shutter speed. With fast moving objects blurring will begin with shutter speeds as high as 1/250s, the longer the exposure time the greater the effect (see Figure 14.18). There will come a point though, where the subject will blur to such an extent that it will become totally unrecognisable. With slower moving subjects such as running water, quite long exposure times, up to 1 second or more can be used successfully. To start with it will pay to take a series of exposures at differing shutter speeds, in order to evaluate the very different results achieved.

The other method of simulating movement with blur is panning, here the subject is followed by the camera during exposure, blurring the background and thus giving the impression of speed. A high shutter speed is not necessary for this method, speeds can be as low as 1/60s once the technique has been mastered, nor is a high ISO film essential as recommended by some sources. Remembering that

Figure 14.18 Here the action has been allowed to blur using a slow shutter speed of $^{1}/_{2}$ second providing some intersting patterns.

the background will not be sharp this allows a shallow depth of field, using an aperture of around *f*/4 or 5.6, to be used quite successfully. Best results are achieved hand holding the camera with anything other than a very long focal length lens. When shooting with a long lens then some sort of camera support will be needed to assist in keeping the camera reasonably steady. A tripod with a panning head

Source: (BAe/Hawker Siddeley Aviation).

Figure 14.19 The ultimate in panning shots, a tremendous sense of movement comes from this photograph of a fast and low flying jet.

could be used but it is probably easier to use a monopod or rifle grip as they allow more freedom. The most difficult task will be keeping the subject sharp, particularly if the direction of movement is not at 90° to the camera, possibly a good case for autofocus (see Figure 14.19). Keeping the subject in the correct position within the frame only comes with practice, at first there is a tendency to pan too fast or too slow.

Freezing the action is the third method of showing movement, but here the suggestion of motion comes from the composition of the picture. A fast shutter speed will normally be required but not a large depth of field, so it does not necessarily follow that a high ISO film is needed. However, if the photographs are to be taken in low light or under artificial lighting conditions then a high speed film will be required. A typical situation would be an athletics meeting where perhaps the personalities are as important as the action. It therefore follows that the photograph needs to be sharp in order to recognise their features. An added problem encountered at such events is that the crowd line is a fair distance from the activities, demanding the use of a long lens, so the use of higher shutter speeds becomes even more important.

The use of a camera support, such as a monopod, will relieve the weight of the camera from the neck and enable one to concentrate on picture taking. Again focusing will be the biggest problem so select the position at which the photograph

Figure 14.20 Pre-focusing on a known position assists in capturing moving subjects. Here the blurring of the wheels and the attitude of the driver give a sense of motion.

is to be taken and pre-focus at that point; it is then just a matter of waiting for the subject to arrive (see Figure 14.20). The use of a motor drive is often advocated for such occasions to ensure capturing the right moment. However, this is no guarantee of success and may just result in the use of a great deal of film.

Another more technical way of showing movement is to use a strobe light which records a series of images onto one frame. Everyone must be familiar with the shot of the golfer swinging at a ball, where some dozen or more positions are recorded. The technique is to set the subject up against a black background with just enough light to frame and focus. The camera is put on a tripod and the aperture set for correct exposure using the strobe light. The shutter is set on brief and the strobe remotely activated by the subject, firing as many as ten or fifteen times a second. High speed flash photographs can be taken of any fast moving object, using a remote sensing device where the subject takes its own picture. With a flash duration as short as 1/50 000 of a second almost everything will record as a sharp image. Strictly speaking this is no longer movement but the recording of an instant in time.

The research notes should show a progression in thought processes towards the final images chosen, including some of the failures. Thumbnail sketches are always worth including in the background notes to show detailed planning, even if the end result bears no resemblance to them.

14.5 Still life and close up

This side of photography is the closest that one comes to painting or drawing, requiring a good imagination and eye for design. This is also the subject that strikes most fear in the hearts of amateurs and many professionals alike. Still life is the one area where the photographer has to come up with the artistic idea and literally build on it. Unlike all other disciplines, where the beauty already exists, with still life it has to be created almost from scratch. The interrelationship between objects must be considered carefully as must their relationship with the background (see Figure 14.21).

Once this decision has been made, lighting must be the next consideration, as with the portraiture this should start off with a single lamp and gradually be built up, if necessary. It may be that a window light and reflector are all that are required to achieve the desired effect. As with all forms of photography, simplicity is the key to good composition; add objects slowly and carefully, taking time to consider whether they do anything for the picture. There is a wealth of inspiration out there in the form of traditional still life paintings as well as photographs.

Close up photography on the other hand tends to be more about recording, although there is scope for artistic interpretation. Beyond a macro lens some specialised equipment will be required in the form of extension tubes, reversing ring or a bellows attachment. Alternatively, one could use a close up lens, but there will be a consequential loss of quality. As with still life a tripod or other form of camera support is essential, when working only a few centimetres away from the

Figure 14.21 Still life shots are all around us, it is a case of keeping a look out for suitable subjects.

Figure 14.22 This flower was photographed using the macro facility on a 70mm lens at 1:6, i.e. 1/6 life size.

subject any slight movement of the camera will result in the loss of the subject from view. It is extremely difficult to carry out close up work when hand holding the camera, apart from which the shutter speeds are likely to be fairly long resulting in camera shake.

In order to record the very fine details, a low ISO film should be used and this in turn will need maximum depth of field to achieve best results. Remember the closer one gets to the subject the shorter the depth of field becomes, requiring the use of the smallest aperture to achieve even a modest depth of acceptable focus. Actual magnification achieved will depend upon the lens used and the amount of extension. The terms used to describe magnification are often confusing, but once explained are easy to understand. On macro lenses and in the tables that come with extension tubes and bellows numbers such as 1:4 can be found, these refer to the amount of magnification achieved or reproduction ratio, in other words how large the image is on film compared to the original. As an example 1:4 means that the image will be one quarter the size of the original subject, so if the object being photographed is 8cm long the image will be 2cm long on film. Therefore, 1:2 means half life size and 1:1 means life size, easily achievable when using extension tubes or bellows units (see Figure 14.22).

When working so close to the subject it may prove very difficult to actually light the object, particularly if working under artificial lighting. This is where the ring flash comes into its own as mentioned in Chapter 8 on flash. Otherwise a series of reflectors may be needed to direct the light onto the subject. There is a marked loss of light when doing close up work, but if the camera's TTL metering system

◀Figure 14.23a

◀Figure 14.23b

Figure 14.23c▶

Figure 14.23a–c For the photo essay the picutres must tell a story; in this sequence the shots show work going on plus an informal portrait.

is being used, there should be no problem in obtaining correct exposure.

As with the portraiture module the workbook for still life and close up photography should show sketches of set and lighting layout, highlight any problems encountered and describe how they were overcome. It is always a good idea to include some of the lesser photographs to illustrate these problems and as a comparison for the final images.

14.6 Photo essay

It is the title of this City & Guilds module that perhaps puts most photographers off attempting it, when in fact it can be one of the most enjoyable. The word 'essay' suggests a lot of writing, but the essay comes from the pictures, with a little help from words. Maybe a change of title to 'picture story' would make it more popular. 'A photograph is worth a thousand words' is often quoted in respect of pictures, and this is probably true of the best images. It therefore follows that a collection of photographs in the form of a story should have a greater impact than the sum of the individual images (see Figure 14.23a-c). Here the photographer is required to tell a story using a sequence of between 8 and 15 pictures, it follows that the photographs must be in a logical order. The subject matter for this module is vast, anything from a 'day in the life of' type of approach, such as a public servant, fireman, policemen, etc., to a more defined 'story' as in the construction of a building or relating a process from start to finish. There is still plenty of scope for artistic interpretation in spite of the fact that events are being recorded. The words should take the form of extended captions or short magazine article. One of the best sources for gaining an idea of photo essay style work is the *National Geographic* magazine. This module must be the result of careful research and planning in order to maximise the overall impact. The workbook must contain a representative selection of the rejected photographs plus a study of a photo-essayist.

Picture stories or sequential photography is also acceptable as part of the GCSE examination. Here it could also take the form of progression of a photographic technique, or the development of a single image through image manipulation. For any form of sequential photography there must be a clear beginning, middle and end, just as in writing.

14.7 History of photography

This City & Guilds module gives the student the opportunity to investigate the development of photographic processes and aesthetic innovation. Only a general understanding and outline is required with no in-depth analysis. The idea is to produce an essay of approximately 3000 words on the development of photography across a wide range of applications, or on one particular aspect. Alternatively the module can look at the growth of particular styles or genres within the medium and their aesthetic impact. One must be prepared to undertake a good deal of research and visit exhibitions in order to achieve a reasonable grade in this

Figure 14.24 Zoos provide easy access to animals for the beginner in natural history photography

module. The marking scheme differs from other modules in so far as there are marks for appropriate use of illustrations and list of sources.

14.8 Natural history

This is the most specialised of the City & Guilds modules and one that needs a great deal of patience and planning. The portfolio should cover both flora and fauna, as the module requires a mix of the two. Locating subject matter will be the result of a lot of hard work, which is only the beginning. Photographing plants is relatively easy but thought must still be given to the laws pertaining to wild flowers, there are also strict laws regarding wild animals which must be followed. The Royal Photographic Society (Nature Group) publish a code of practice which starts 'There is one hard and fast rule, whose spirit must be observed at all times. The welfare of the subject is more important than the photograph.' This sums up a general approach very neatly.

Certain rare plants and animals are covered by very strict legislation and guidance on this can be obtained from either your local natural history trust, Wildlife Trust or English, Scottish or Welsh Nature.

The Royal Society for the Protection of Birds will give advice on the photography of birds and list those endangered species that require a licence before photographs can be taken. English Nature is the controlling body that may or may not issue that licence, separate offices exist for Scotland and Wales.

Having located your subject then work must begin on preparing the site for photography. A wind shield may be needed to prevent plants moving in the breeze, this can also act as a reflector. When photographing wildlife some form of hide will need to be constructed, having obtained permission from the landowner. Remember that any permanent structure will announce the presence of wildlife to less scrupulous people. Wild animals have very keen hearing and even the noise of the shutter firing will scare them. Most of the noise when taking a picture with an SLR is that of the mirror going up, some cameras offer the facility to lock the mirror in the up position, but this means that the subject cannot be viewed through the lens. With the camera set up on a tripod, all that remains is to wait, one may be there hours for no result at all, so patience is a virtue.

Of course there are easier ways of photographing animals which are perfectly acceptable for the portfolio. One is to visit a zoo or wildlife park (see Figure 14.24) where the animals are used to human activity and having cameras thrust at them. Another is to take the animals to a studio and photograph them under controlled conditions; this will require a licence.

The workbook must contain evidence of an understanding of the laws regarding wild animals and plants and show a sympathetic approach to the subjects. There should also be some research into the various aids available, even if these were not used in the production of the portfolio.

14.9 Black and white

As already stated, to achieve success in black and white photography one has to be able to switch out the colour mode and think in terms of tonal ranges. There are filters available which reduce colours to a series of brightness ranges and are certainly worth investing in to start with. If one elects to undertake black and white for either GCSE or City & Guilds, then one must be prepared to put a lot more thought and work into the pictures.

There are three City & Guilds modules concerned with black and white photography, the first of which is the 'Introduction to Black and White'. Here the student is taken through composition, film characteristics and processing, contact printing and enlarging. The portfolio must consist of at least five definitive black and white photographs which represent the student's best interpretation of the medium (see Figure 14.25). The workbook must contain all preparatory work, including a series of exercises showing an understanding of the principles and techniques involved, plus contact sheets of all films taken for the course. Suggested exercises include the making of photograms, selection and evaluation of images from the contact sheets (these should include examples of with and without filters, showing an understanding of their use), one negative printed onto different grades of paper, local printing control and multiple printing. Faults in negatives and prints should be identified and if one has produced examples during the course, then these should be included. Beyond this there should be a study of black and white work from one or more well known photographers, plus an evaluation of images in both colour and black and white. Evaluation may prove very difficult if this is the first venture into the realms of black and white. Though not a requirement for the GCSE, these exercises will prove very useful for all students if undertaken before photography starts.

The next module in the series is the 'Art of Black and White' where the student uses several techniques to inject mood into the photographs; these can include exposure/development manipulation, to change the grain structure and contrast, and multiple printing. The majority of portfolio images will of course be the result of good lighting and composition (see Figure 14.26). Photographs used for the Introduction module will not be of a high enough standard to be used again in the Art of Black and White module.

Perhaps one of the most interesting of these modules is 'Image Derivation', where the photographer takes continuous tone negatives and derives a number of different images from them. Acceptable techniques within the range are solarisation, bas relief, lith transfer, toning and printing on coloured paper (see Figure 14.27). The portfolio must not just consist of a series of derived images for their own sake, but each picture should work well in the particular method undertaken. As with the Art of Black and White module a new set of photographs will need to be taken for this module.

The workbooks for these modules should take the form of a working manual describing each stage in detail, particularly the production of the portfolio prints; this will make a useful reference source in the future.

Source: ('A' grade GCSE, Nicola Kent).

Figure 14.25 More imagination and a willingness to experiment are essential for success at the higher levels of black and white.

Figure 14.26 Progressing through black and white towards more artistic images is the aim of the City & Guilds Art of Black & White module.

Source: ('A' grade GCSE, Flora Westwood).

Figure 14.27 This very striking image is a lith transfer from a standard black and white negative. Simple picture structure is essential for it to work successfully.

15 Examination requirements

Once enrolled on a photography course, your first priority must be to make sure that you understand the syllabus. This should be explained in detail by your tutor in the first lesson, but it is advisable to obtain a copy of the syllabus so that you can refer to it throughout the course.

For the GCSE Photography exam a number of projects will have to be undertaken on given themes, such as architecture, abstracts or people and a selection of prints presented. For the various City & Guilds modules the portfolio has to be carried out on a chosen theme - not just landscape, but something in the landscape, not just portraiture, but eyes in portraiture, for instance.

15.1 Planning and research

Before undertaking any photography the subject matter needs to be researched. This will involve looking at how other photographers have approached the subject and analysing their work. This exercise will prove very useful as it should give one inspiration and ideas. One does not have to look very hard in order to find material, every newspaper and magazine is full of photographs which fall into a number of different categories. Beyond this most non-fiction books will be well illustrated, with travel books containing a large amount of landscape and building photographs. The next line of research will probably be photographic books, either profiles of famous photographers or works on particular disciplines.

Then one needs to think carefully about possible locations that will provide suitable subject matter (see Figure 15.1). Initially these need to be local sites that are easily accessible, so that a number of reconnaissance and photographic visits can be undertaken. Should the location be at some distance, then a study of the weather forecasts will be required to ensure the right kind of lighting for the subject and avoid a wasted trip. Time of day will also be important so knowing the aspect of the subject is essential - if sunlight only illuminates it in the morning there is no point in arriving after lunch. For landscape photography a basic knowledge of map read-

Source: ('A' grade GCSE, Louisa Taylor).

Figure 15.1 Thorough research and planning are essential to find suitable subject matter for the chosen theme. This windmill could provide images for a number of different disciplines, such as buildings and abstracts.

ing, such as understanding contour lines, is useful to help identify suitable locations.

Having completed the research a statement of intent then has to be made, i.e. why you chose the particular subject or theme, how you intend to approach that subject and where likely locations are to be found. All of this appears as part of the coursework notebook for both GCSE and City & Guilds and carries as much as 25% of the overall mark. The research notes can be illustrated with cuttings and photocopies of pictures, and individual pictures commented upon.

15.2 Technical quality

With any mechanical process technical quality must constitute a fair proportion of the marks, and this is the case with both series of exams. Technical quality covers camera techniques such as sharpness of the image, appropriate use of shutter speeds, appropriate use of apertures to give correct depth of field and choice of film (see Figure 15.2).

For the GCSE, students are required to process and print all their own work, whereas many of the City & Guilds modules accept commercially processed prints. Where the student has to undertake the work themself, then print quality comes into the mark scheme. This includes not only straight prints but also all manipulated images for the Image Derivation and Constructed Images courses. Finally,

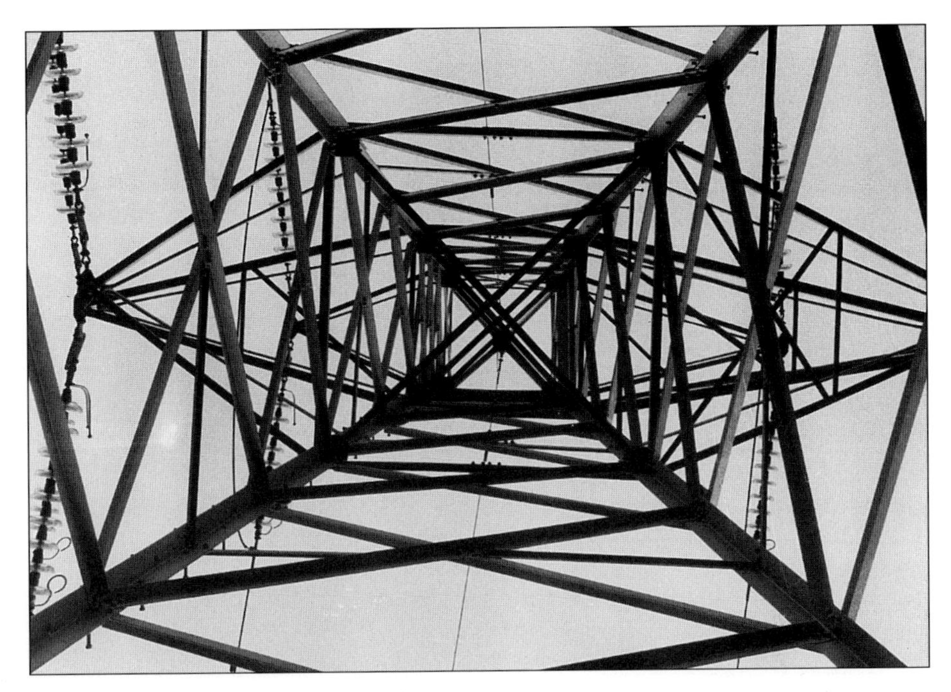

Source: ('A' grade GCSE, Sarah Prag).

Figure 15.2 Technical quality is important for all photographic exams and here the image is sharp from top to bottom and has been well printed.

skills in presenting the portfolio are also taken into consideration and these include mounting and retouching.

15.3 Visual quality

With a visual medium it is to be expected that visual quality will account for the largest proportion of marks, and this is true in both GCSE and all City & Guilds modules. 'Visual quality' covers composition of the photograph including line, tone, colour and all the other points of composition (see Figure 15.3). Visual continuity will also be taken into account, i.e. how one photograph follows on from the previous one. This linking can be achieved through colour, shape or related objects within the scene. Disjointed and unrelated images make for a weak presentation. The overall visual effect of the portfolio will be included in this section, so thought must be given as to how the images are going to be presented. The workbook can take the form of a separate A4 loose leaf binder or be included as part of the whole portfolio. The final prints can be mounted individually on good quality board or put into a portfolio case, much will depend on the finished print size. For the preparatory work enprints of 7 × 5in prints are adequate, for the GCSE a maximum size of 10 × 8in is recommended. The City & Guilds do not stipulate a maximum size, but for the majority of the modules 7 × 5in prints presented in an A4 portfolio are acceptable. Cost must be a consideration with large

Source: ('A' grade GCSE, Kirsty Mackay).

Figure 15.3 Visual quality must be given top priority in a visual medium, here excellent composition and mood have gone into the production of this image.

Figure 15.4 Evaluation can prove difficult, but by applying the basic rules of composition and technical quality it becomes a simple objective task.

good quality colour prints being very expensive, as are the portfolio cases. Remember the bigger the print the more obvious the mistakes.

15.4 Evaluation

With all City & Guilds modules the portfolio must be accompanied by a workbook; as already stated this should contain all research and planning notes, plus the statement of intent with individual evaluation of the photographs and overall evaluation of the project. The GCSE also requires notes on planning and experimental work, plus an evaluation of the pictures. This category will carry a minimum of 10% of the marks, so it is an important part of the overall presentation.

Evaluating one's own work is quite difficult to begin with and many students find it hard to achieve objectively (see Figure 15.4). However, with time the task becomes easier and there is a risk that the student will go the other way and be too critical of their work. The idea is to highlight the faults and areas for improvement, not to subject the pictures to a negative critique; there may well be extenuating circumstances that can be put forward, such as poor weather and immovable unwanted objects. It is a good idea to get a 'cold' appraisal of work from someone completely detached, then explain the thinking behind the pictures and see if they come up with a different viewpoint.

15.5 Other requirements

The GCSE and some of the City & Guilds modules require a personal study into an aspect of photography or a photographer's work. The study into an aspect of photography should be a personal analysis of one area, such as fashion or portrait photography and look at the development of styles and prominent figures involved. This could be an historical overview or concentrate on one particular period.

Looking at the work of an individual photographer the student should try not to be influenced by opinions of biographers and editors, although there will inevitably be some historical background notes which will have to be sourced from books. This could cover the life's work of an individual or just a specific period. Alternatively, one could look at the work of an influential group such as the Photo-secessionists.

For the GCSE these studies should normally be around 1500 words. The City & Guilds recommend about 1000 words, though many students become really enthused with the project and produce very wordy pieces. Cuttings and photocopies from magazine and books may be used to illustrate the piece and individual pictures commented on.

The personal study is marked separately for the GCSE and is worth a greater percentage of the overall mark, whereas for the City & Guilds it can be part of the planning and research or marked under its own category.

The human animal is the only species that appears to need some form of creative outlet, be it music, dance or art, and photography fills this need for far more people than any other medium. It has been said that photography freed art from the need to record and allowed it greater expression, thereby elevating it to a higher plain. With the advent of electronic imaging perhaps photography, too, will be given a new lease of life.

Glossary

Aberration: Fault in a simple lens which causes an unsharp or distorted image.
Accelerator: A chemical in developers, also known as the alkali, which speeds up the action of the developing agent.
Ambient light: The light already illuminating a subject, such as daylight, artificial light or a mix of both.
Angle of view: The angle of acceptance of a lens - how much it sees, differs with the focal length of lens.
Aperture: The hole in the lens created by the iris diaphragm controlling the amount of light that passes through to the film. Defined in terms of *f*/numbers and called stops.
ASA: American Standards Association, a system of defining film sensitivity now going out of use.

B: Brief, shutter speed setting allowing the shutter to remain open for extended times by maintaining pressure on the shutter release button.
Backlighting: Where the light source is behind the subject.
Ball and socket: A type of tripod head which allows the camera to be moved through three planes simultaneously.
Barn doors: A fitting put over a studio flash or light having four flaps which can be adjusted to control the light.
Burning in: Printing technique where a small area of a print is given more exposure than the rest of the print.

Cable release: Accessory used in conjunction with a tripod to fire the cameras shutter without touching it, thus avoiding camera shake.
Camera movements: Used in large format cameras where the lens and film panels can be moved on four axes to control or create distortion in the image.
Camera obscura: Latin for 'dark room', originally a darkened room with a small aperture in one wall allowing an image of the scene outside to pass onto the opposite wall and be drawn.

Cassette: A light tight container for 35mm film.
Catchlight: The all important highlights which give life to the subject's eyes.
Changing bag: A light tight bag to enable film to be removed from the camera or cassette and loaded into a processing tank.
Close up lens: A supplementary lens fitted to the front of a standard lens, shortening the focal length, and allowing the camera to be focused closer than would otherwise be possible.
Colour temperature: The colour of a light source measured in Kelvins.
Compound lens: A lens made up of several simple elements designed to eliminate or minimise aberrations.
Compur shutter: A shutter that is fitted between the lens elements.
Contact print: A print from a negative or strip of negatives made by placing the negative directly onto printing paper and exposing it to light.
Contrast: The ratio between the lightest and darkest parts in a scene or on the print.
Contre-jour: From the French 'against the light', simply taking pictures into the light.
Converging verticals: Where vertical lines taper, caused by looking up at buildings, etc. making them appear to fall over.
Cropping: Adjusting the composition by excluding parts of the image during printing or by cutting the print before display.

Dedication: Term used to describe a flashgun that is designed to operate with a specific make and model of camera, particularly for TTL flash metering and high synchronisation shutter speeds.
Depth of field: The distance in front and behind the point of critical focus that is in acceptably sharp focus.
Depth of focus: The amount by which the film can move in the camera and still produce a sharp image.
Developer: A mix of chemicals that change the latent image on negatives or prints into a visible one.
Developing agent: The chemical ingredient that changes silver halides into metallic silver to form an image.
Dichroic fog: A greenish staining of the emulsion caused by developer contaminated with fixer.
Differential focus: Using a small depth of field and critical focusing to highlight a subject.
DIN: A German method of expressing film sensitivity, being replaced by the ISO system.
Dioptre: Unit of measurement used to describe the magnifying power of a close up lens.
Dodging: Printing technique where part of the image being printed receives less exposure than the rest.
Double exposure: Putting two images on the same piece of film or print.

Emulsion: The light sensitive layer on which the image is formed on negatives and prints.

Enlarger: The piece of equipment used to make prints of varying sizes from negatives.
Exposure: The action of light on a sensitive material.
Exposure latitude: The amount by which an emulsion can be over or under exposed and still give an acceptable result.
Exposure meter: An instrument used for measuring light levels to calculate exposure of film.
Extension bellows: A bellows unit of variable length that fits between the lens and camera body for macro photography.
Extension tubes: Short tubes fitted between the lens and camera body to enable macro photography to be undertaken.

***f*numbers:** The sequence of numbers used to define the amount of light passing through a lens.
Film retriever: A device for extracting the leader of a 35mm film from its cassette.
Film speed: A term used to describe the ISO rating of a film, slow: ISO25 - 80, medium ISO100 - 200 and fast ISO400+.
Filter factor: The amount by which exposure has to be increased to allow for the density of the filter.
Fixer: The chemical used after development that desensitises the emulsion allowing it to be viewed in normal lighting.
Flare: Non-image forming light which enters the camera and causes a loss of contrast and creates hexagons on the image.
Flash synchronisation speed: The fastest shutter speed that can be used with a flashgun.
Focal length: Distance between the lens and film plane when focused at infinity.
Focal plane shutter: A shutter that is situated immediately in front of the film, found on most SLRs.
Fogging: Accidental exposure of the sensitive material to light or extended development (chemical fog).

Grain: Minute particles of metallic silver that form the processed image.
Grey card: A sheet of mid-grey card that reflects 18% of the light that falls upon it, used to calculate accurate exposures.
Guide numbers: An indication of the power output of a flashgun.

Halation: A halo created around a point light source in the emulsion.
High key: A portrait lighting technique where the subject is dressed in light clothing, placed against a light background and well lit.
Highlights: The brightest parts of a scene.
Hotshoe: The fitting on top of the camera with electrical contacts for the flashgun.
Hyperfocal distance: The point of focus at which optimum depth of field is obtained.

Incident reading: A method of taking a light reading from the light source by using an exposure meter and invercone.
Infra-red: Radiation beyond the red band of the spectrum, invisible to the eye, used to record images on black and white and colour infra-red films.
Instant return mirror: The mirror used for viewing in SLRs which hinges up for exposure and then returns to its original position.
Iris diaphragm: A series of thin blades that form the aperture in a lens.

Kelvins: Unit of temperature used to measure the colour of light, with its zero at -273°C.
Key light: The main light in any lighting set up from which the exposure reading should be taken.

Latent image: The invisible image formed on light-sensitive material after exposure.
Line/lith film: Very high contrast black and white film with almost no grey tones, only sensitive to blue and green light.
Low key: A lighting technique in portraiture where the subject is placed against a dark background with minimal lighting.

Macro-photography: Photography at very close quarters using a macro lens and/or extension tubes, giving up to 1:1 magnification.
Mirror lock: A device found on some SLRs that enables the mirror to be locked up before long exposures to prevent camera shake.
Monochrome: One colour, largely associated with black and white film but going out of favour.

Newton's rings: Rings or patterns created when two glass or glass and film surfaces come into contact, usually signifying presence of moisture.

One shot: Refers to developers that are used once only and then discarded.
Orthochromatic: Film only sensitive to blue and green light that can be processed in red light.
Over exposure: Allowing too much light to reach the sensitive material.

Pan and tilt: A type of tripod head, adjustable in three planes.
Panchromatic: Film sensitive to all colours of light.
Panning: Following the subject's movement with the camera and exposing the film during the operation, renders the subject sharp and background blurred.
Parallax error: Where the viewing and taking lens of a camera see a slightly different aspect of the scene.
Photogram: A print made by placing objects onto printing paper and exposing to light.
Photomicrography: Photography undertaken through a microscope.
Pinhole camera: A simple form of box camera with a pinhole instead of a lens.
Preservative: The chemical in developers that prevents oxidation.

Primary colours: Red, green and blue light which when mixed form white light.
Pull processing: Decreasing development time to correct for over exposure.
Push processing: Increasing development time to correct for under exposure.

Red eye: Red eyes in colour photographs caused by flash reflecting off the retina of the eye.
Refraction: The change in direction of light when it enters another medium obliquely.
Resolving power: The ability of the lens and film to record fine detail.
Restrainer: Chemical ingredient in developers that prevents unexposed silver halides from being developed.
Reticulation: Crazing of film emulsion due to sudden large changes in temperature during processing.
Retouching: The art of removing unwanted blemishes on film and prints by painting on dyes and/or knifing.
Reversal film: Another name for transparency/slide film.

Safelight: A lamp used in processing and printing which does not affect the emulsion, different colours are required for various emulsions.
Selenium cell: Light-sensitive cell used in light meters, does not require a battery to operate.
Silver halides: The light-sensitive silver salts in emulsions.
Slide film: Another term for transparencies.
SLR: Single lens reflex, a type of camera.
Snoot:: Conical tube that fits over a flash head or light to concentrate it into a spot.
Soft box: A tent like structure that fits over a studio flash spreading the light over a large area.
Soft focus: A deliberate act of making a sharp image diffused by use of a filter or special soft focus lens.
Solarisation: A printing technique where the print is partially developed and then subjected to a very short exposure to white light.
Spotting: A misleading term for retouching.
Stop bath: Chemical used to arrest development, used after developing and before fixing.
Synchronisation: The term used to describe the camera shutter operating a flashgun.

Test strip: A series of short exposures on film and paper used to ascertain best exposure.
Time exposure: An exposure of long duration used with the B setting on a camera.
TLR: Twin lens reflex, a type of roll film camera.
Tonal range: The range of grey tones between black and white to be found in both subject and image.

Transparency: A positive image on film either in colour or black and white, usually projected onto a screen.
TTL metering: The method of taking an exposure reading through the lens of a camera.

Ultraviolet: Radiation beyond the violet band of the spectrum, visible to film emulsions, the scattering of which causes hazy horizons.
Uprating: Exposing film at a higher ISO setting than that suggested, i.e. ISO400 at 1600, used in conjunction with push processing.

Wetting agent: Used after washing a film to help prevent drying marks.

Zone system: An exposure system devised by Ansel Adams which requires a great deal of pre-visualisation on the part of the photographer. Used in conjunction with special processing techniques requiring the whole film to be exposed in the same way. It splits up the tonal range into 10 zones from black to white. Best used with sheet film from large format cameras.